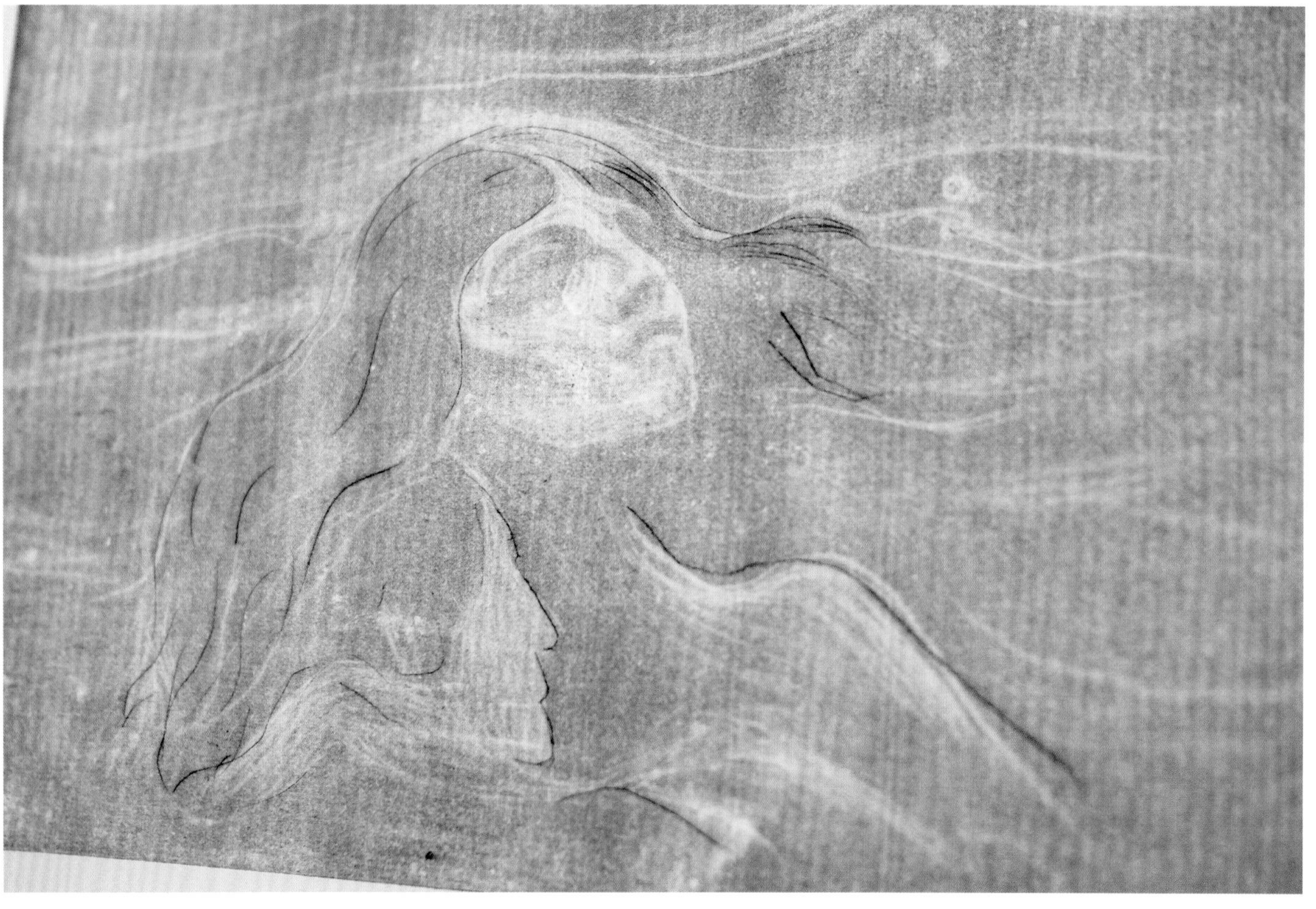

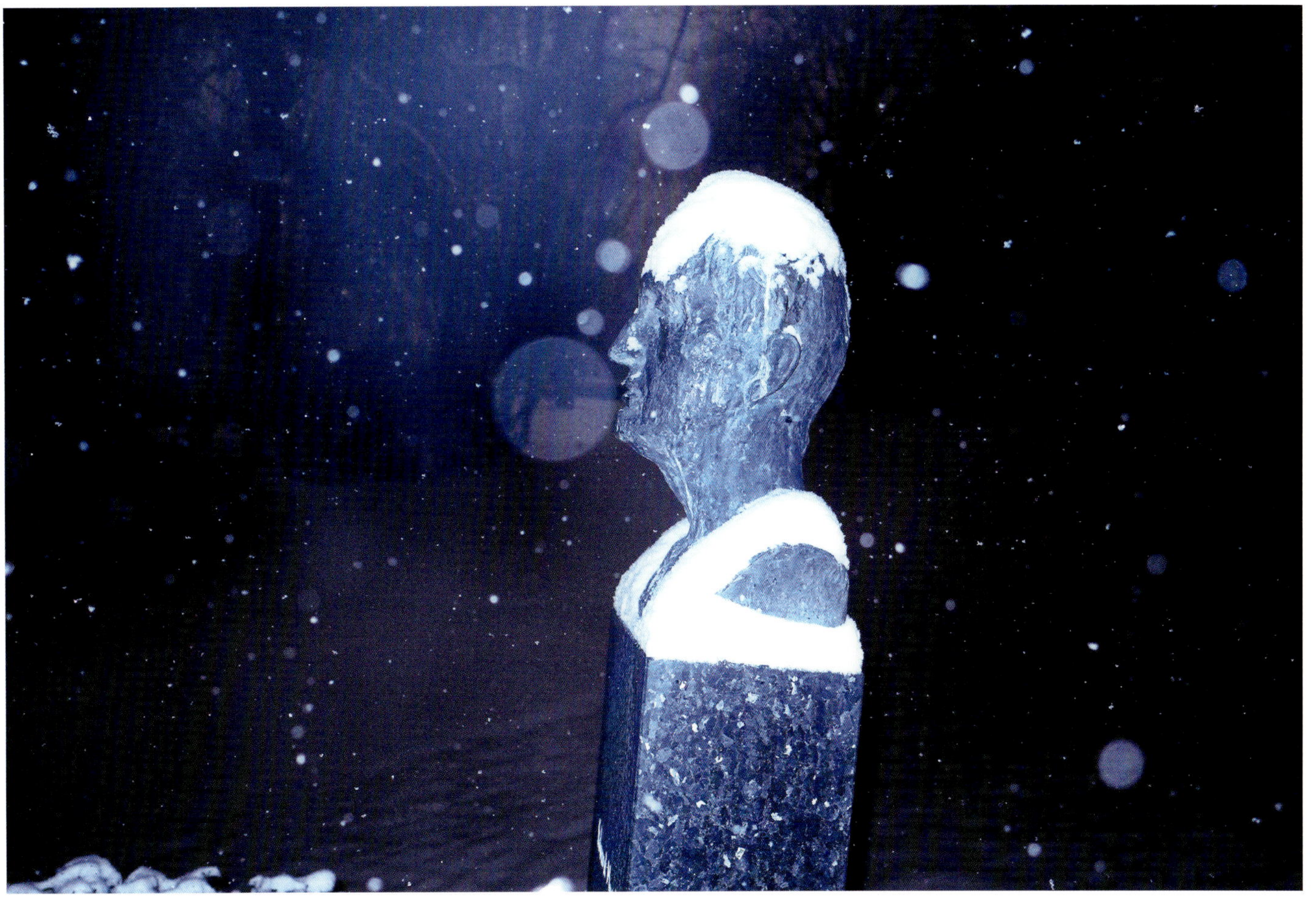

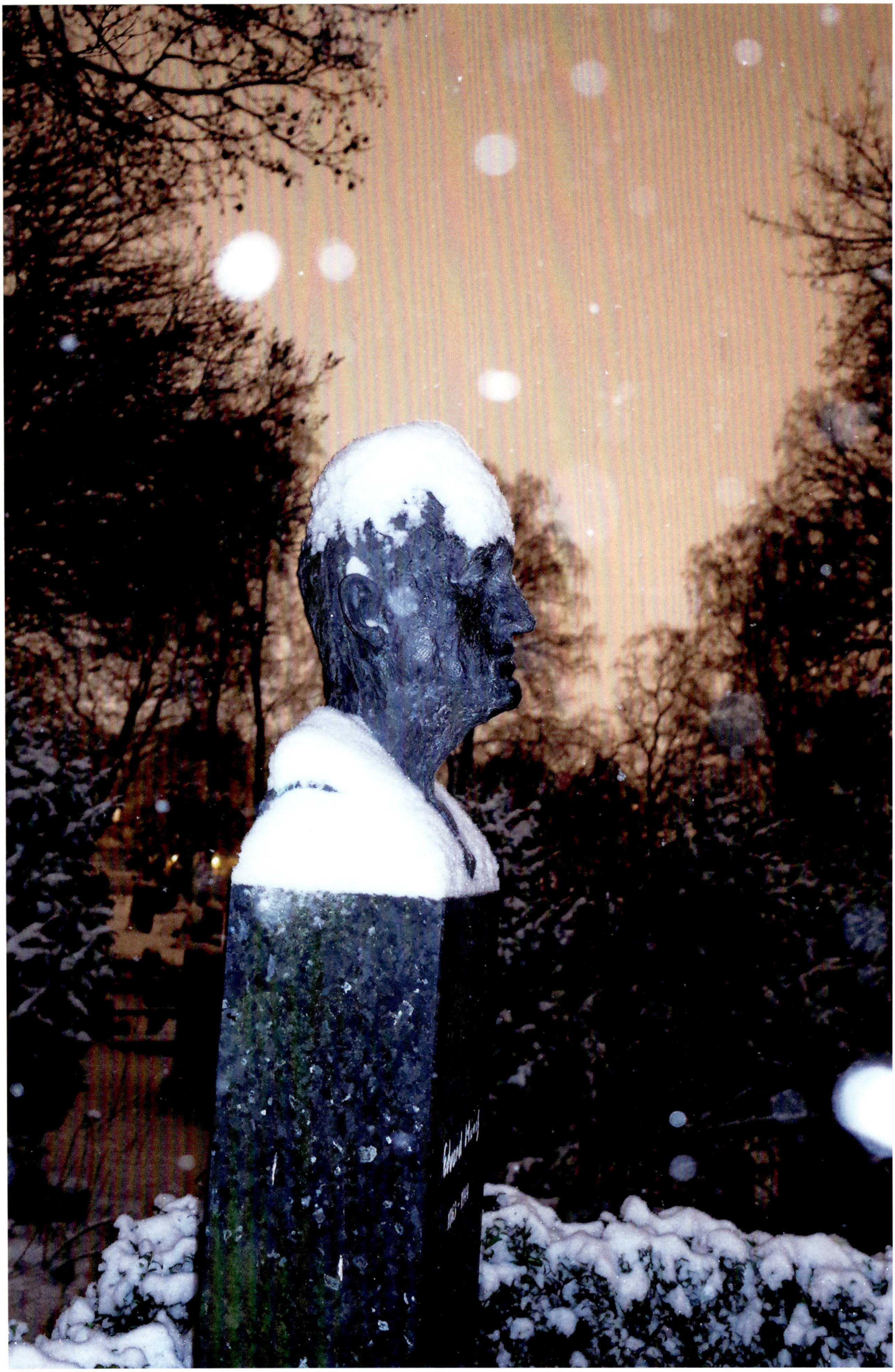

MORTEN ANDERSEN

SATYRICON & MUNCH

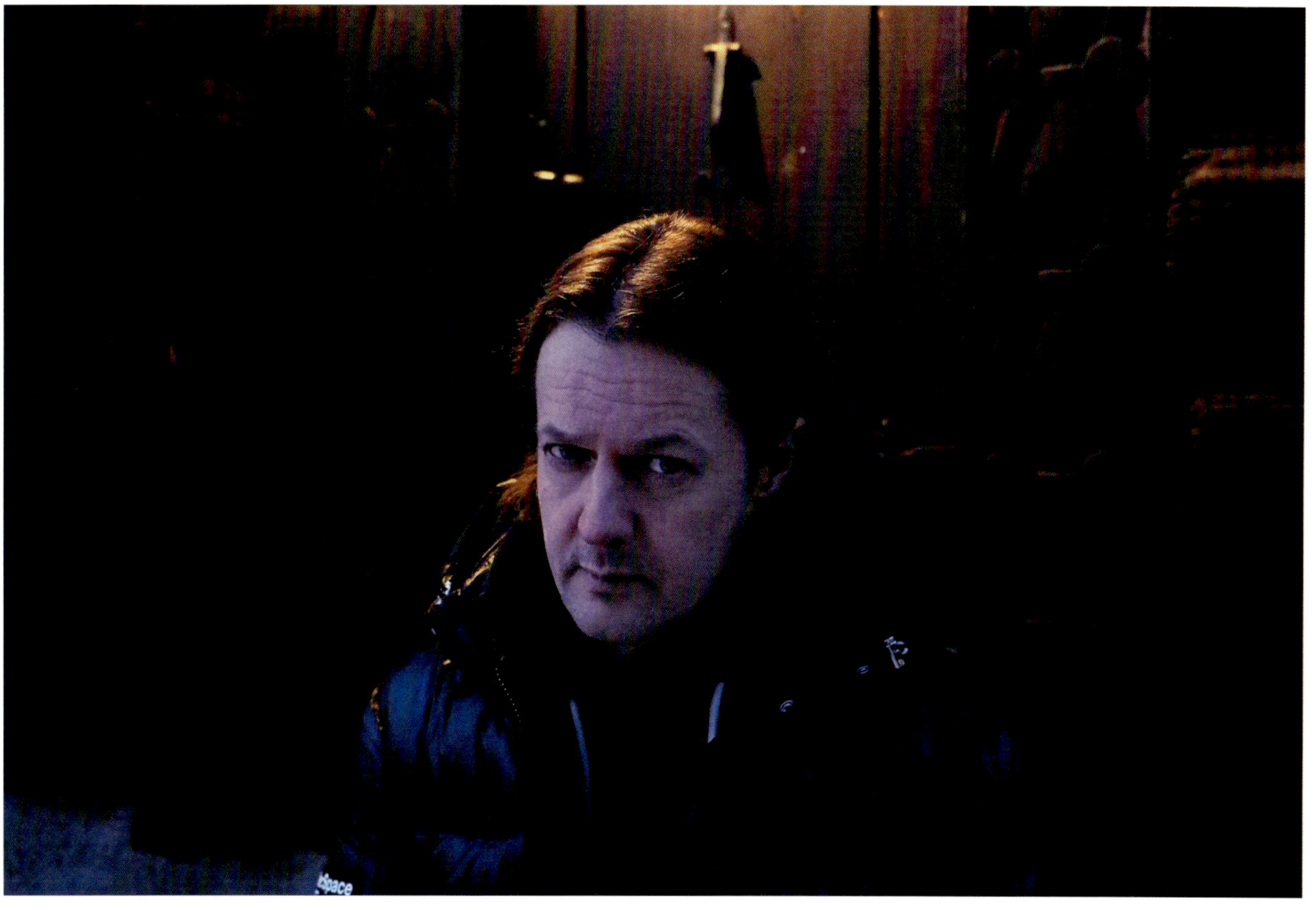

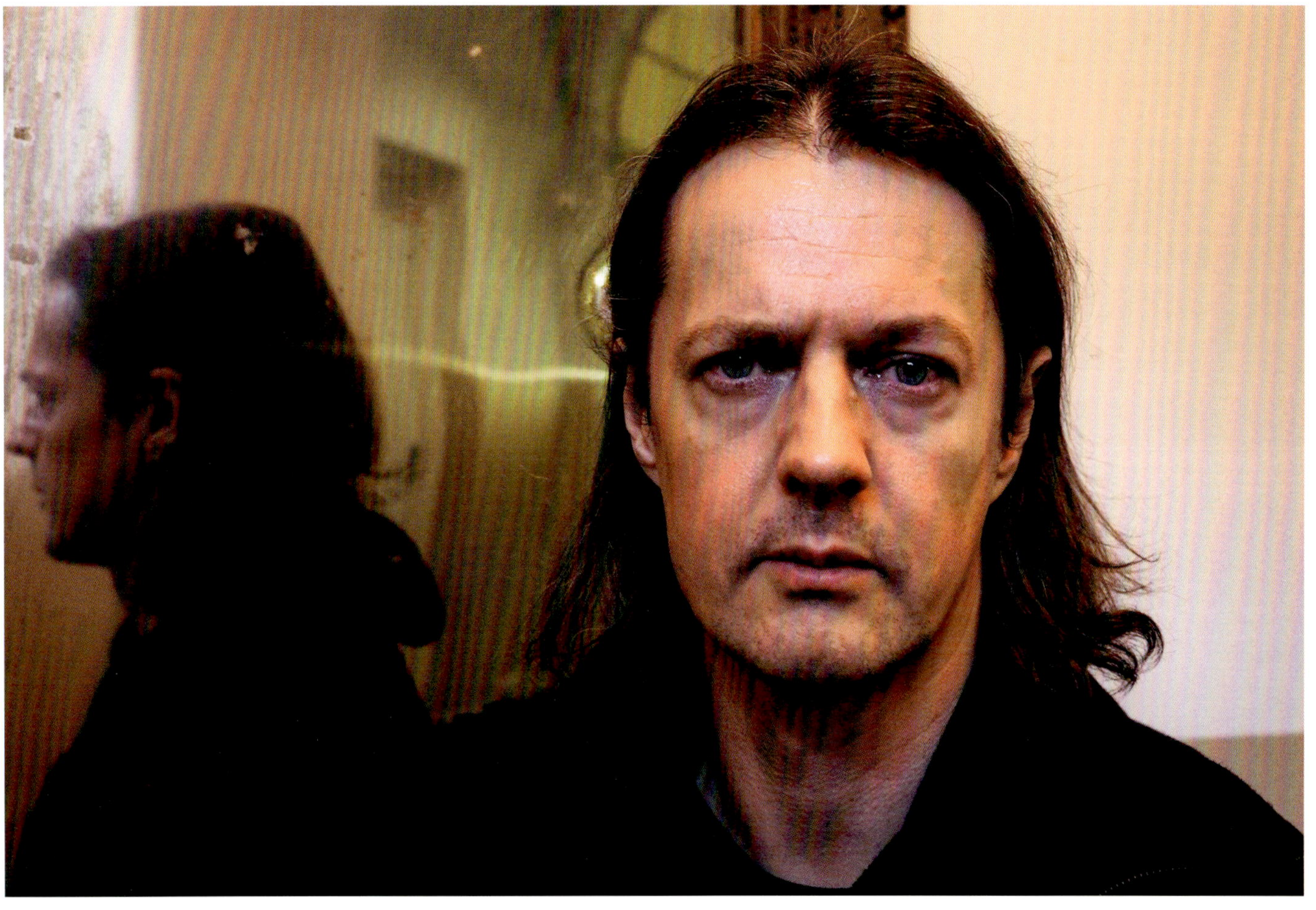

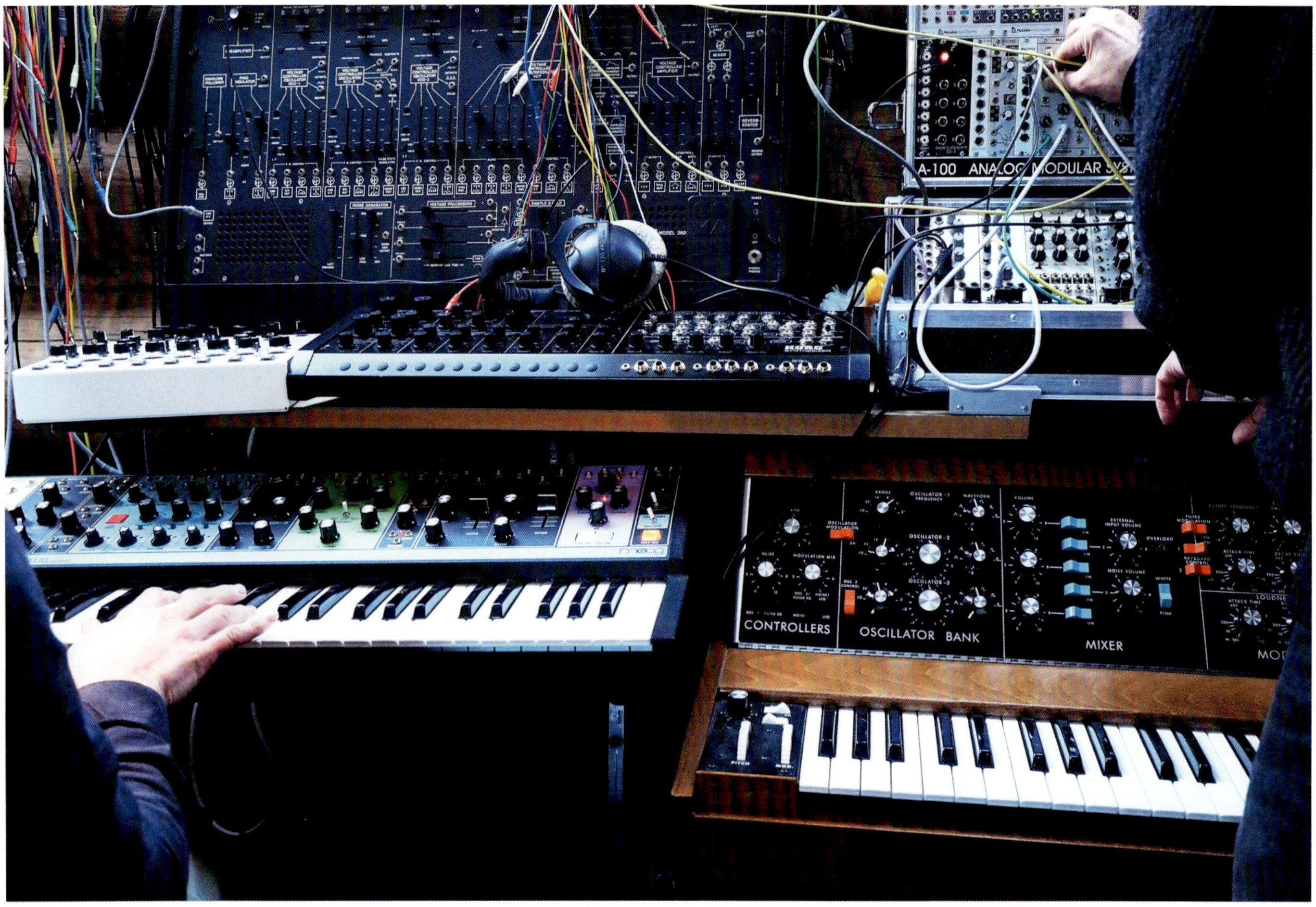
CONTROLLERS
OSCILLATOR BANK
MIXER

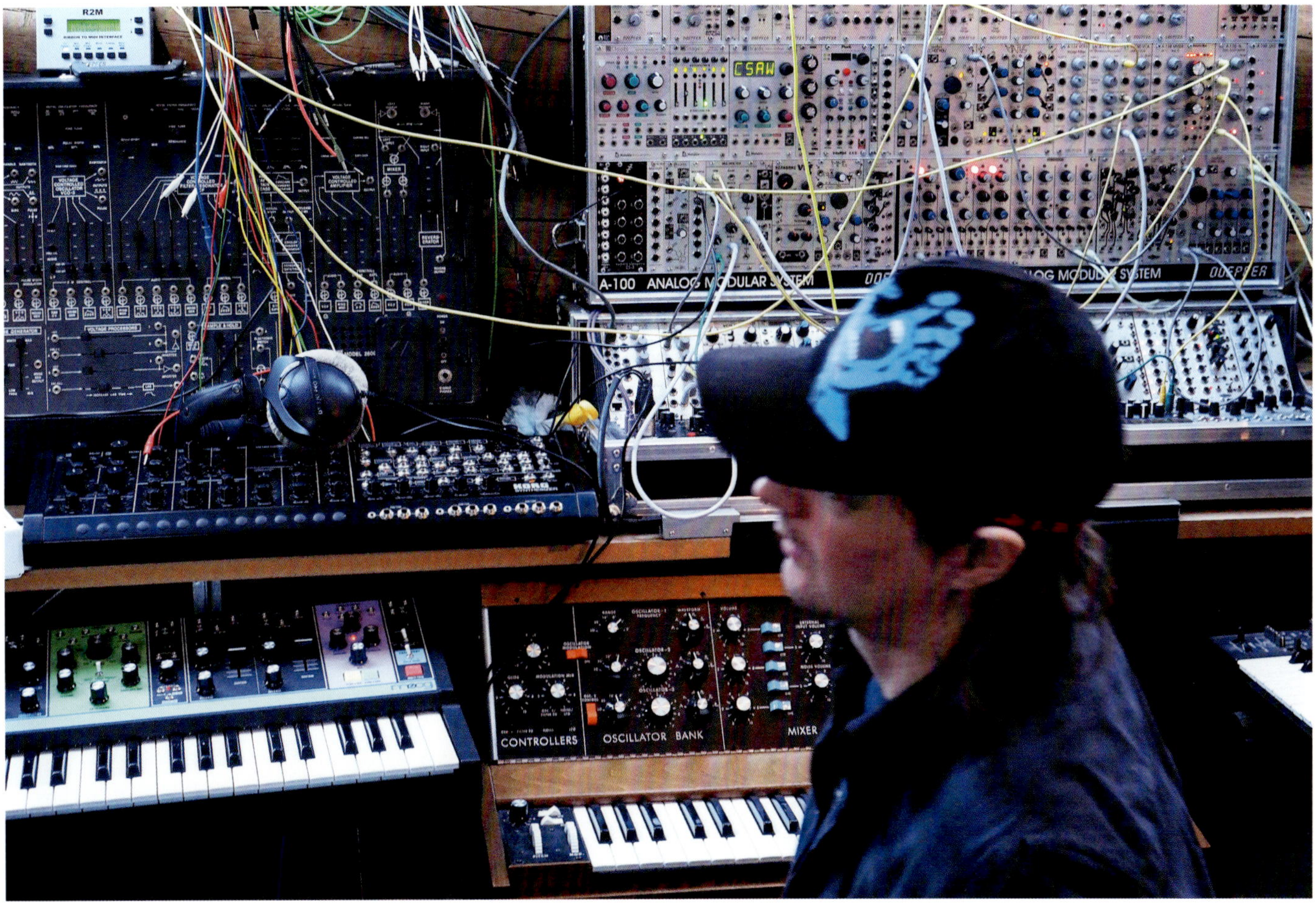
R2M
CSAW
A-100 ANALOG MODULAR SYSTEM
CONTROLLERS
OSCILLATOR BANK
MIXER

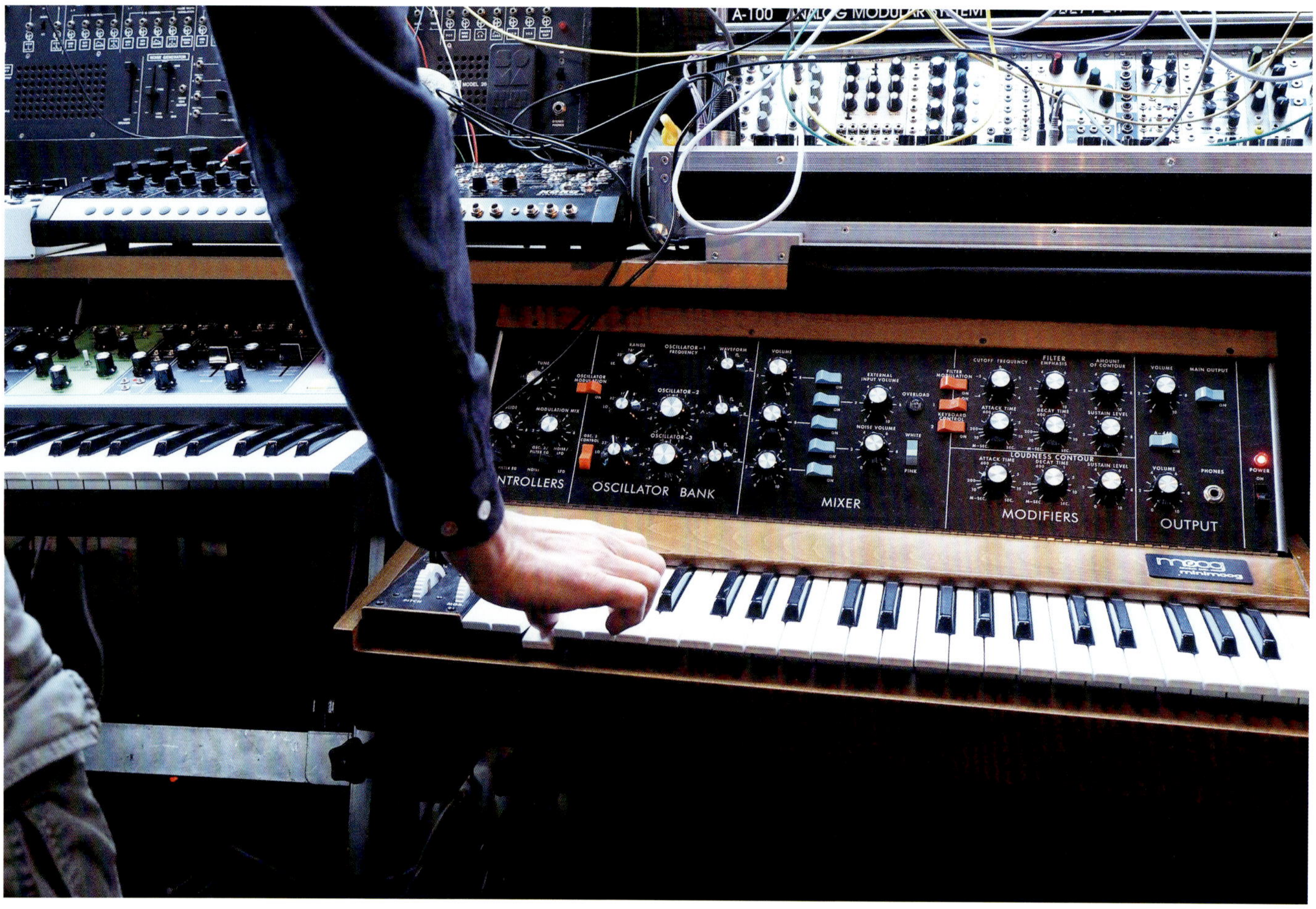
OSCILLATOR BANK
MIXER
MODIFIERS
OUTPUT

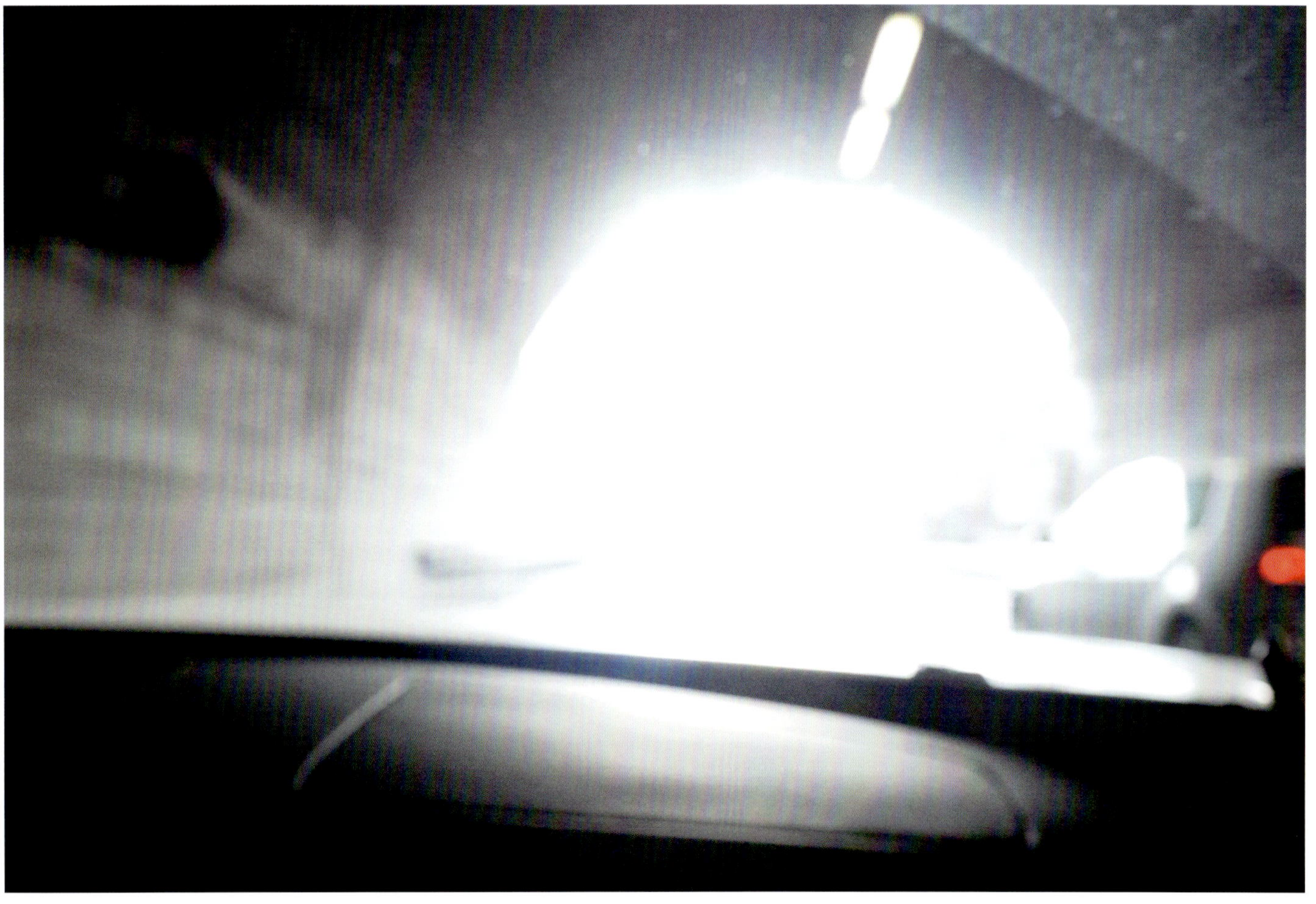

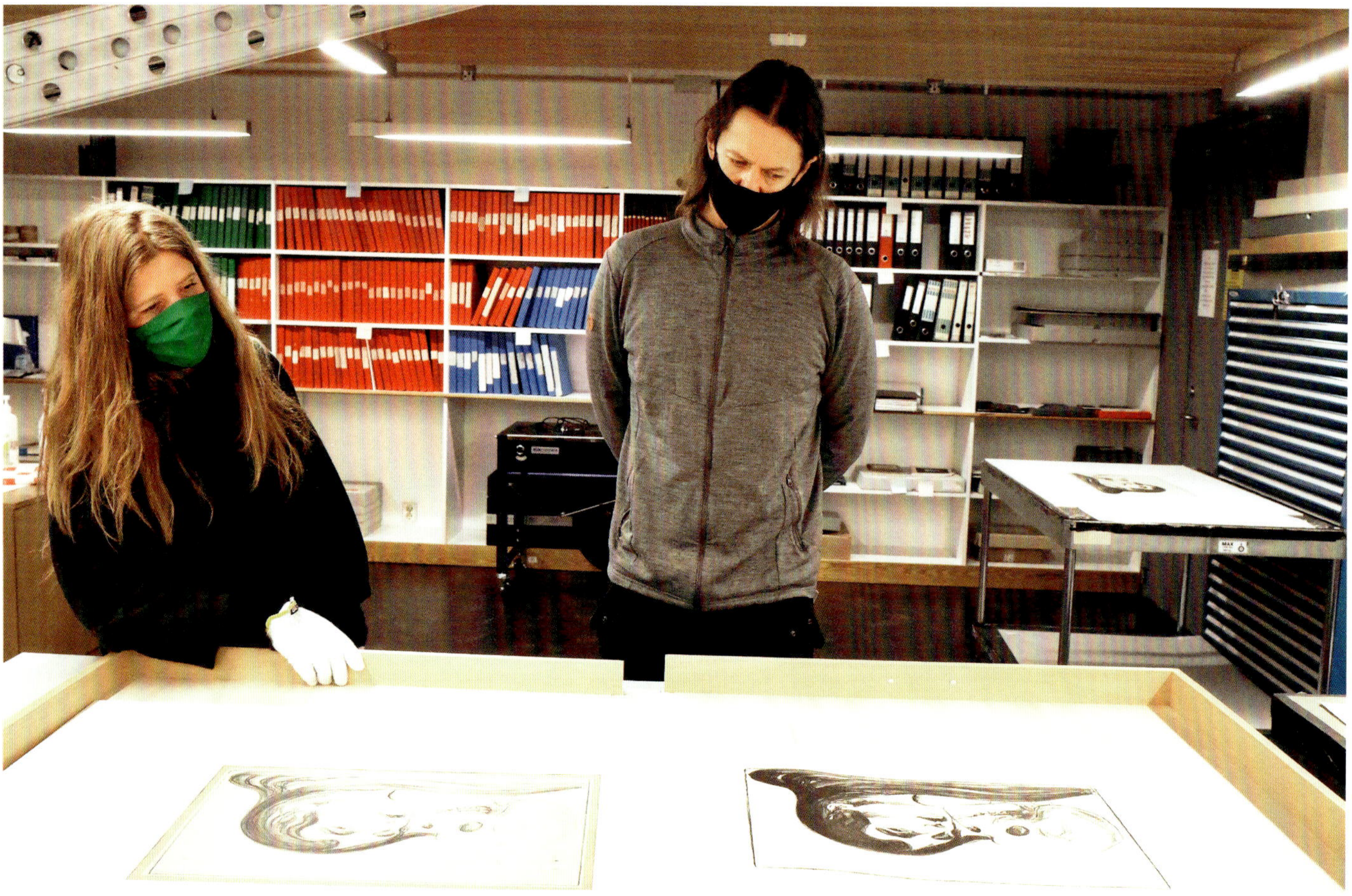

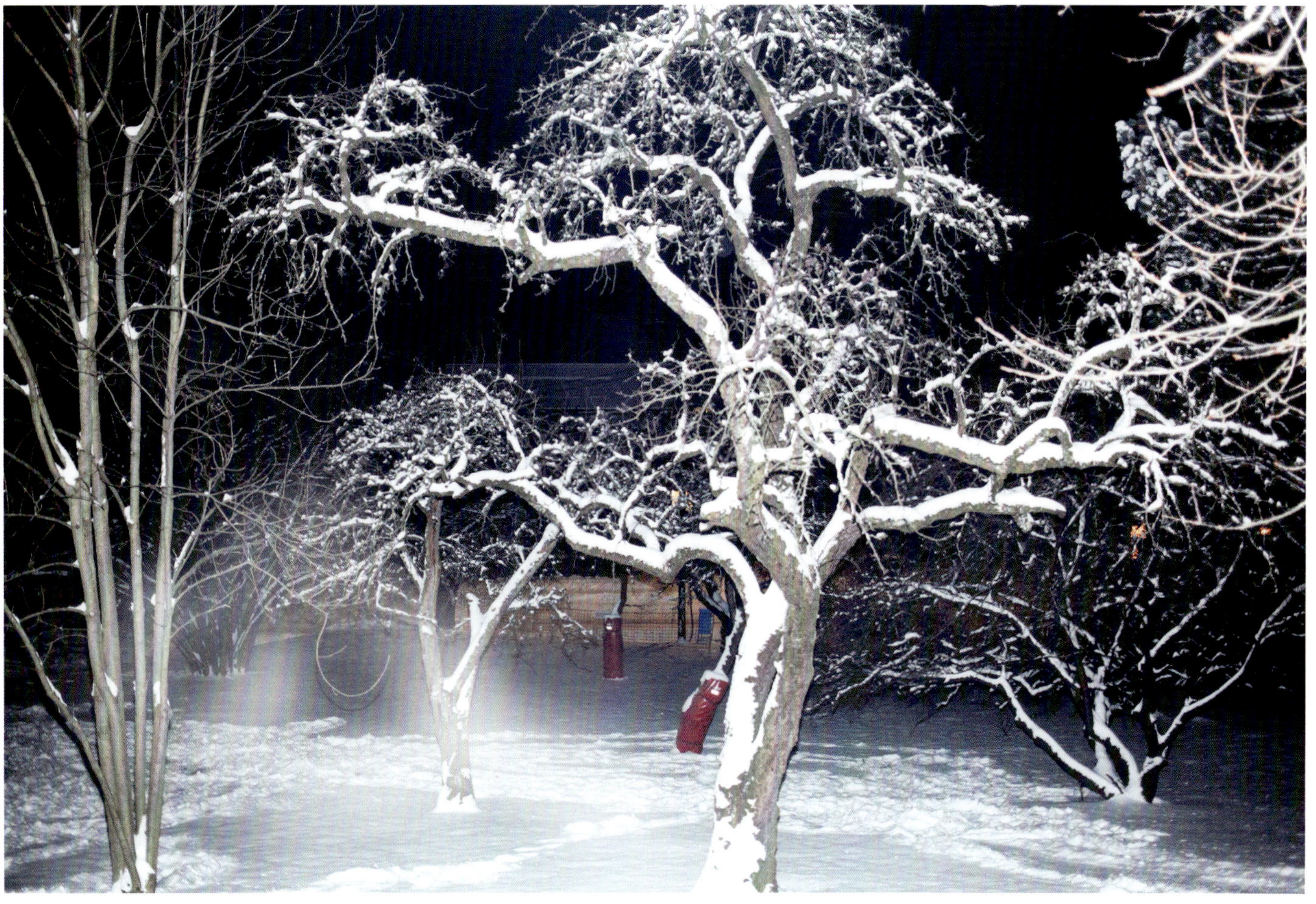

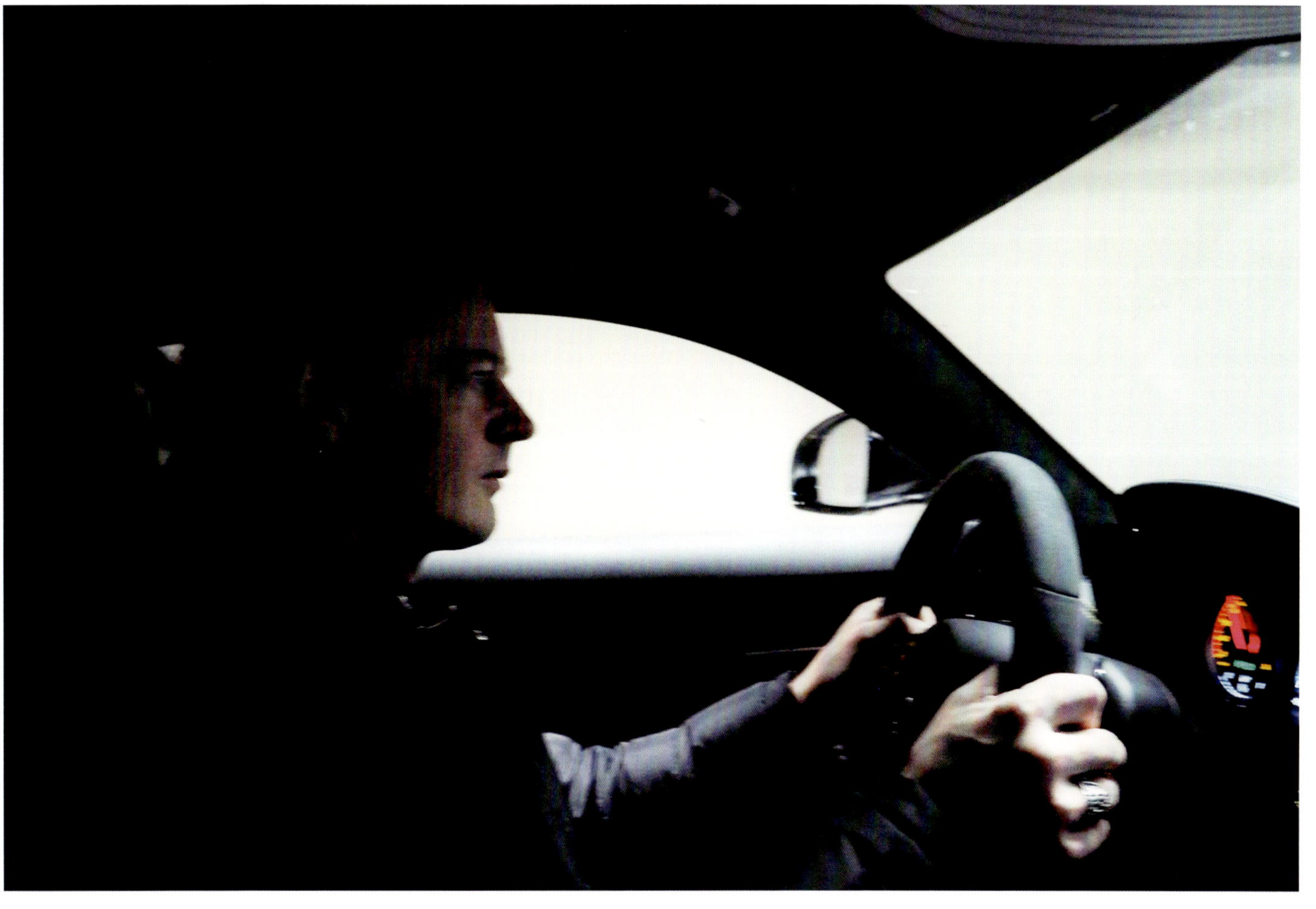

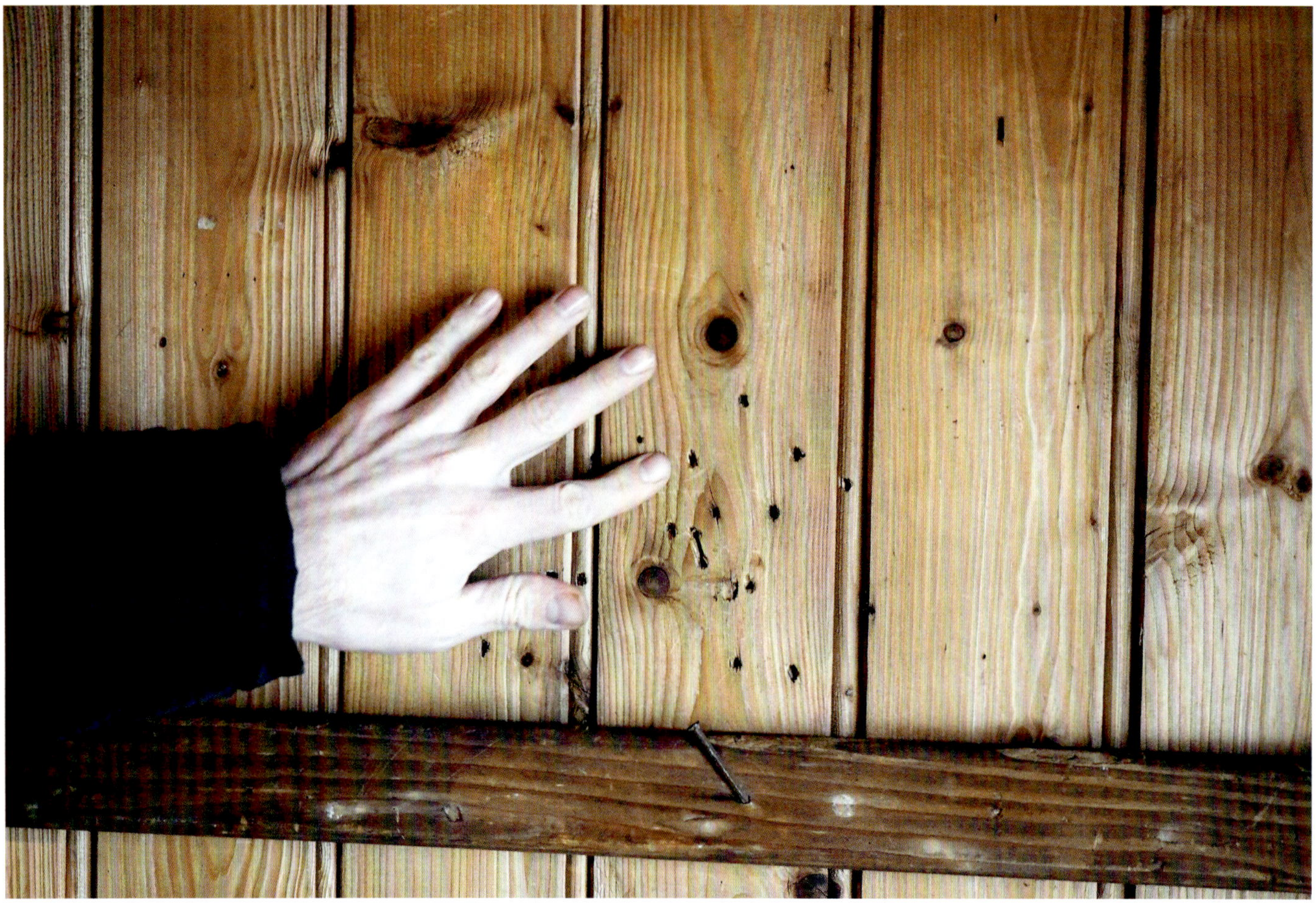

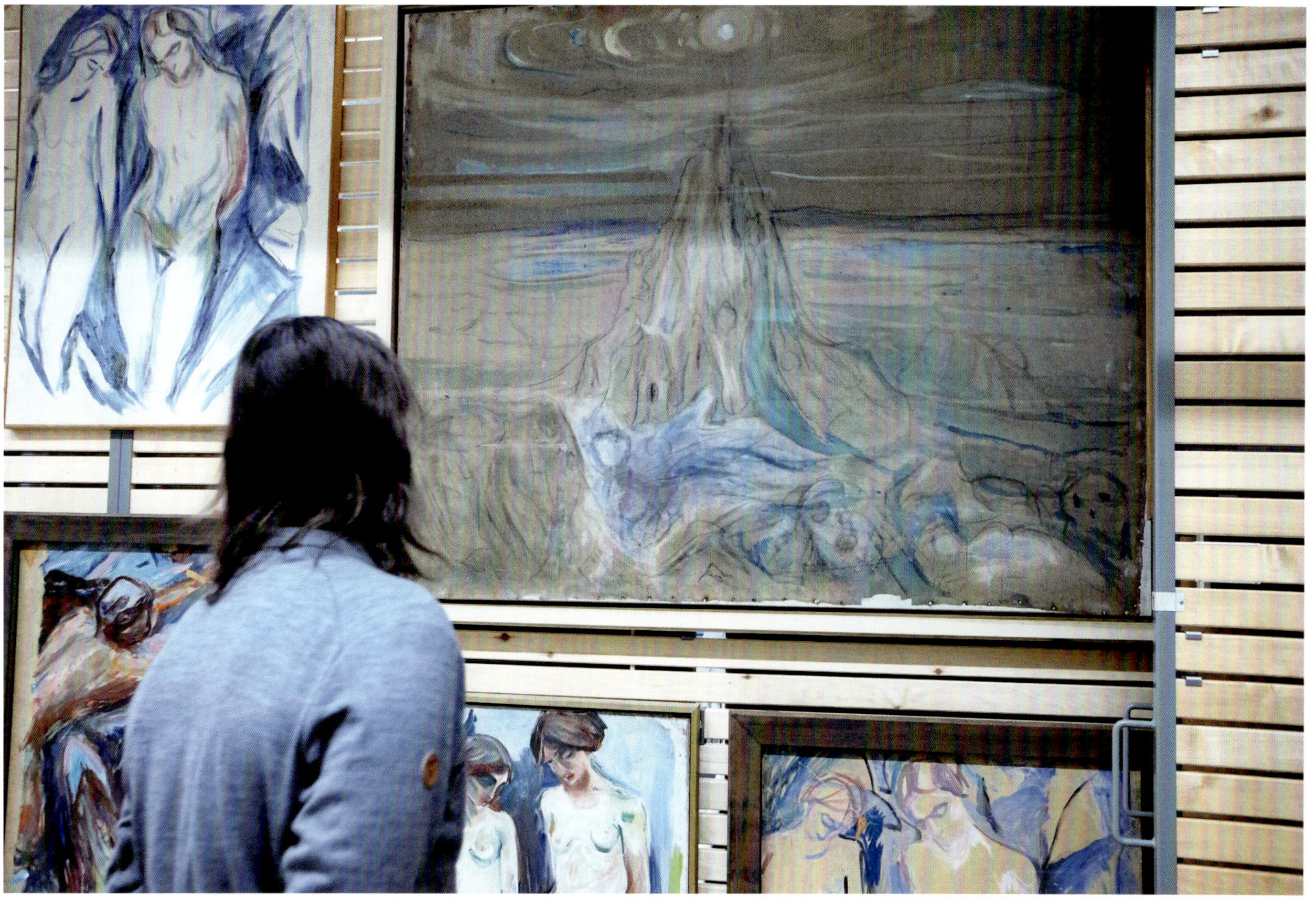

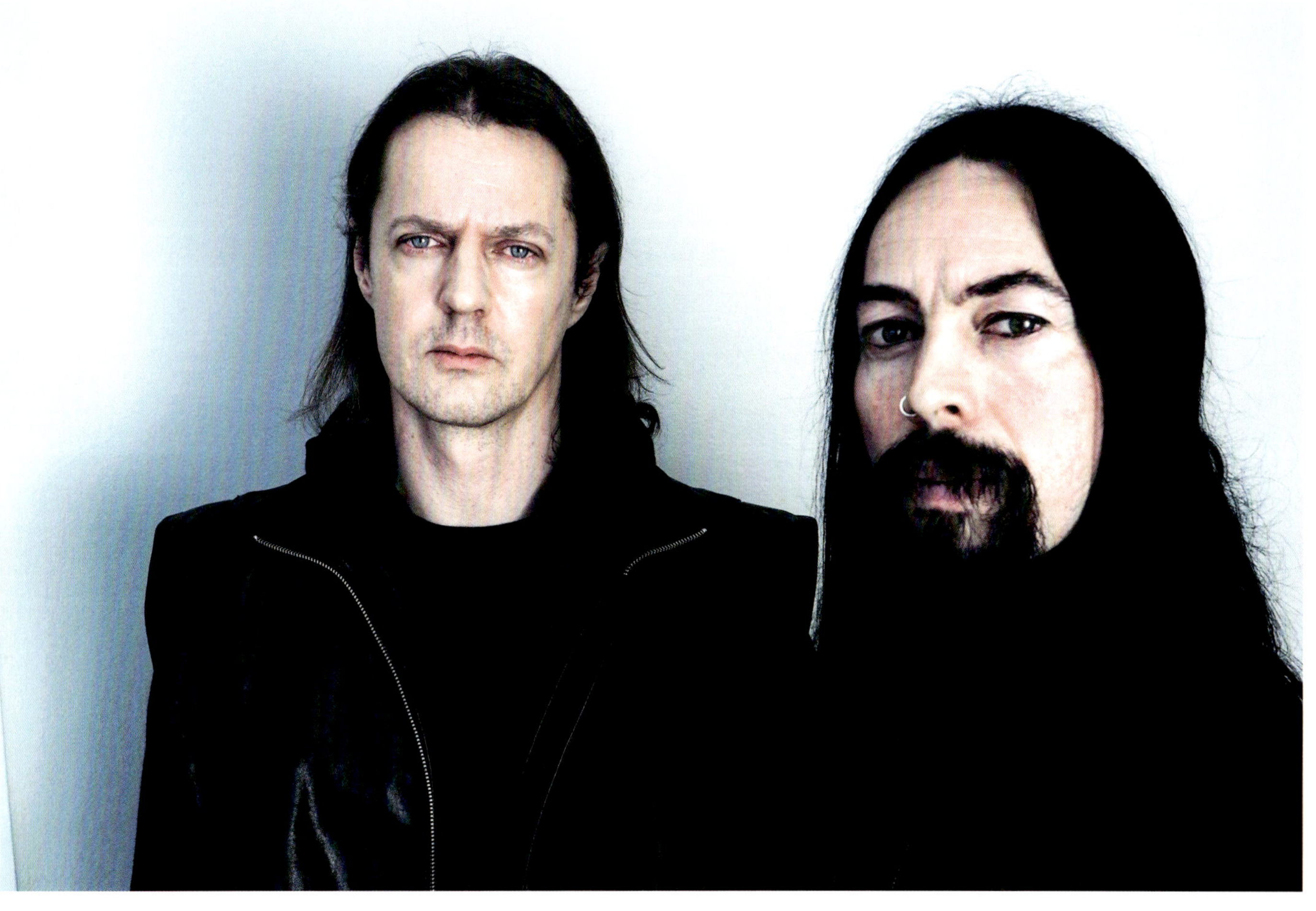

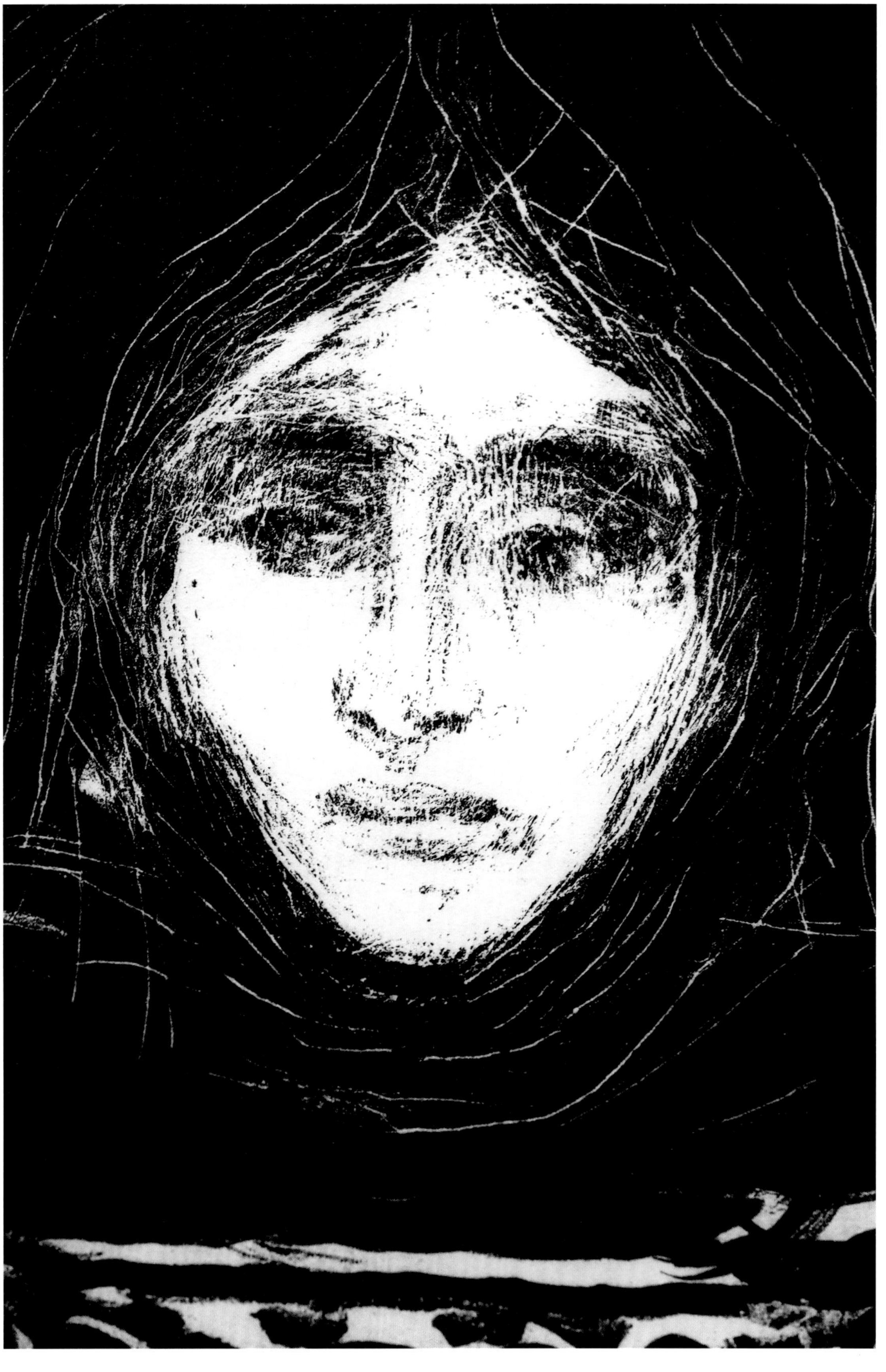

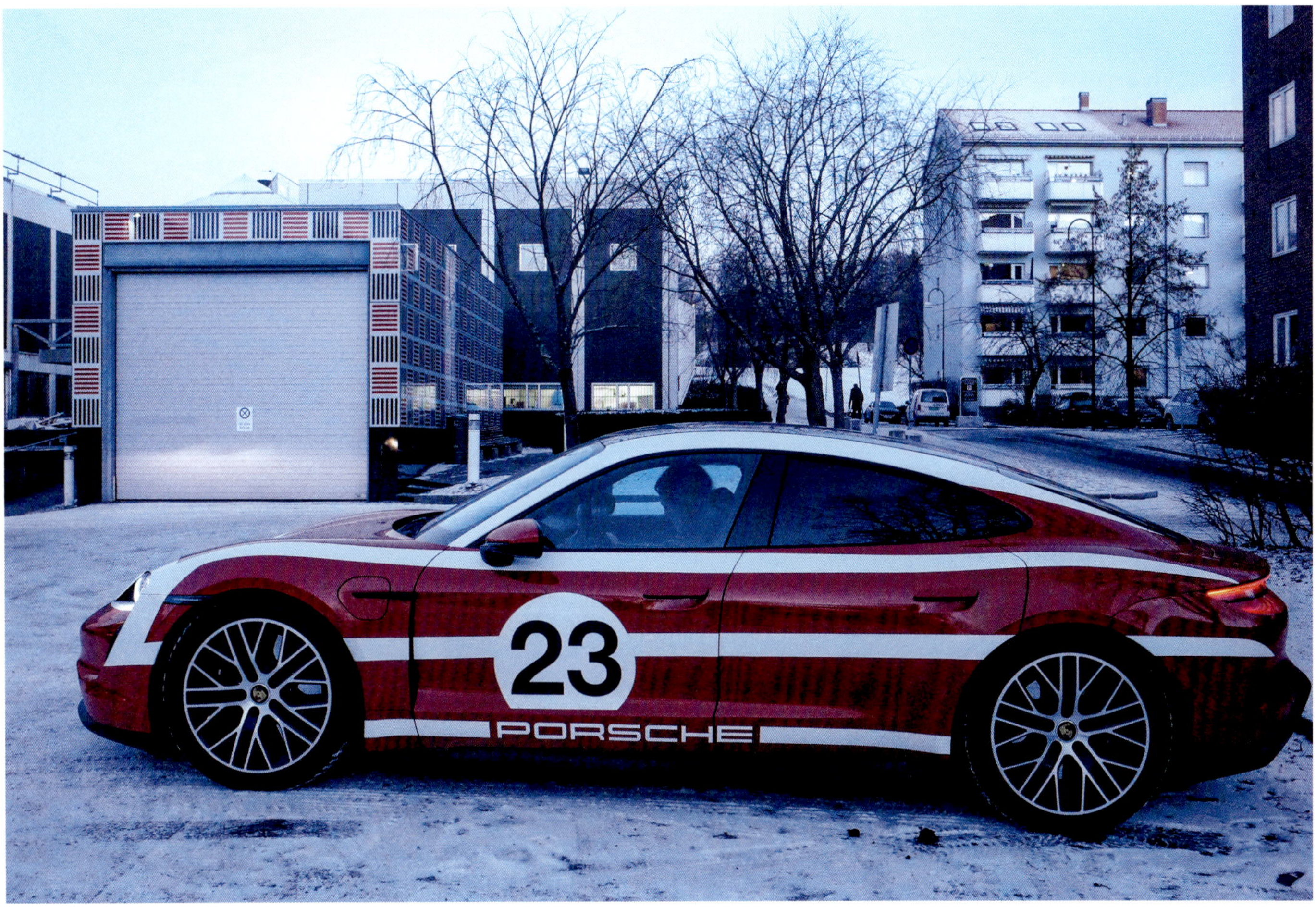
23
PORSCHE

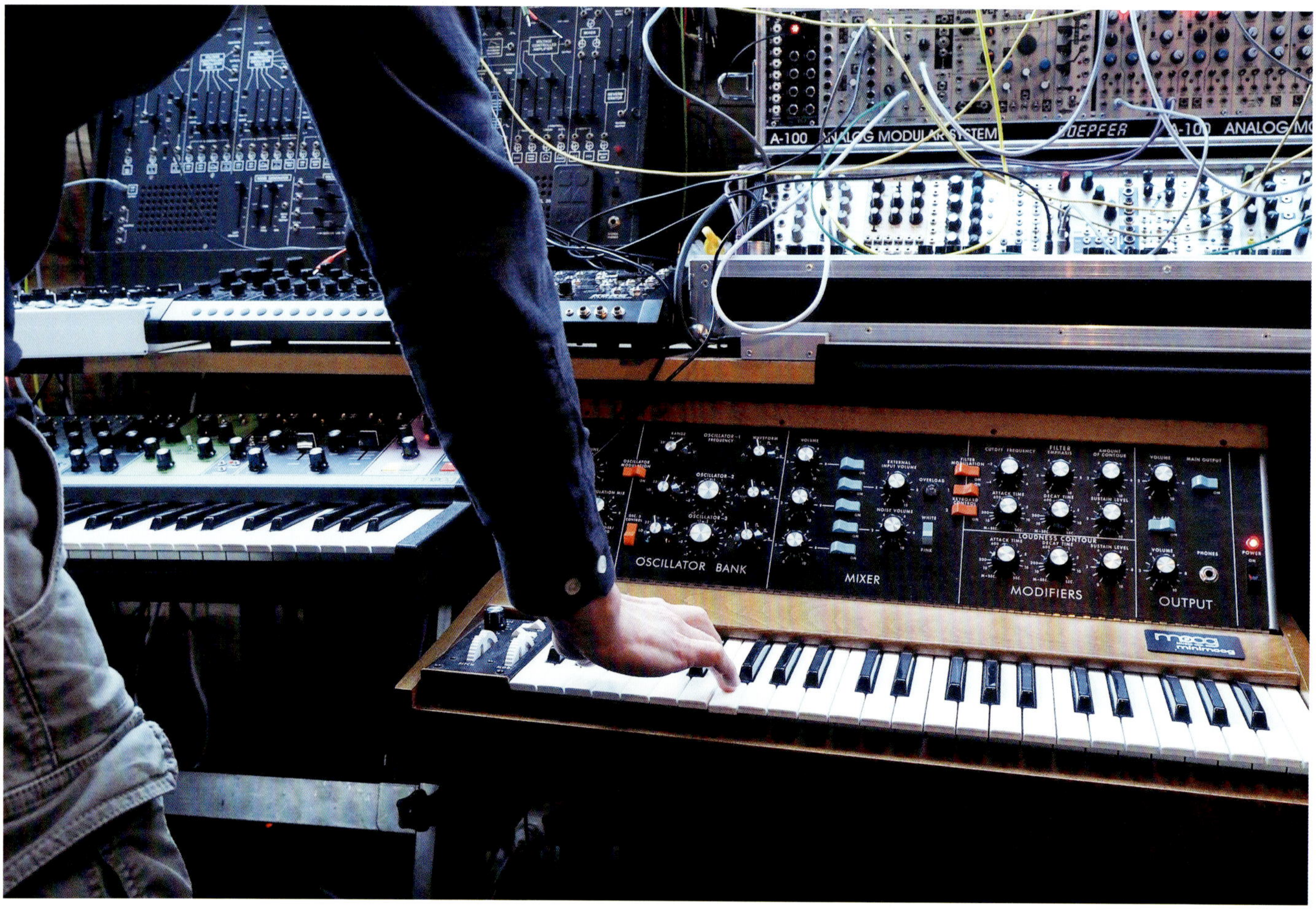
A-100
DOEPFER
OSCILLATOR BANK
MIXER
MODIFIERS
OUTPUT

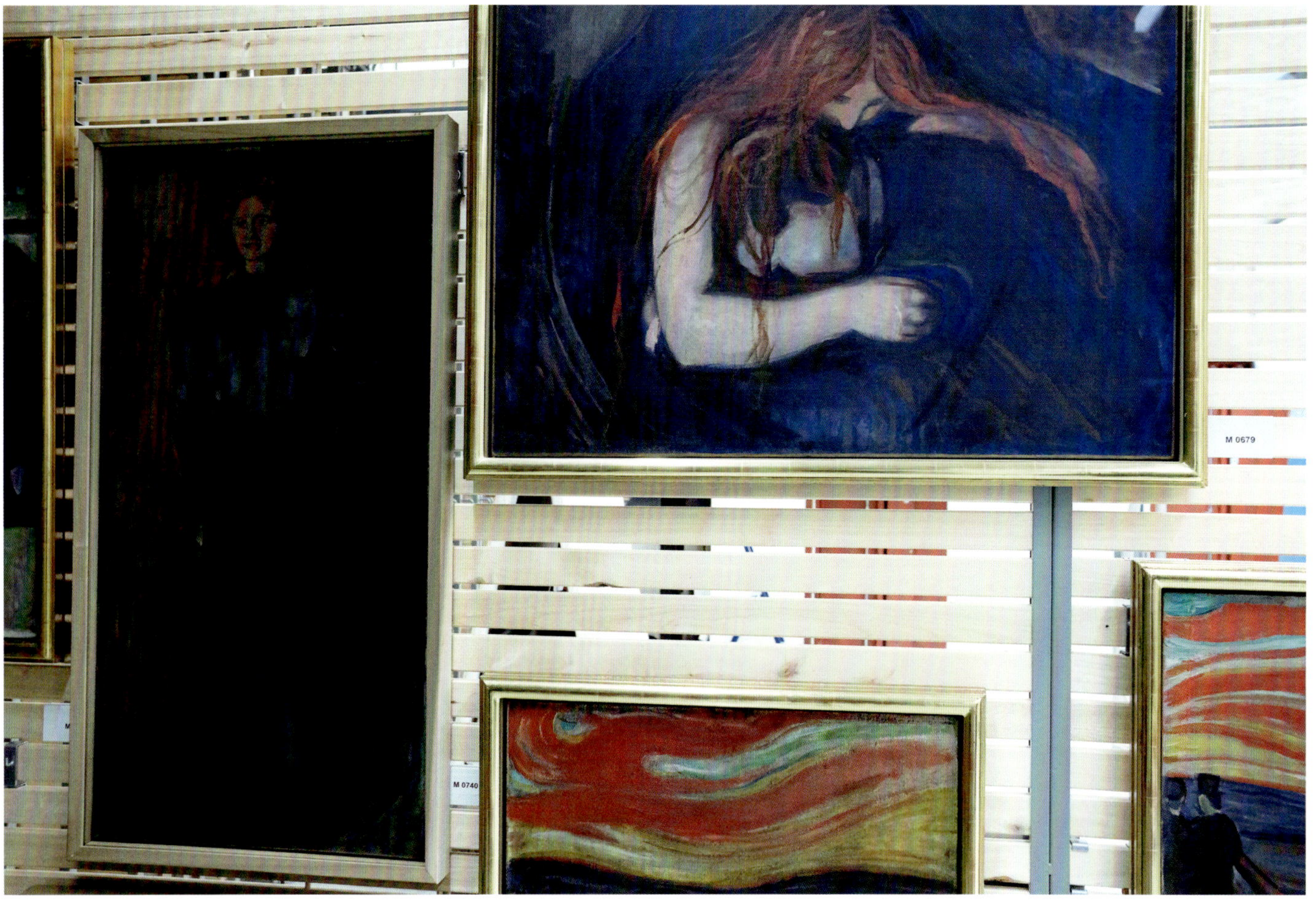
M 0679
M 0740

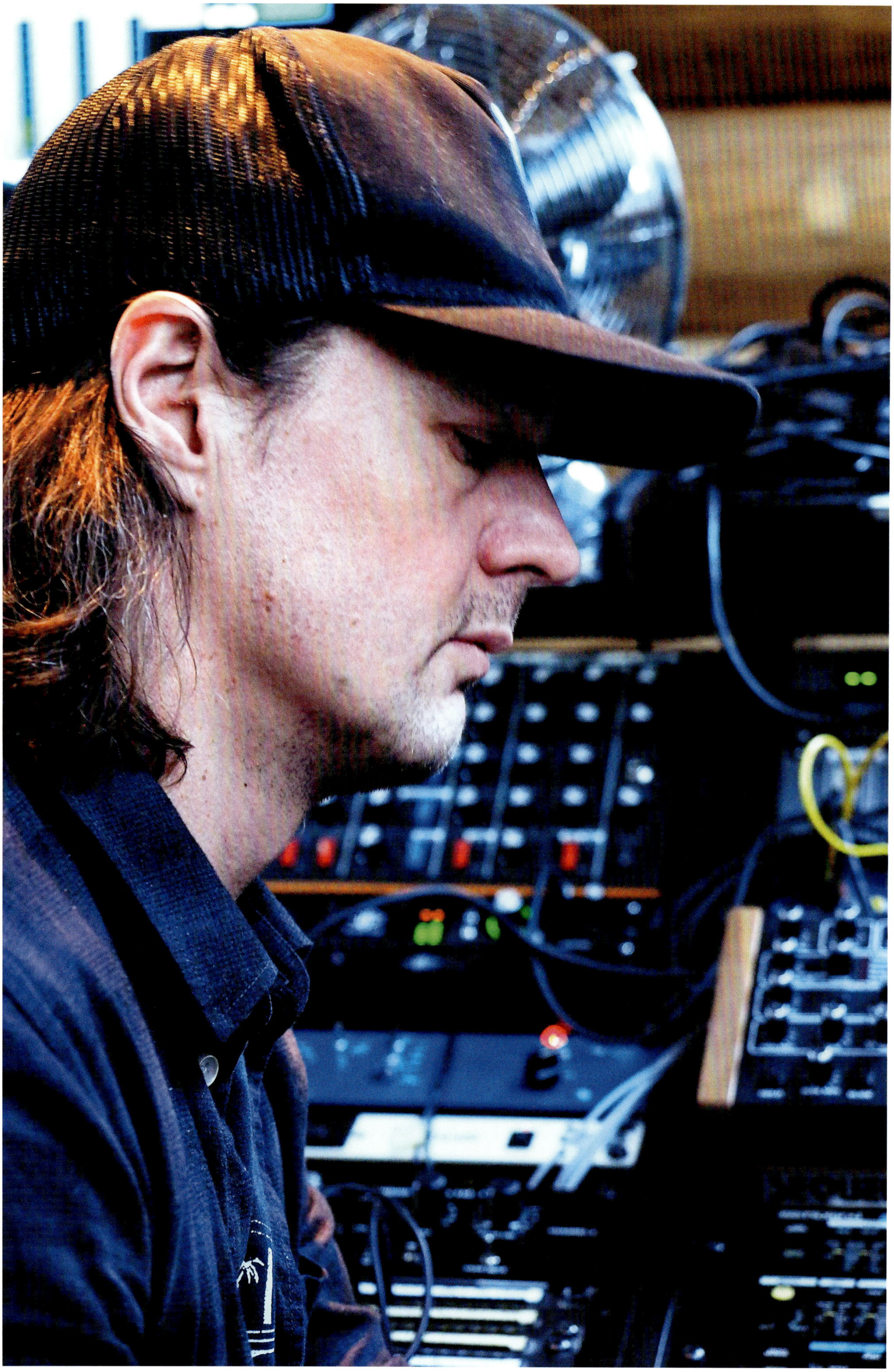

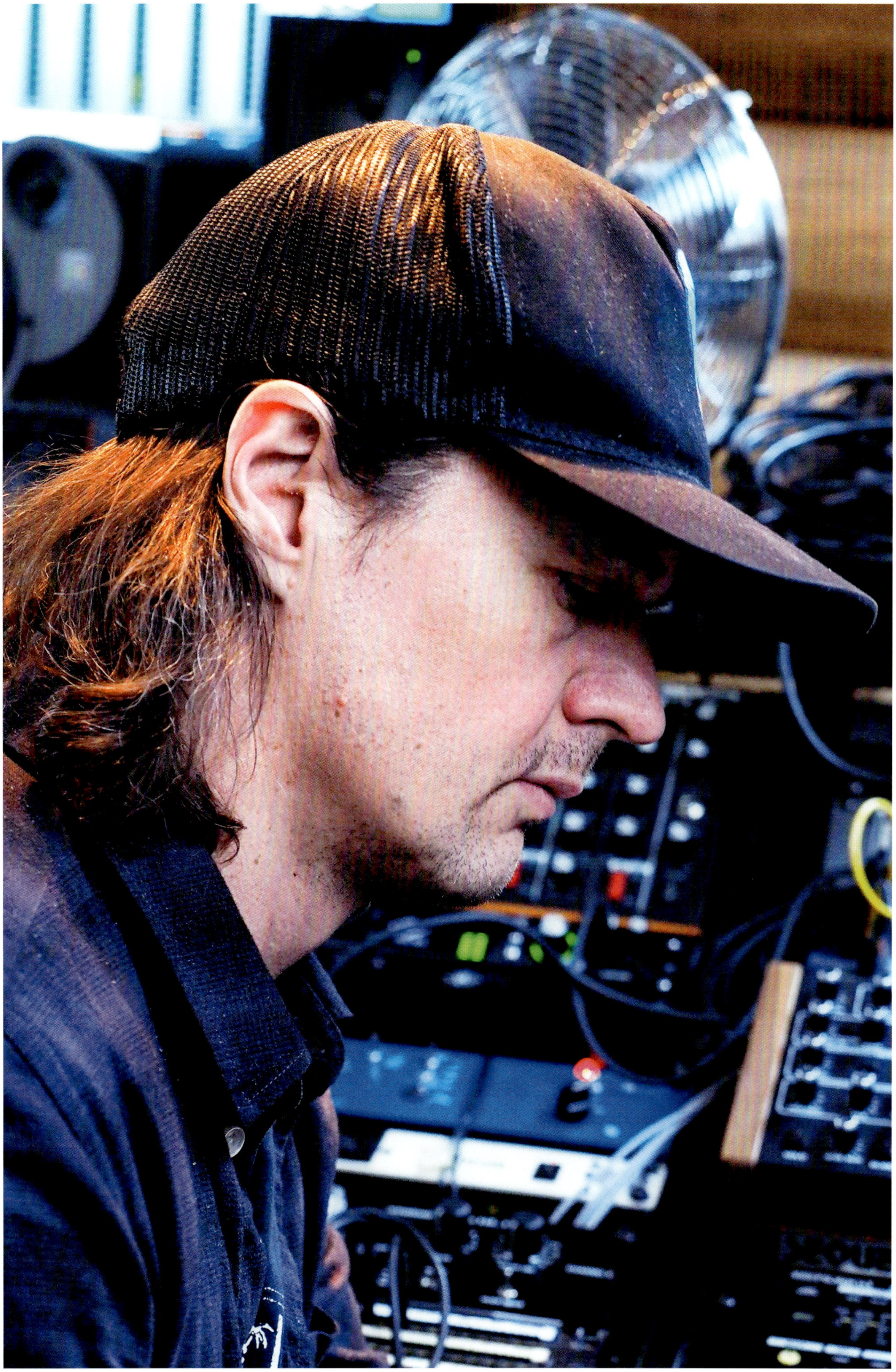

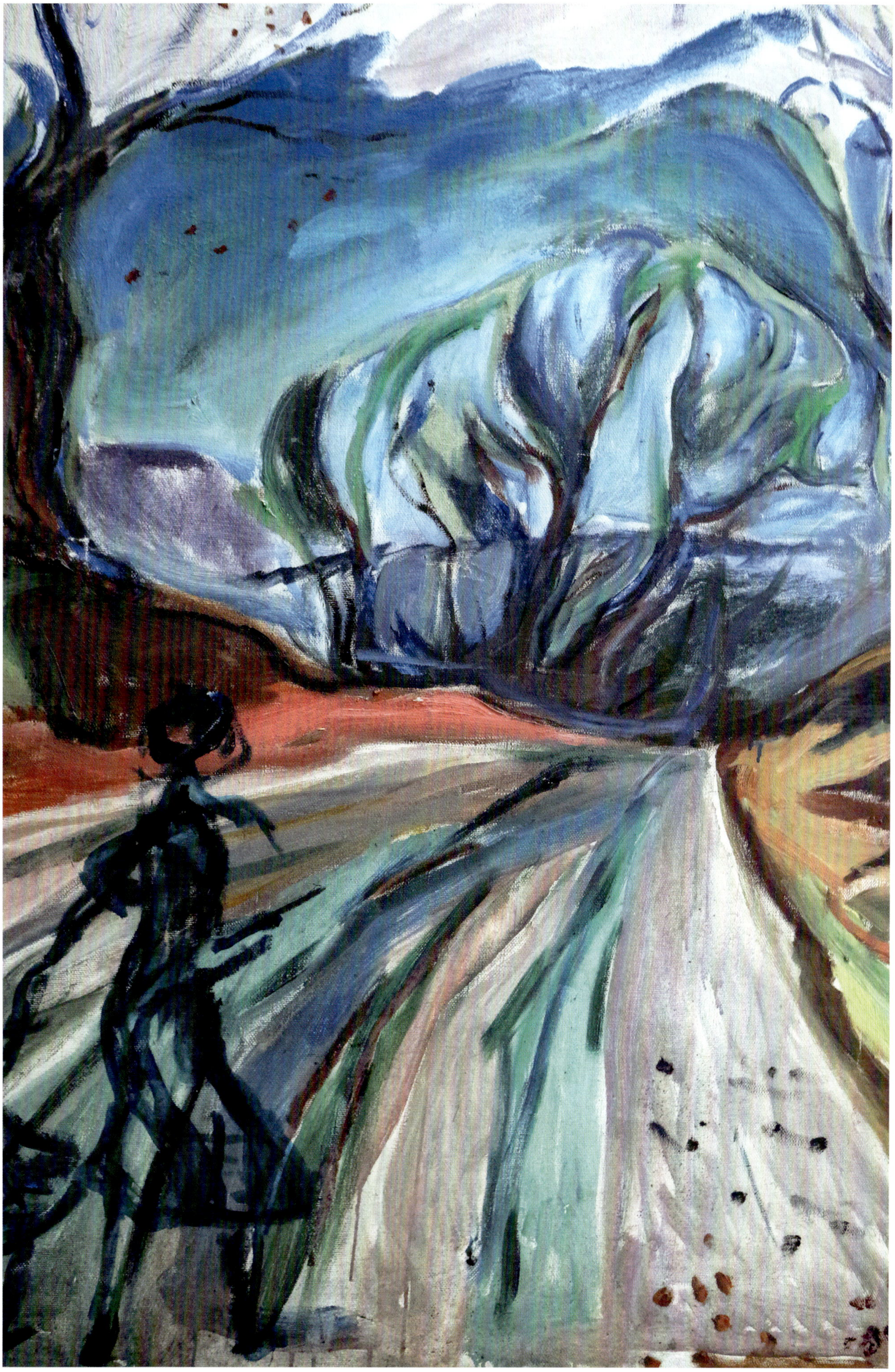

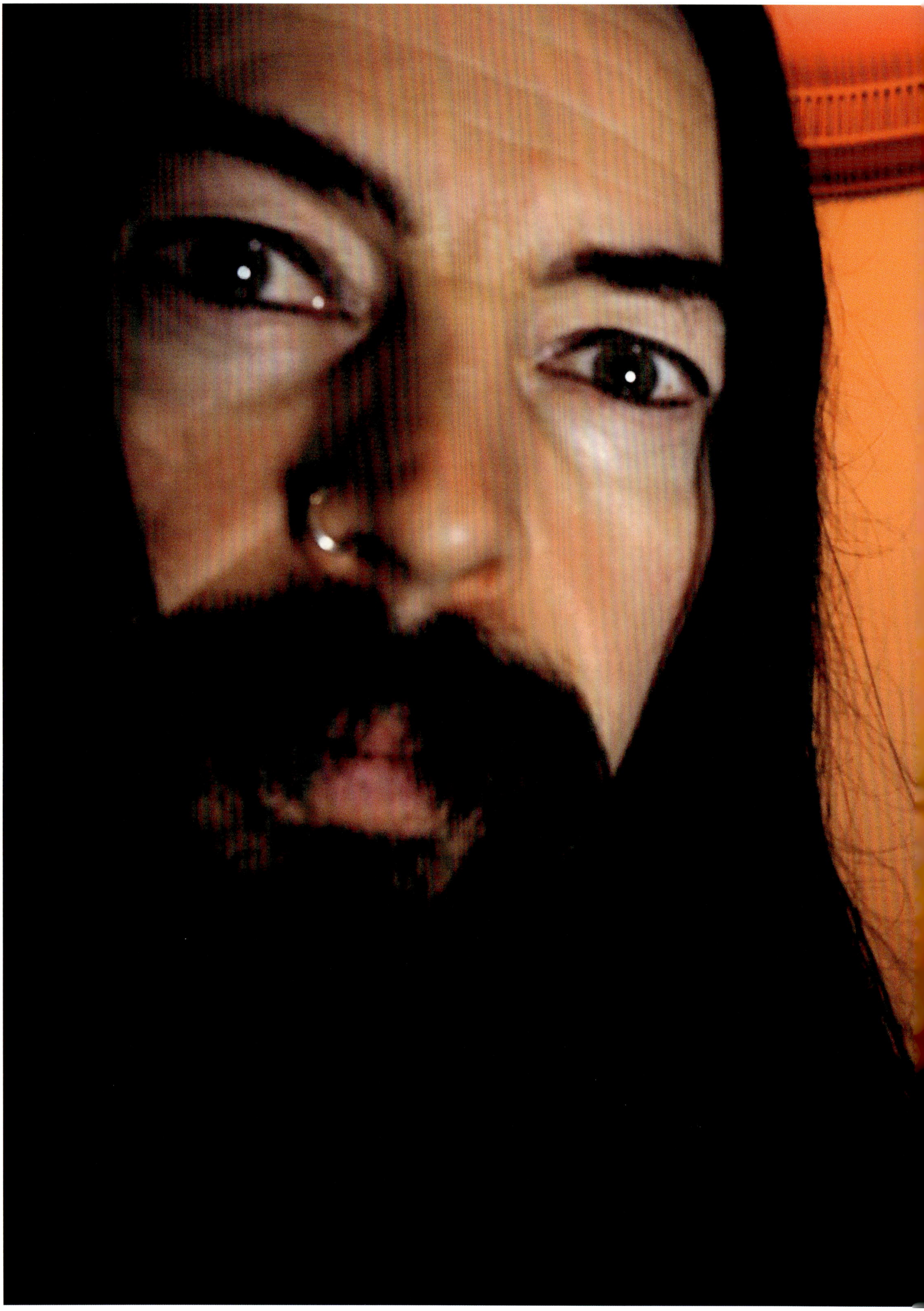

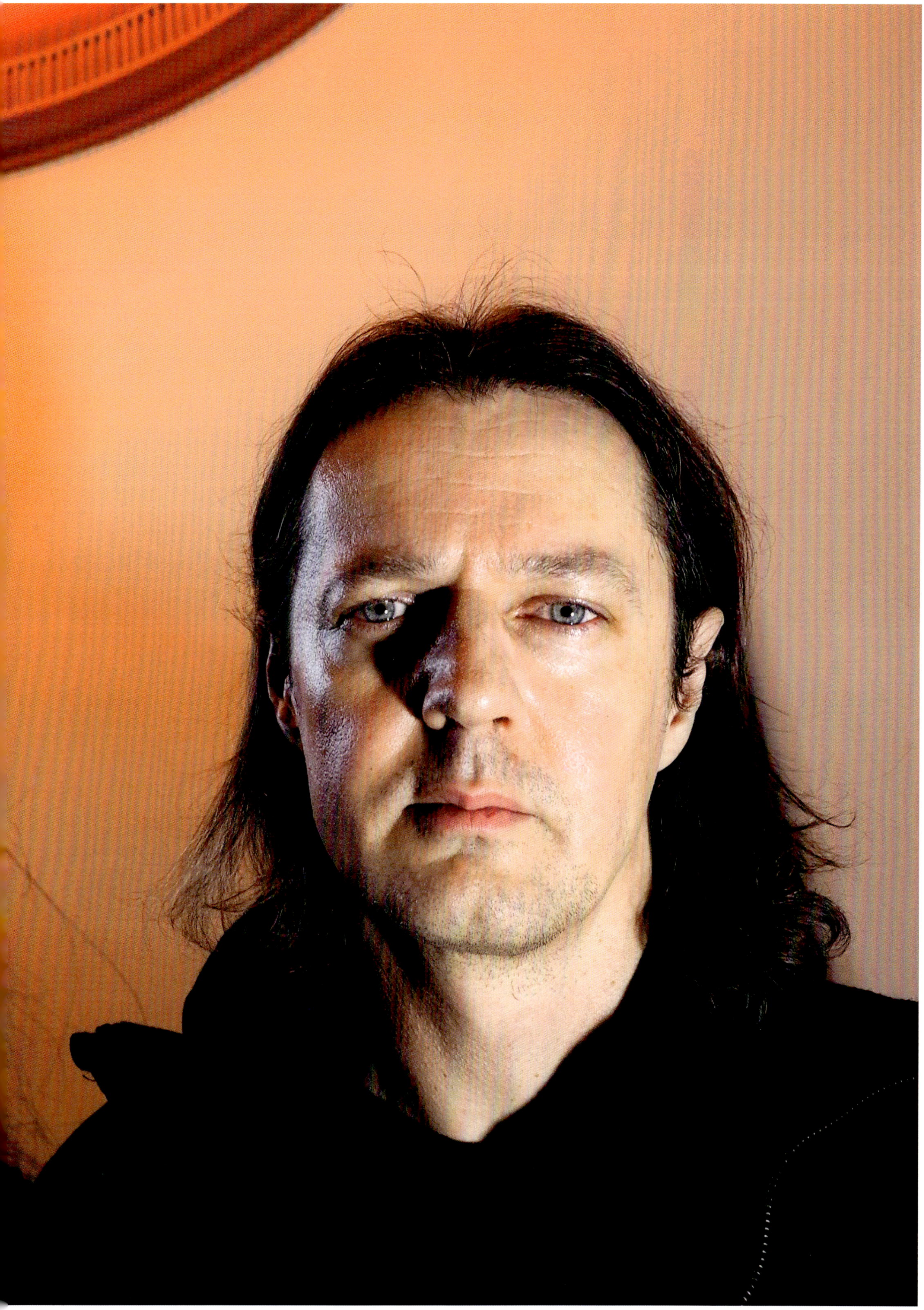

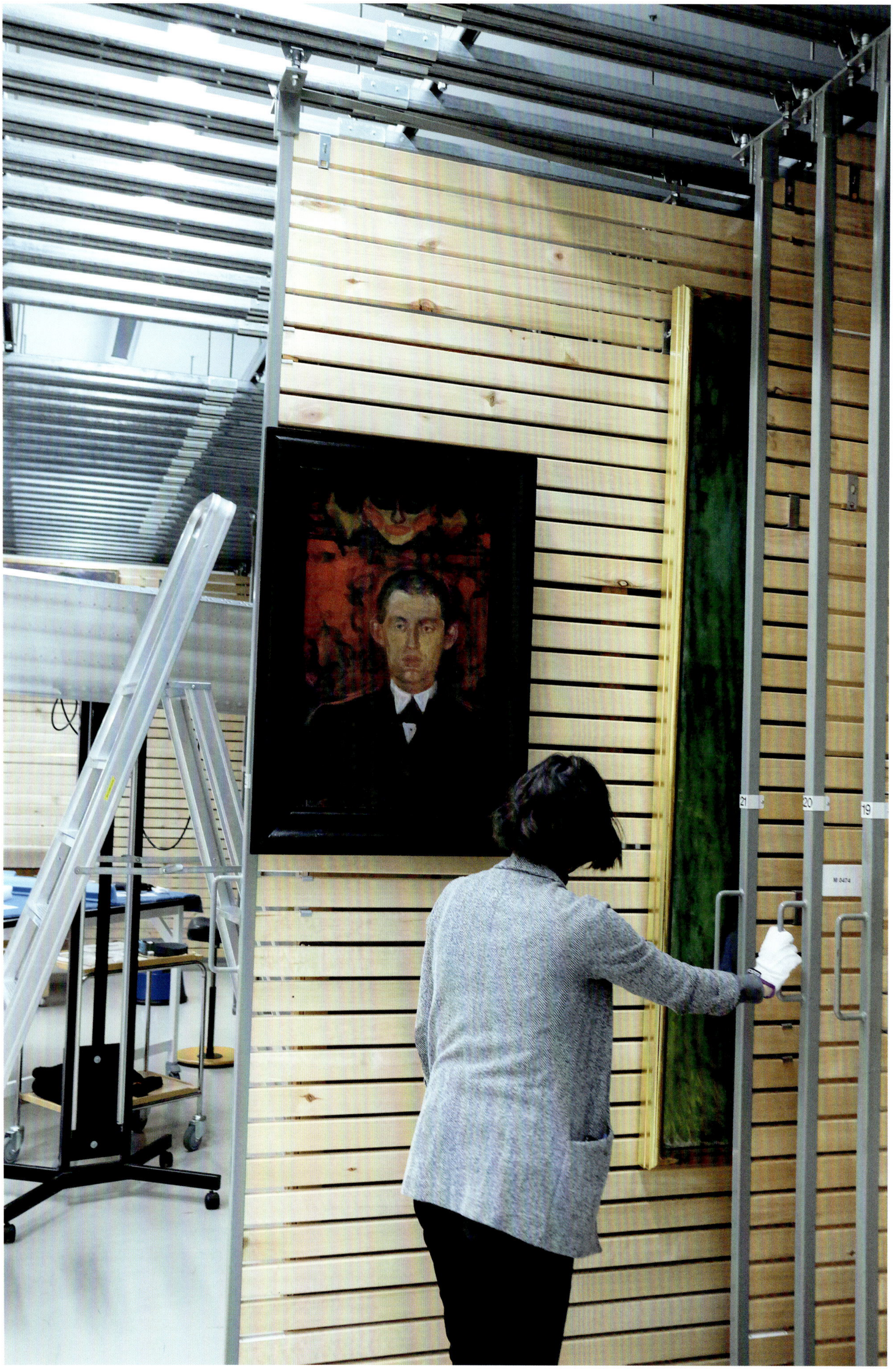

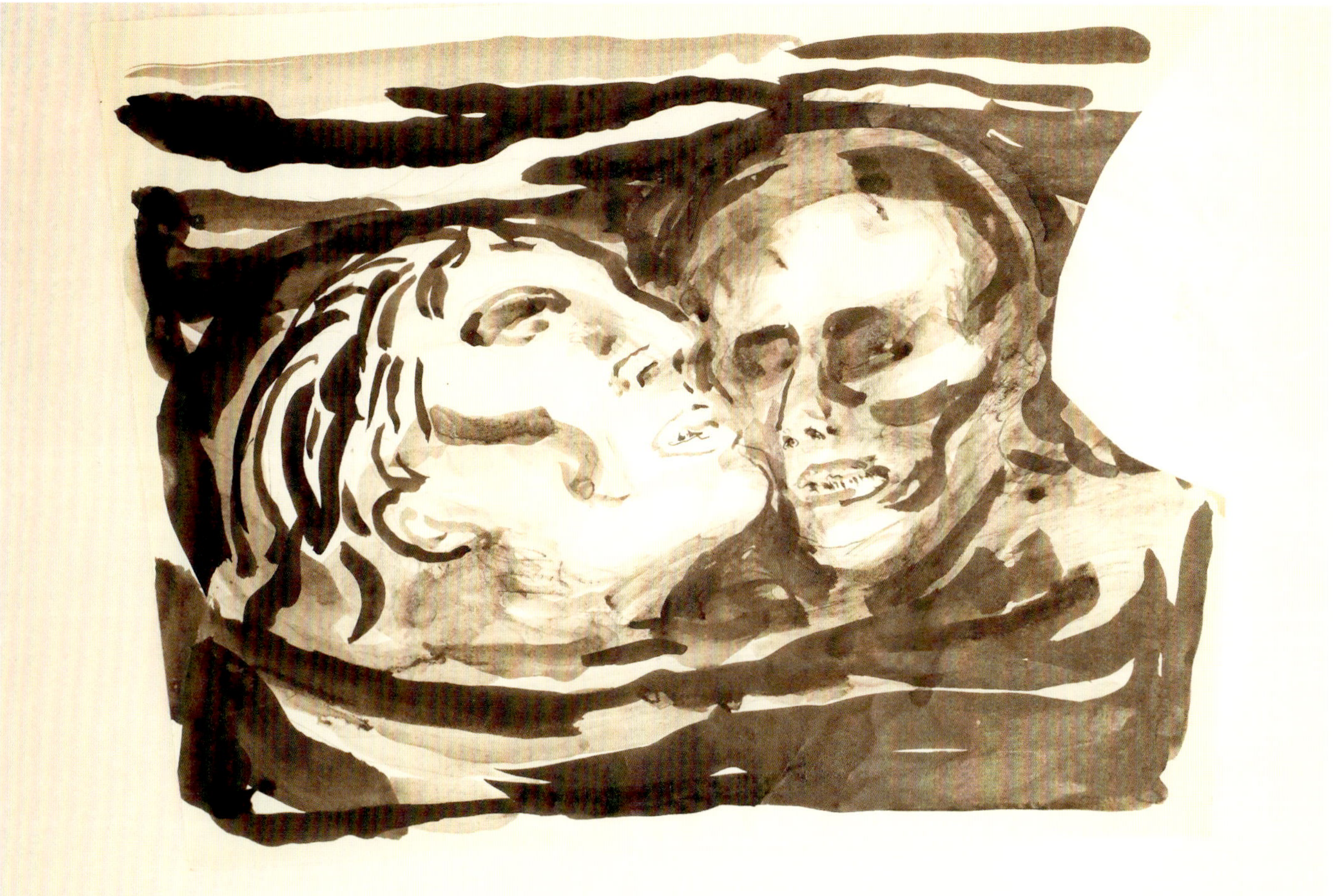

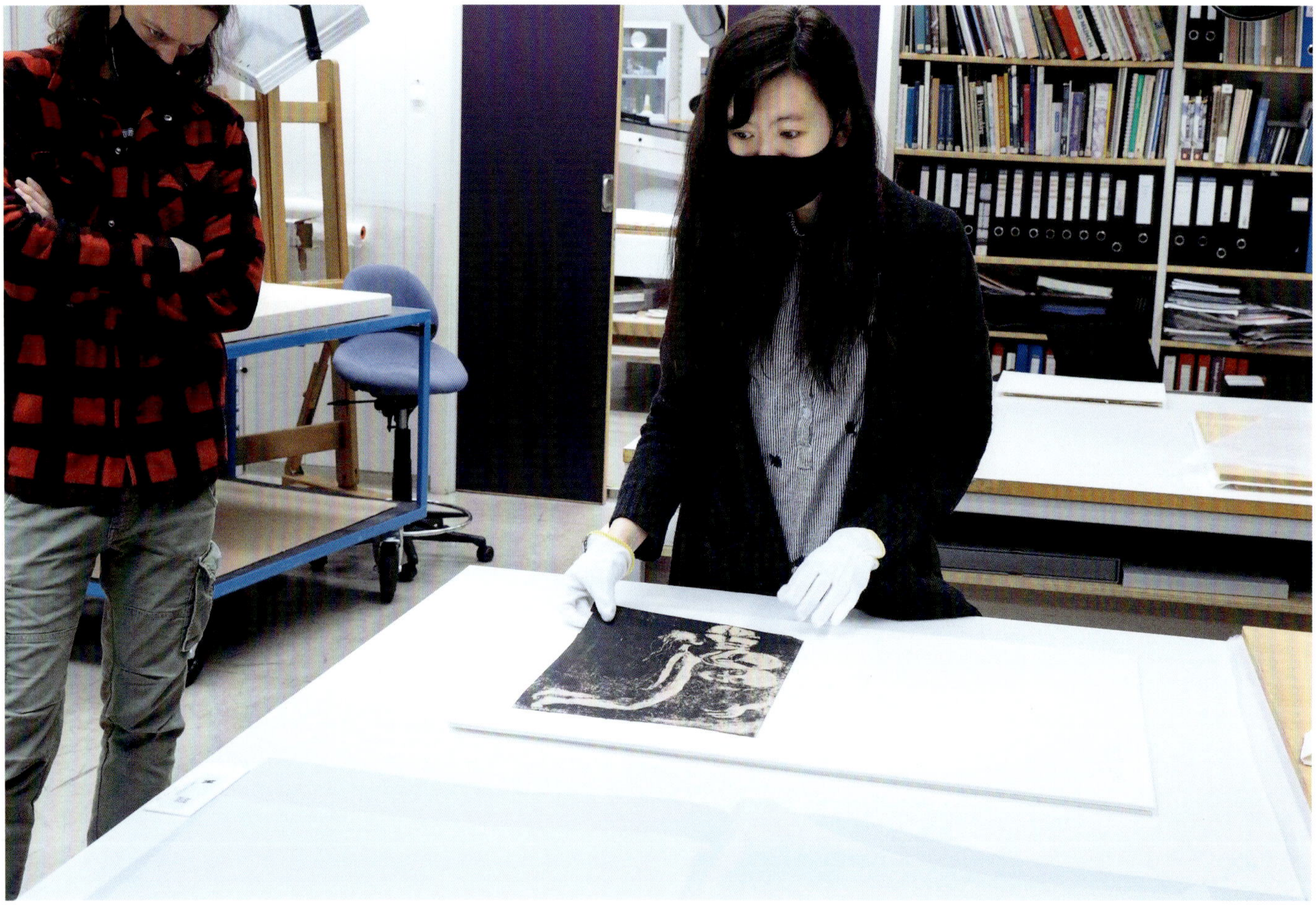

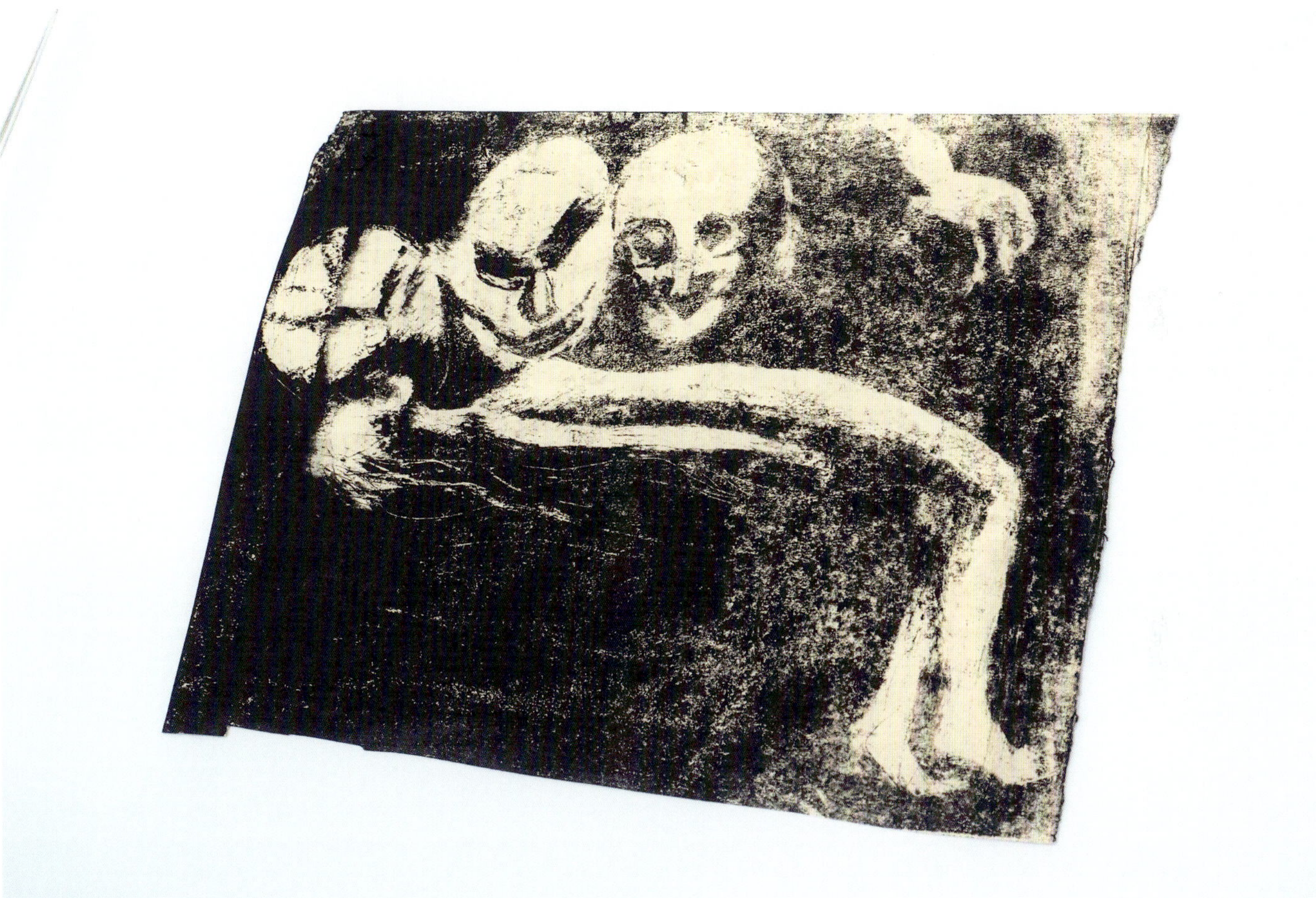

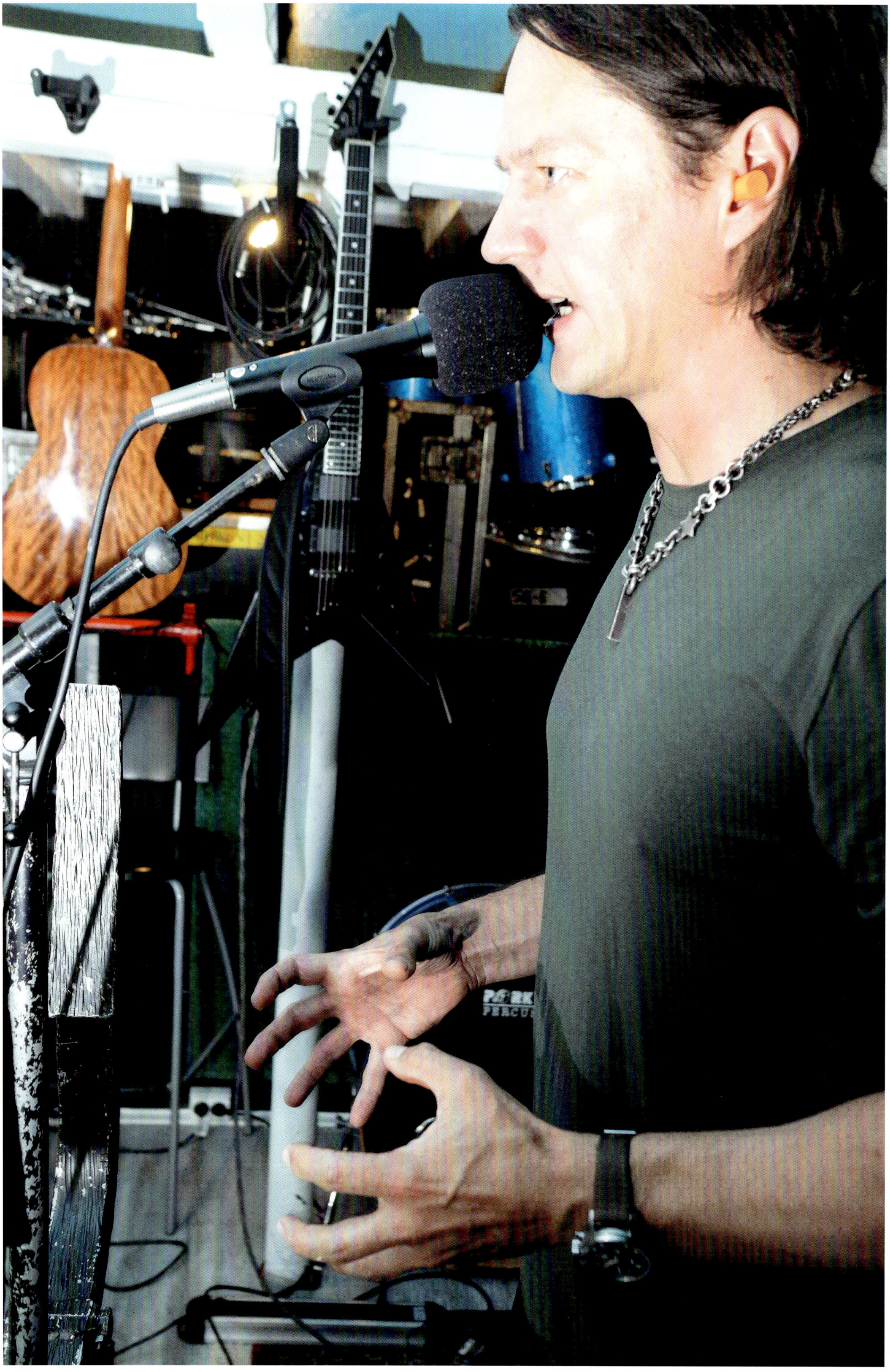

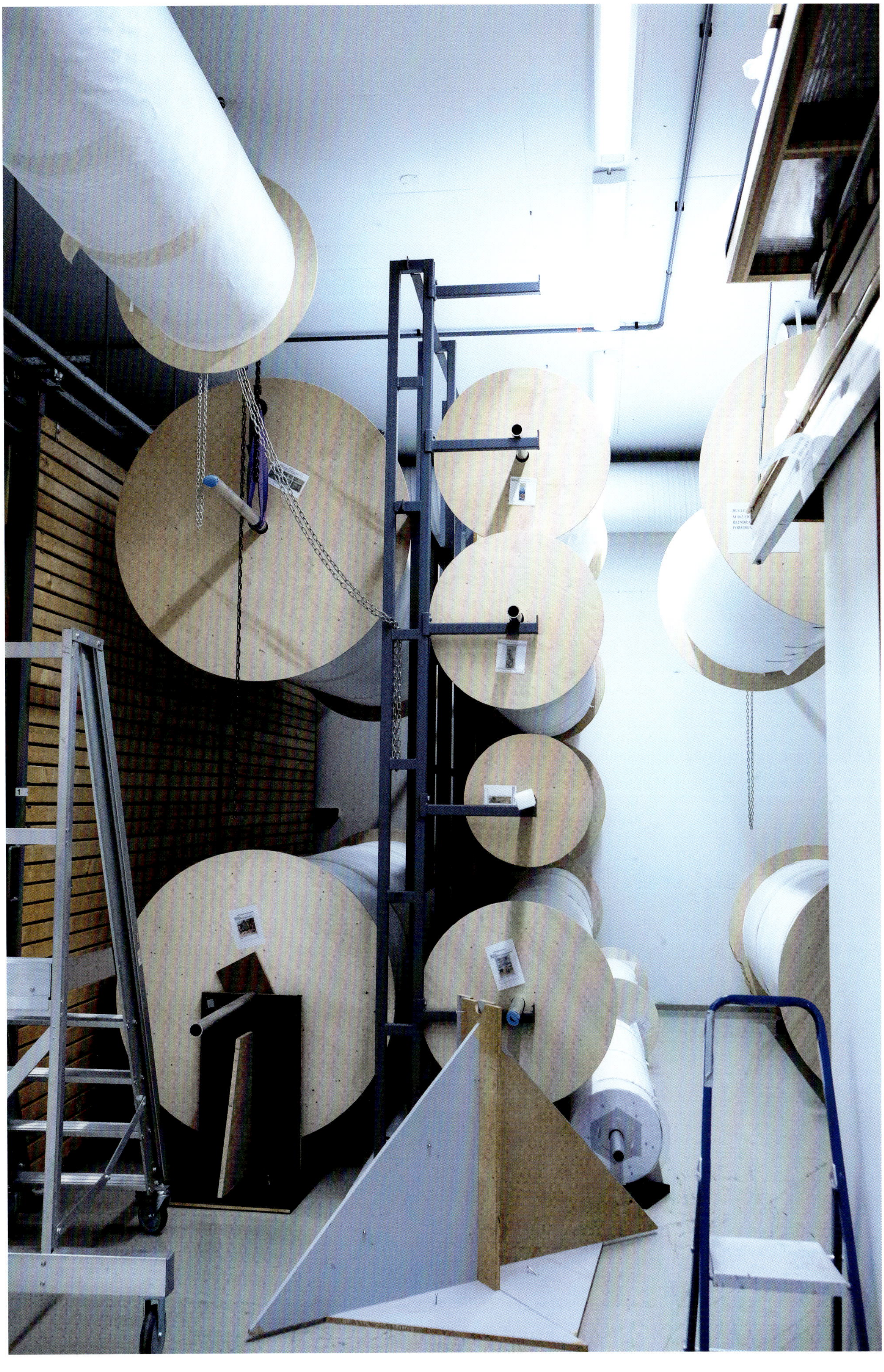

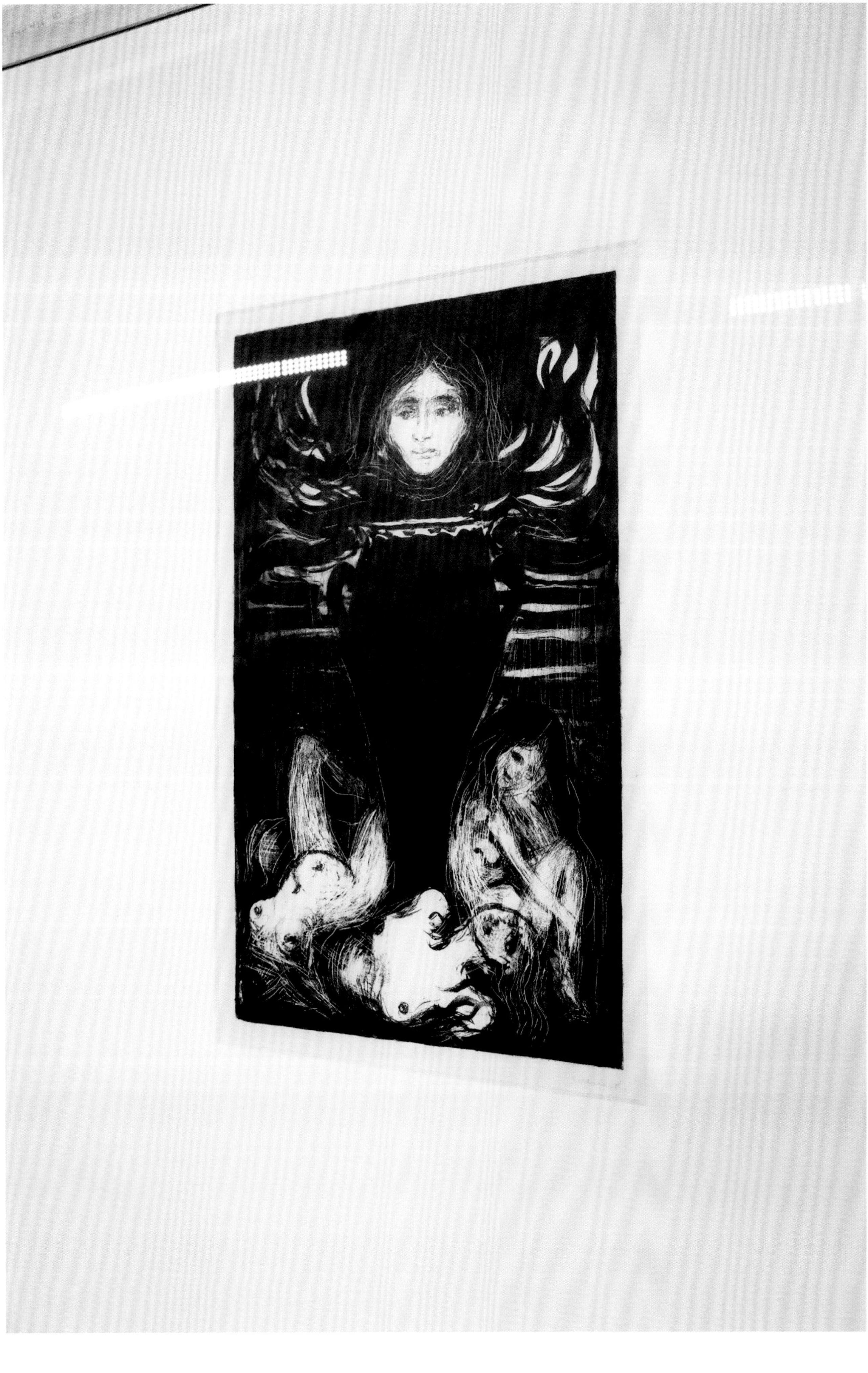

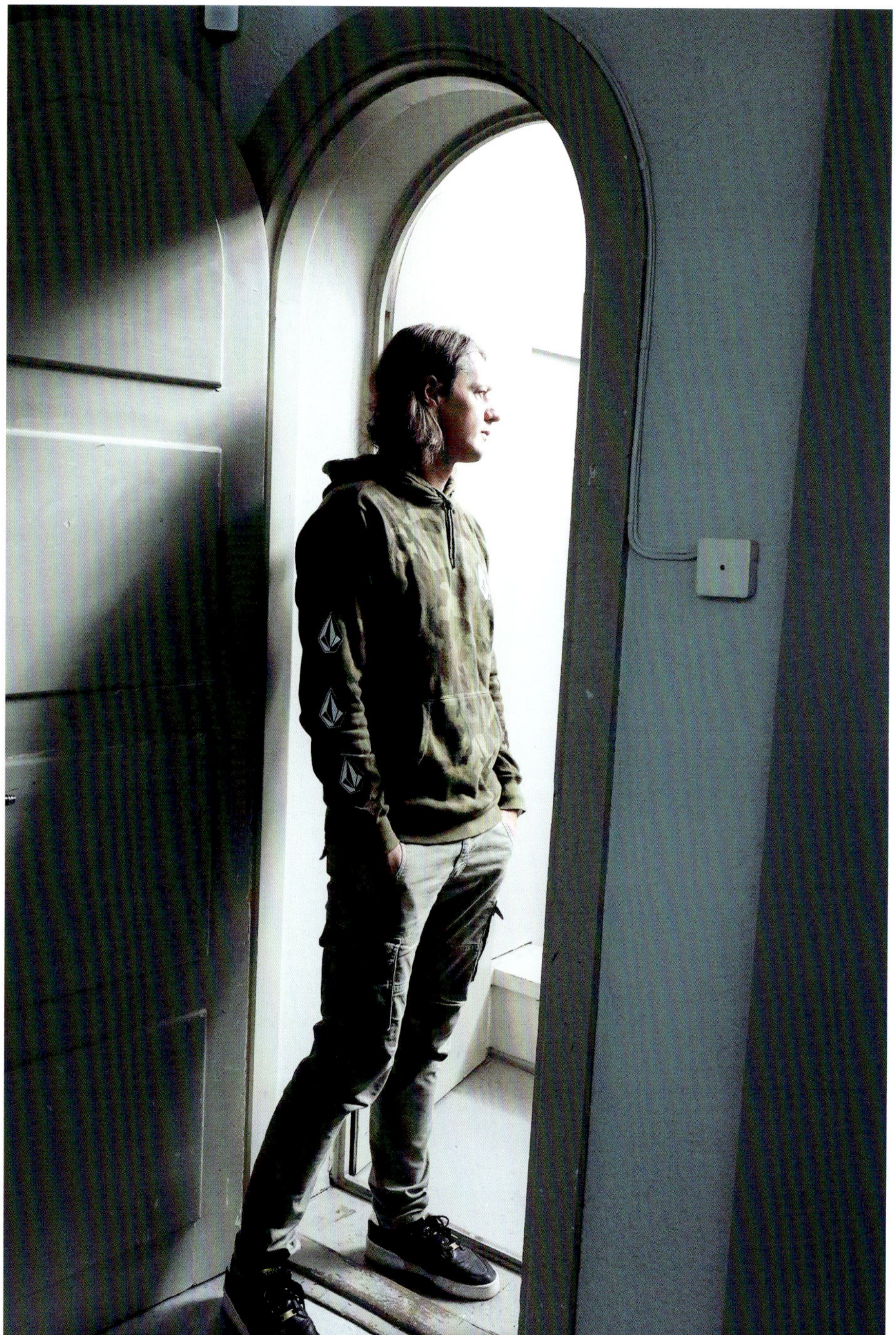

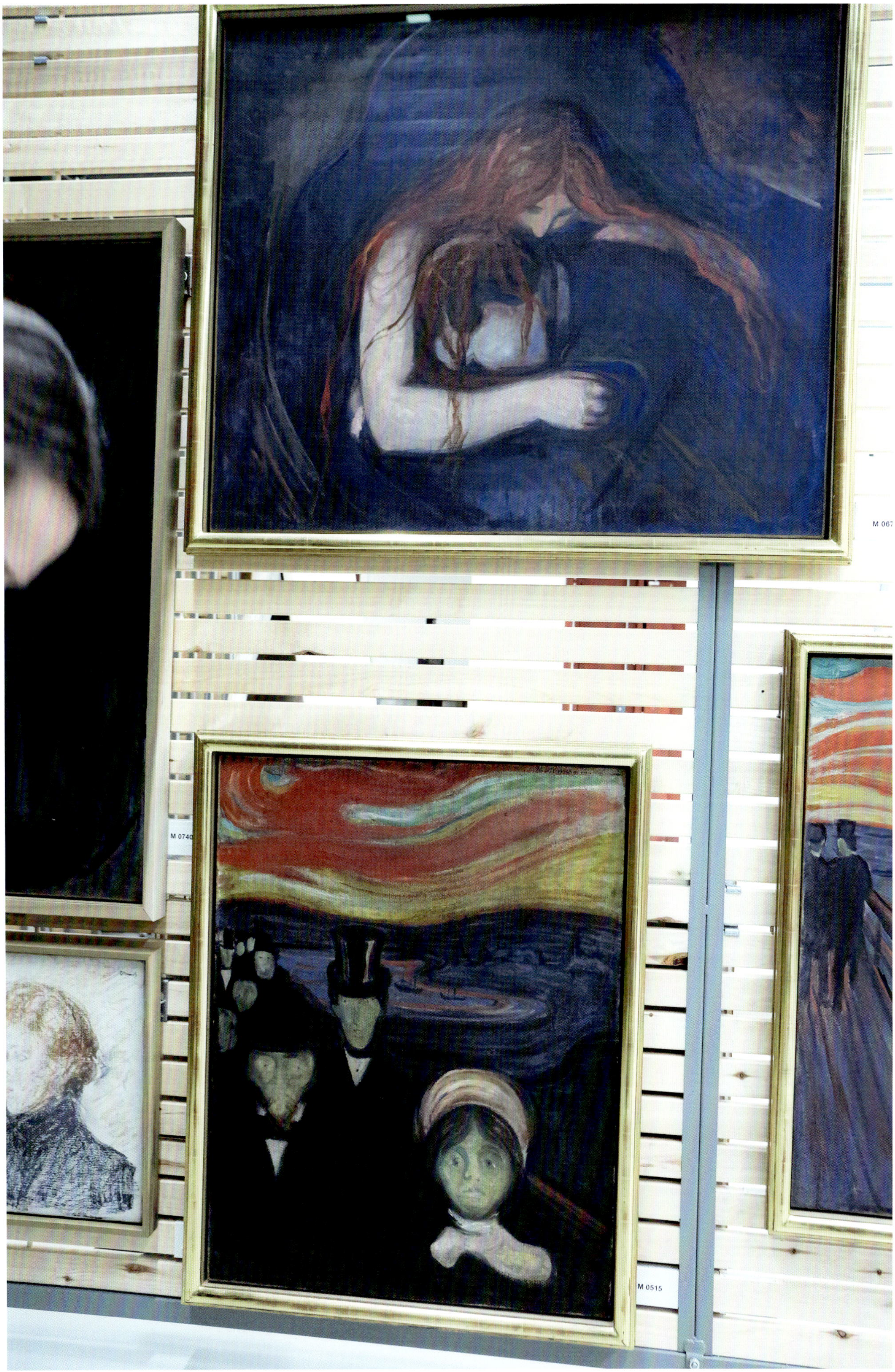

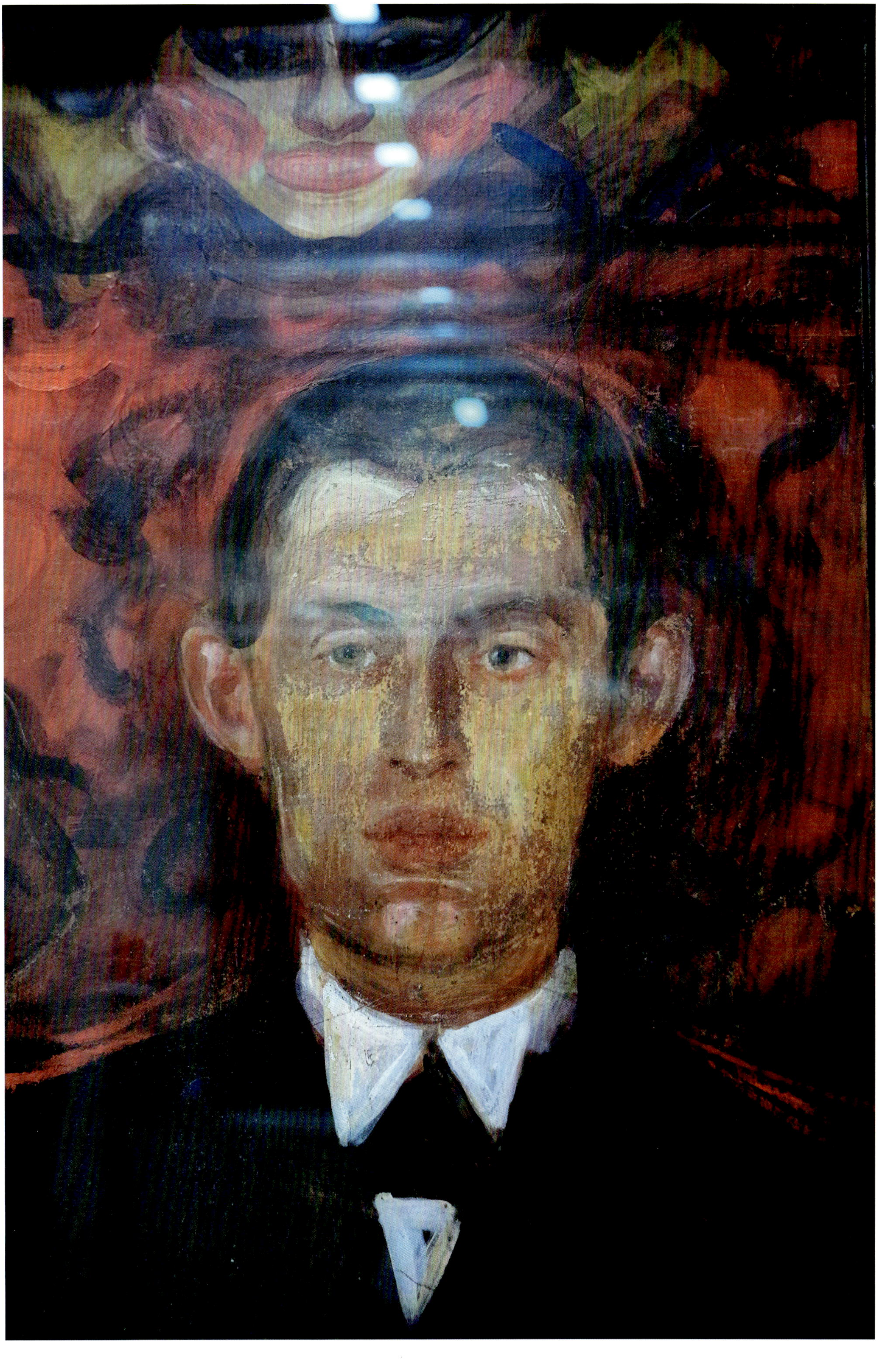

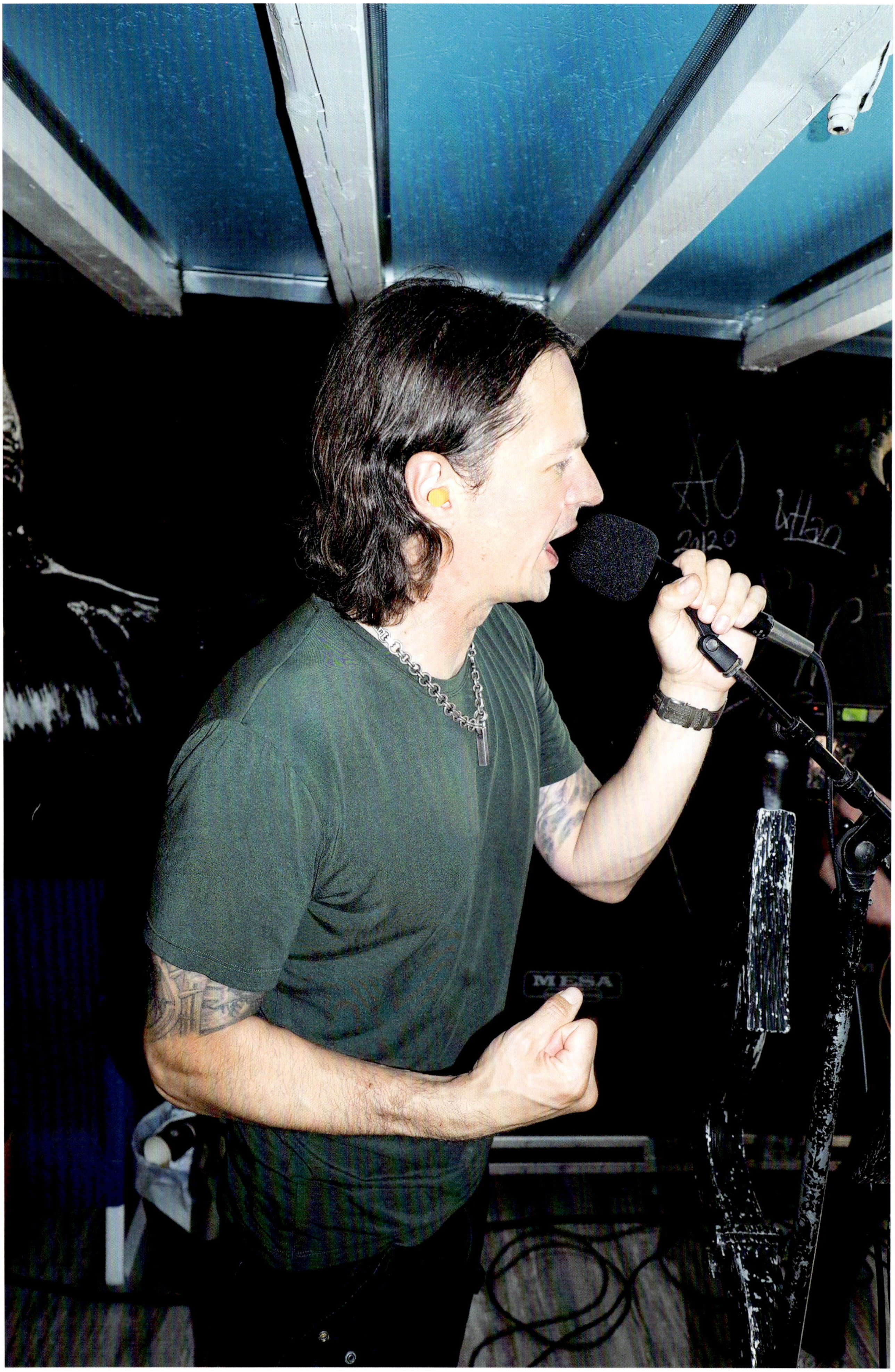

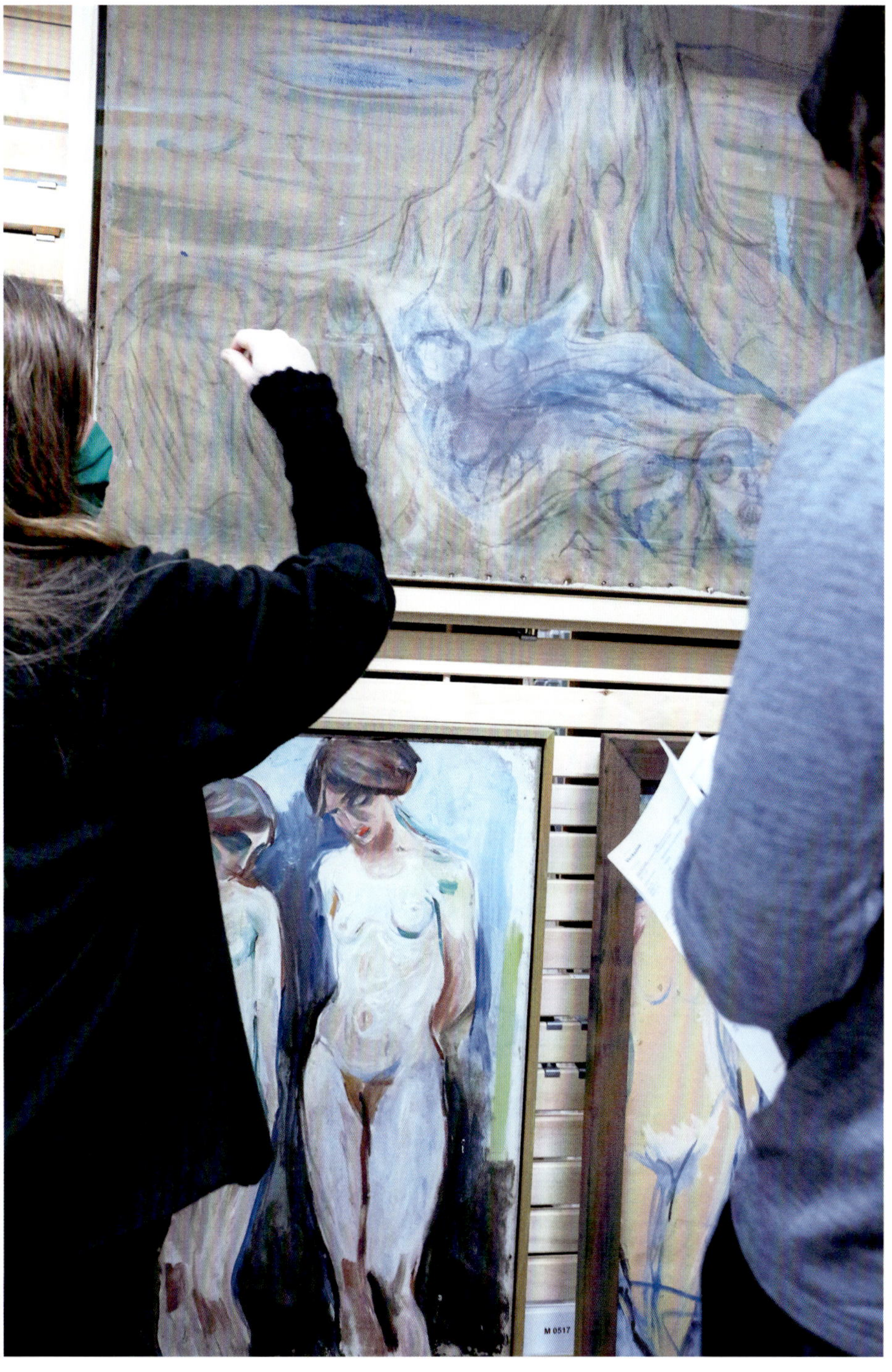

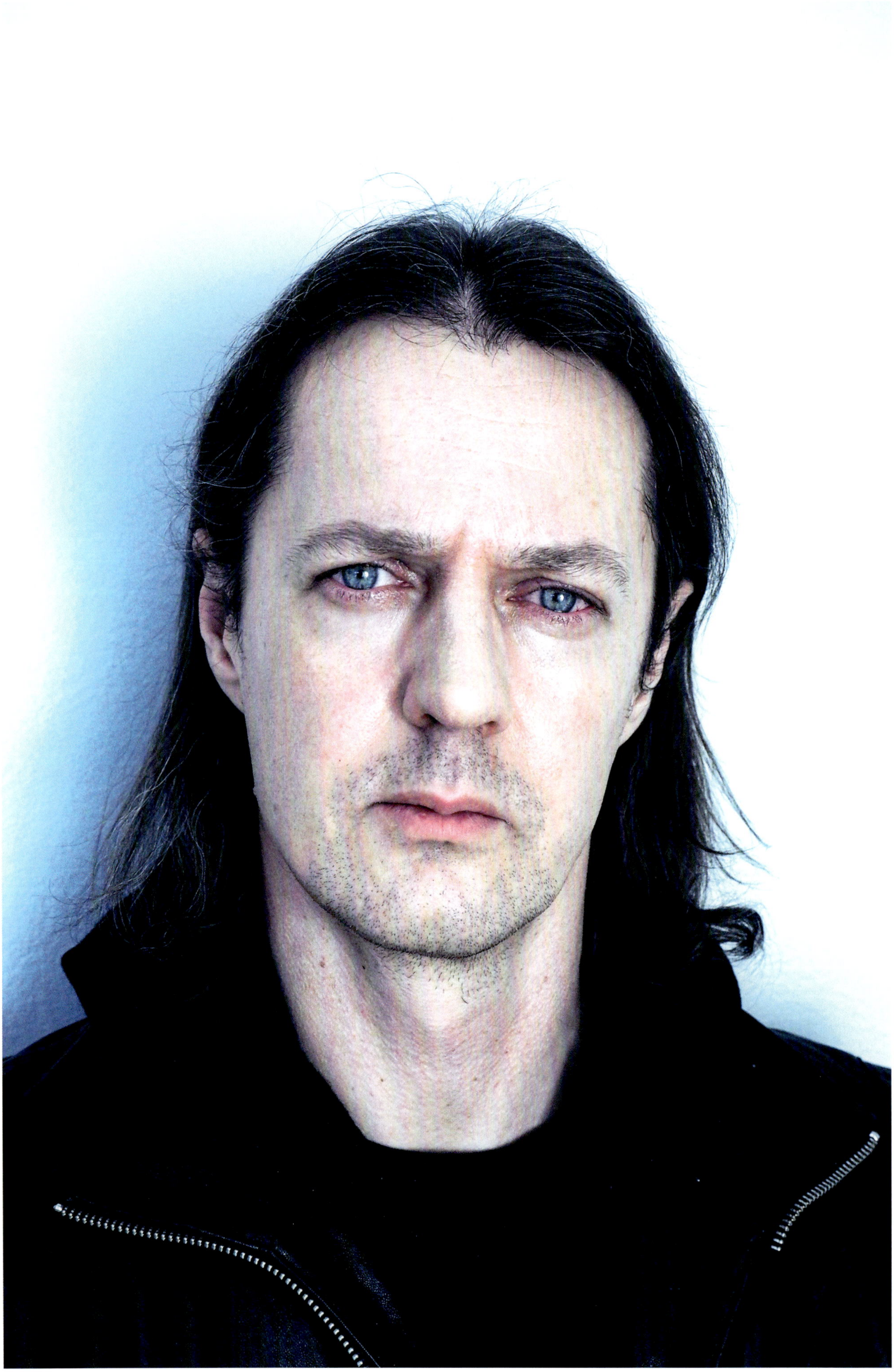

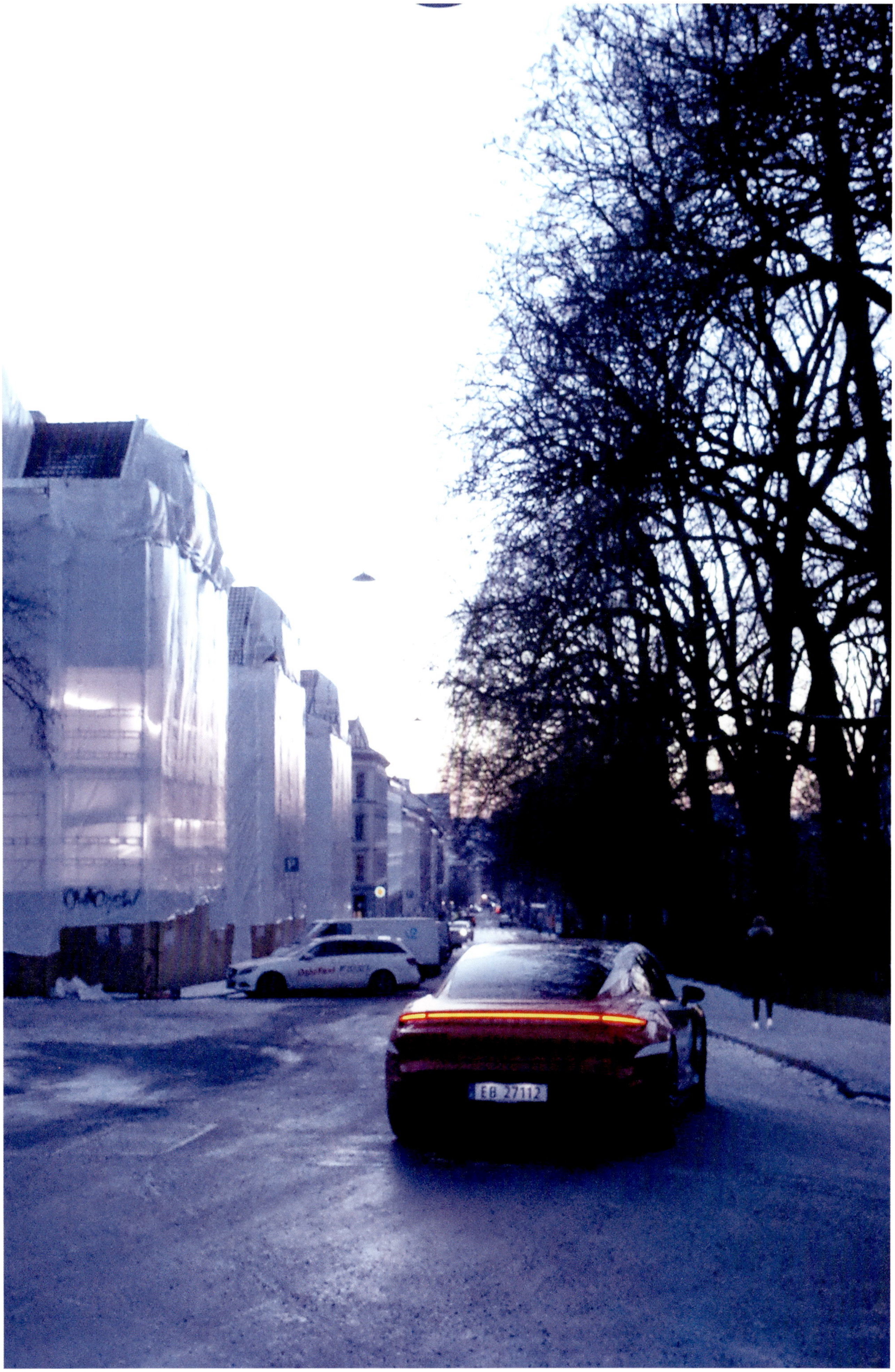
EB 27112

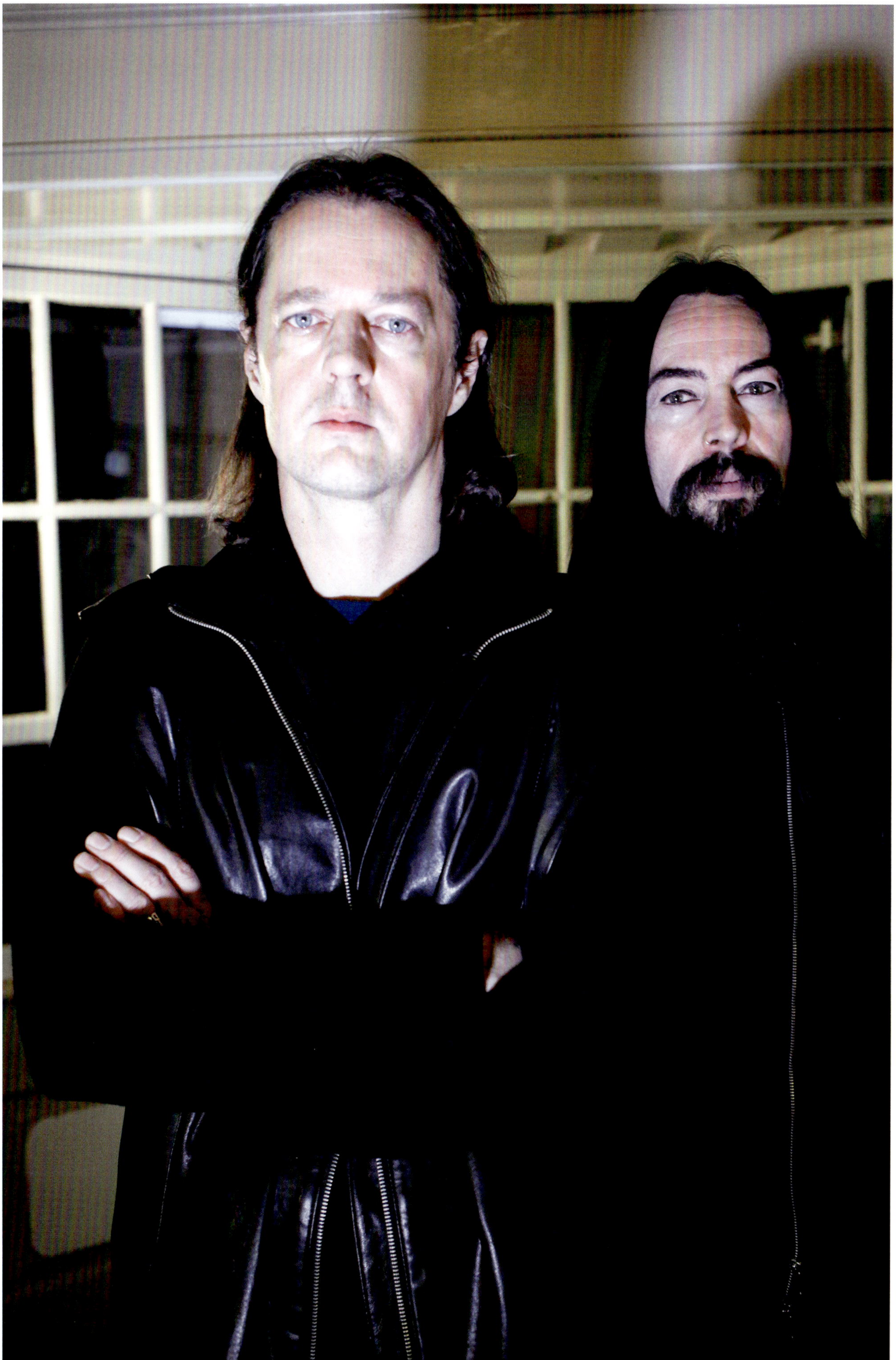

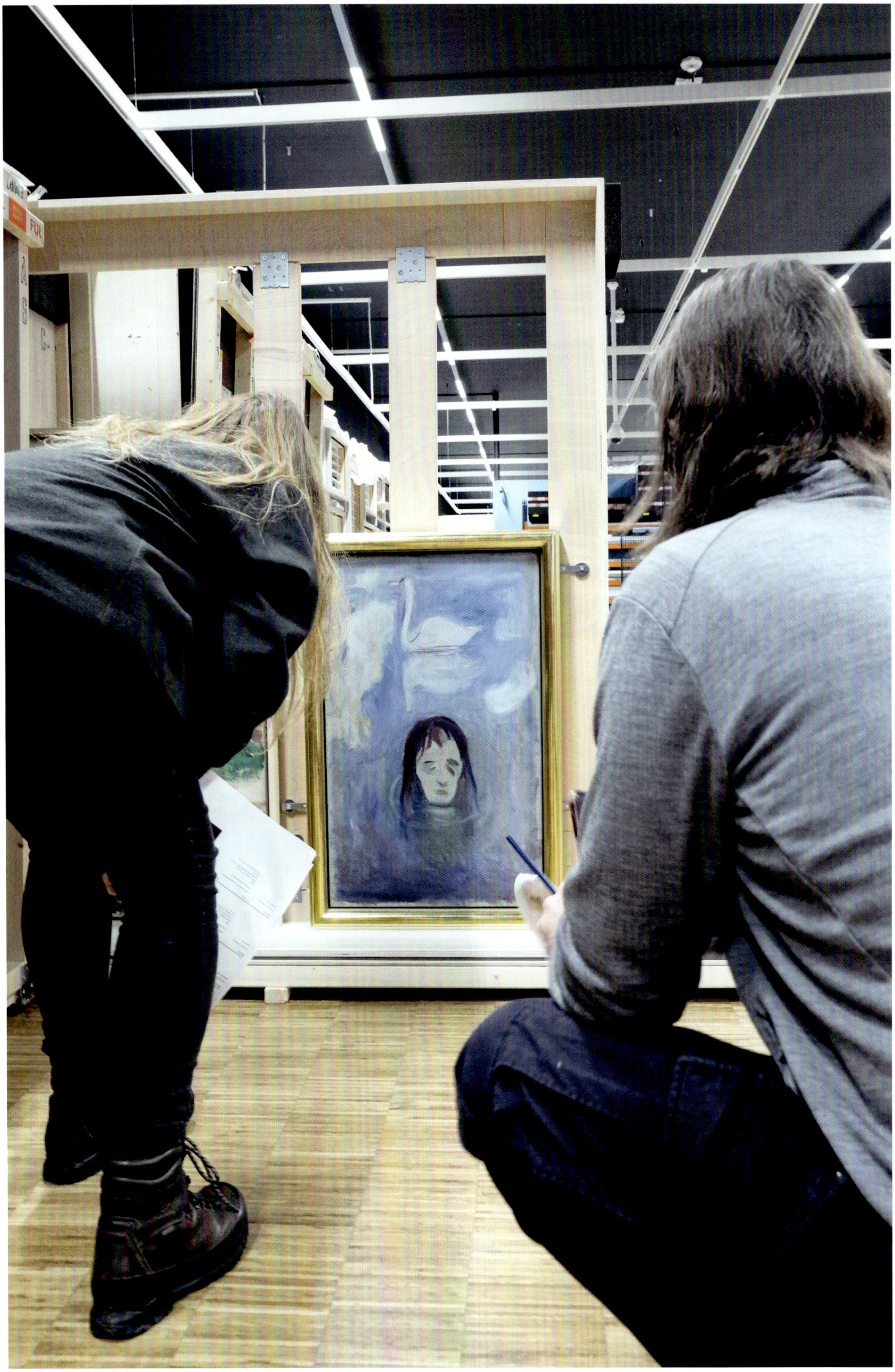

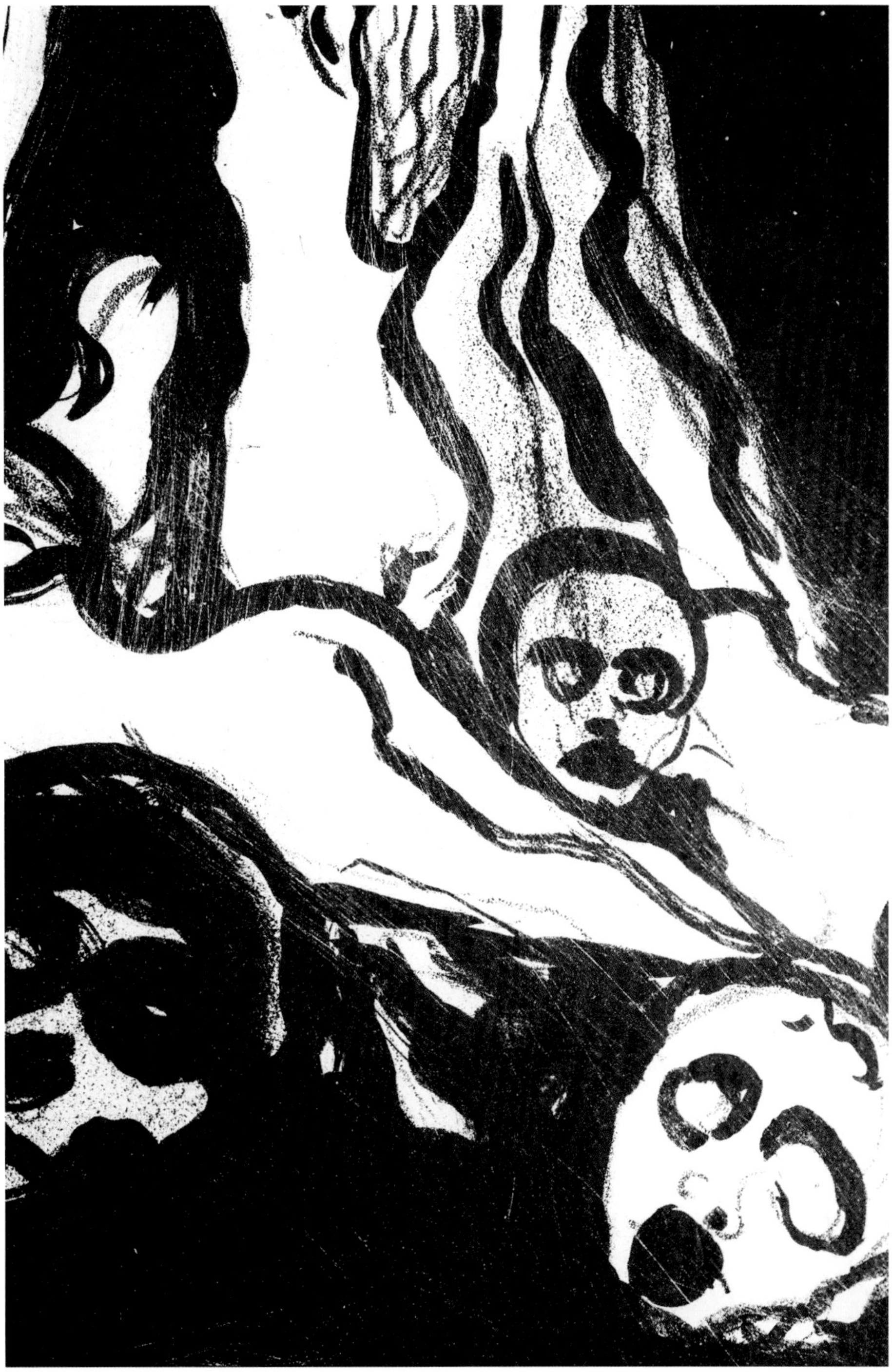

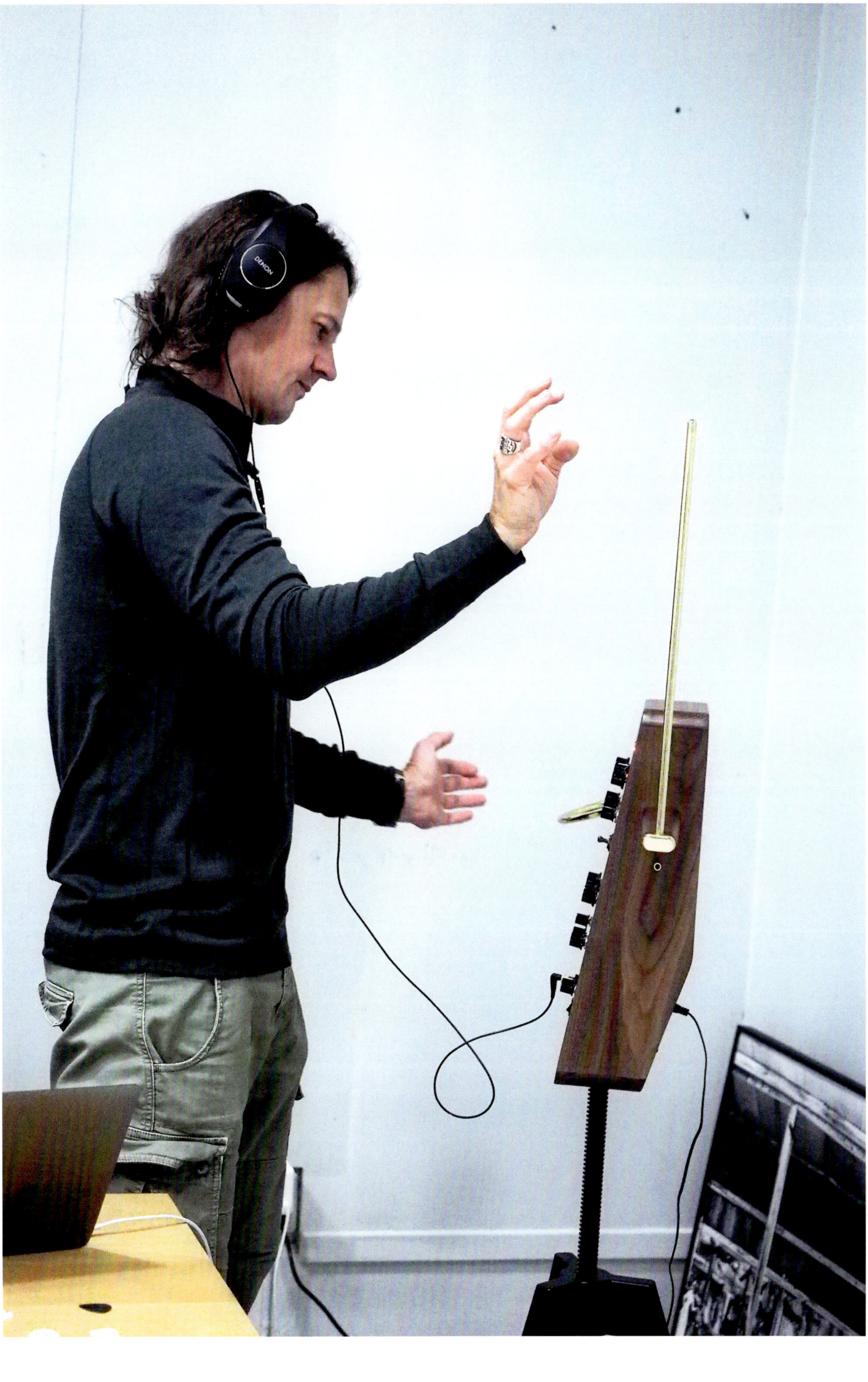
DENON

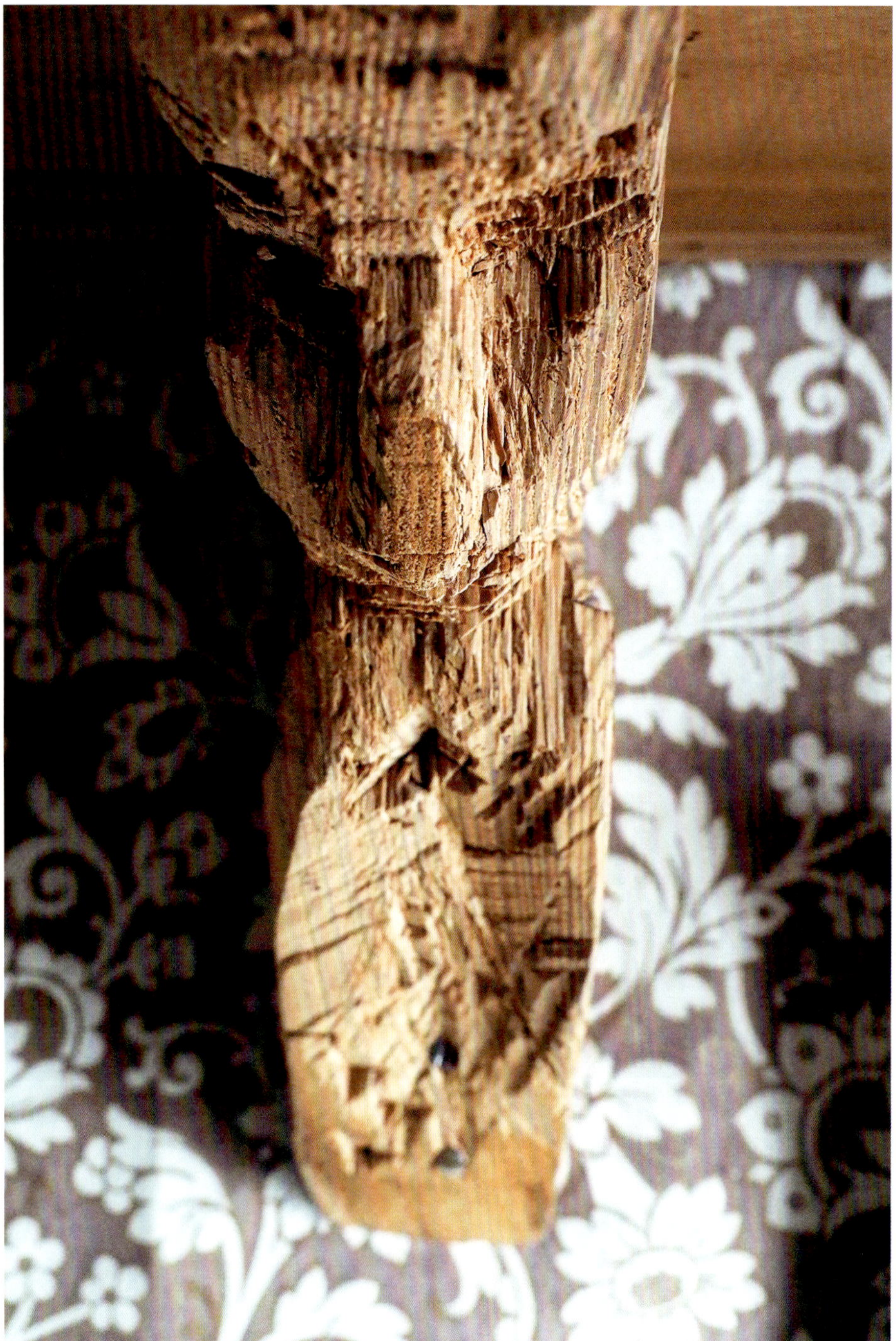

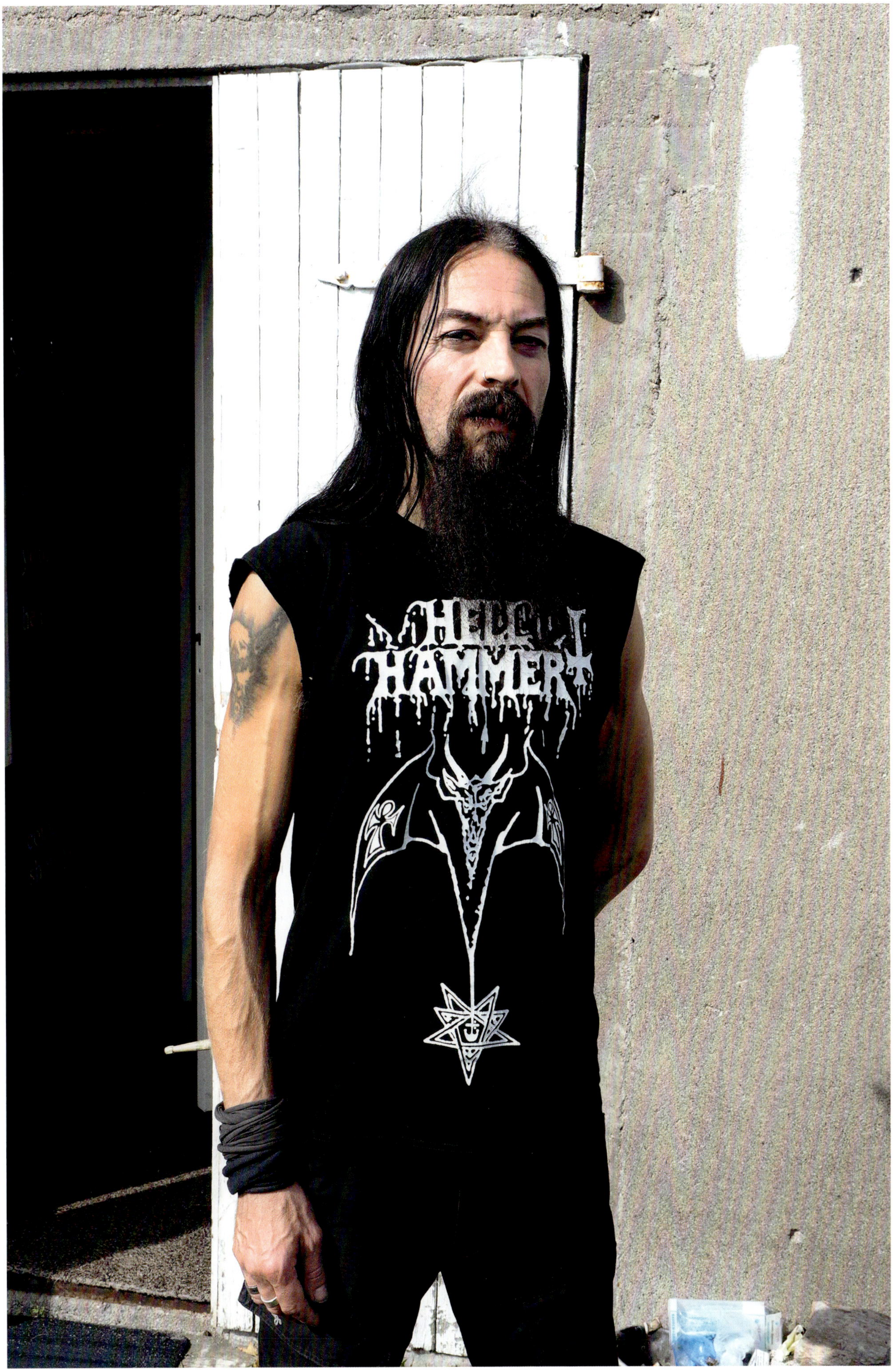
HELLHAMMER

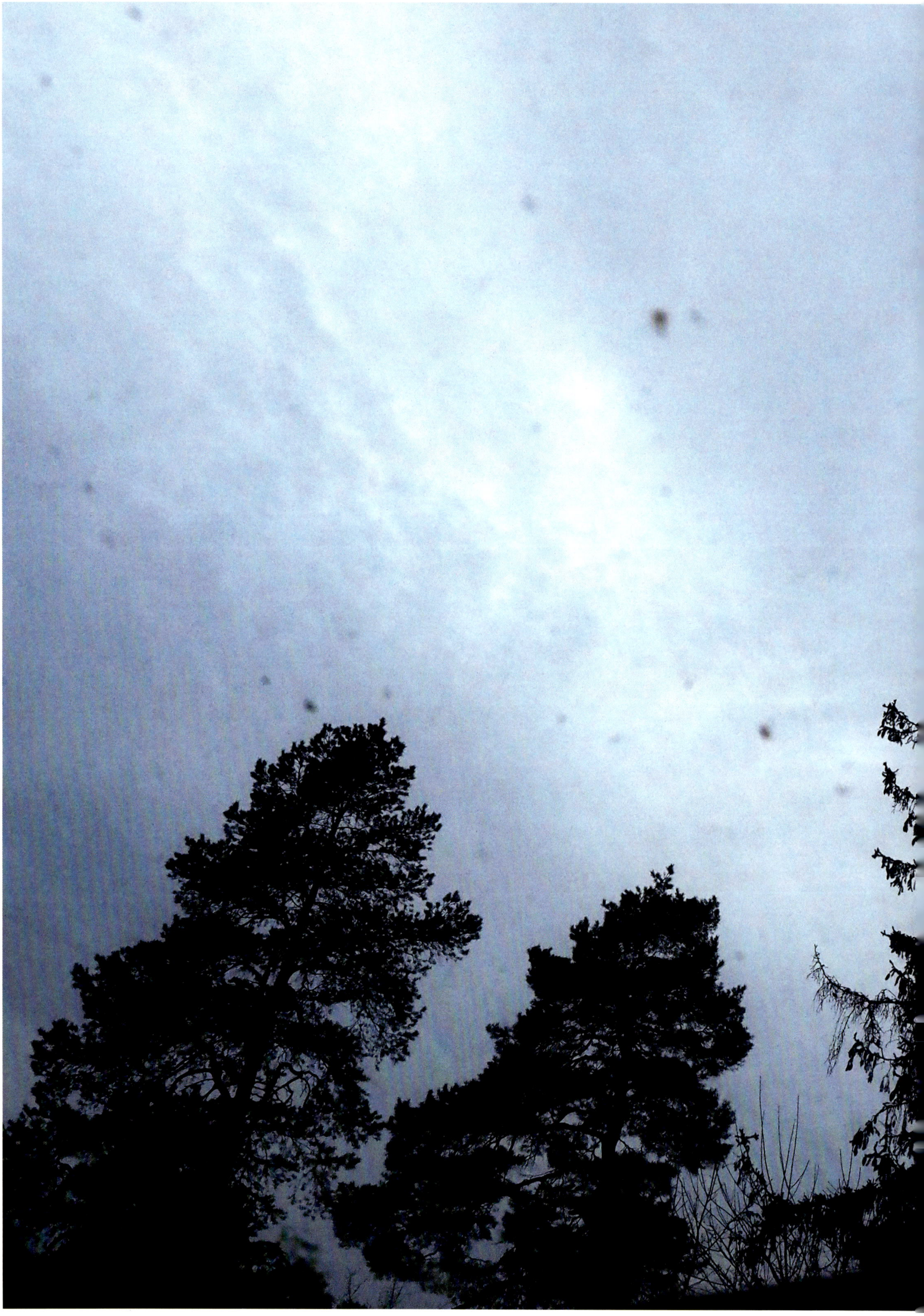

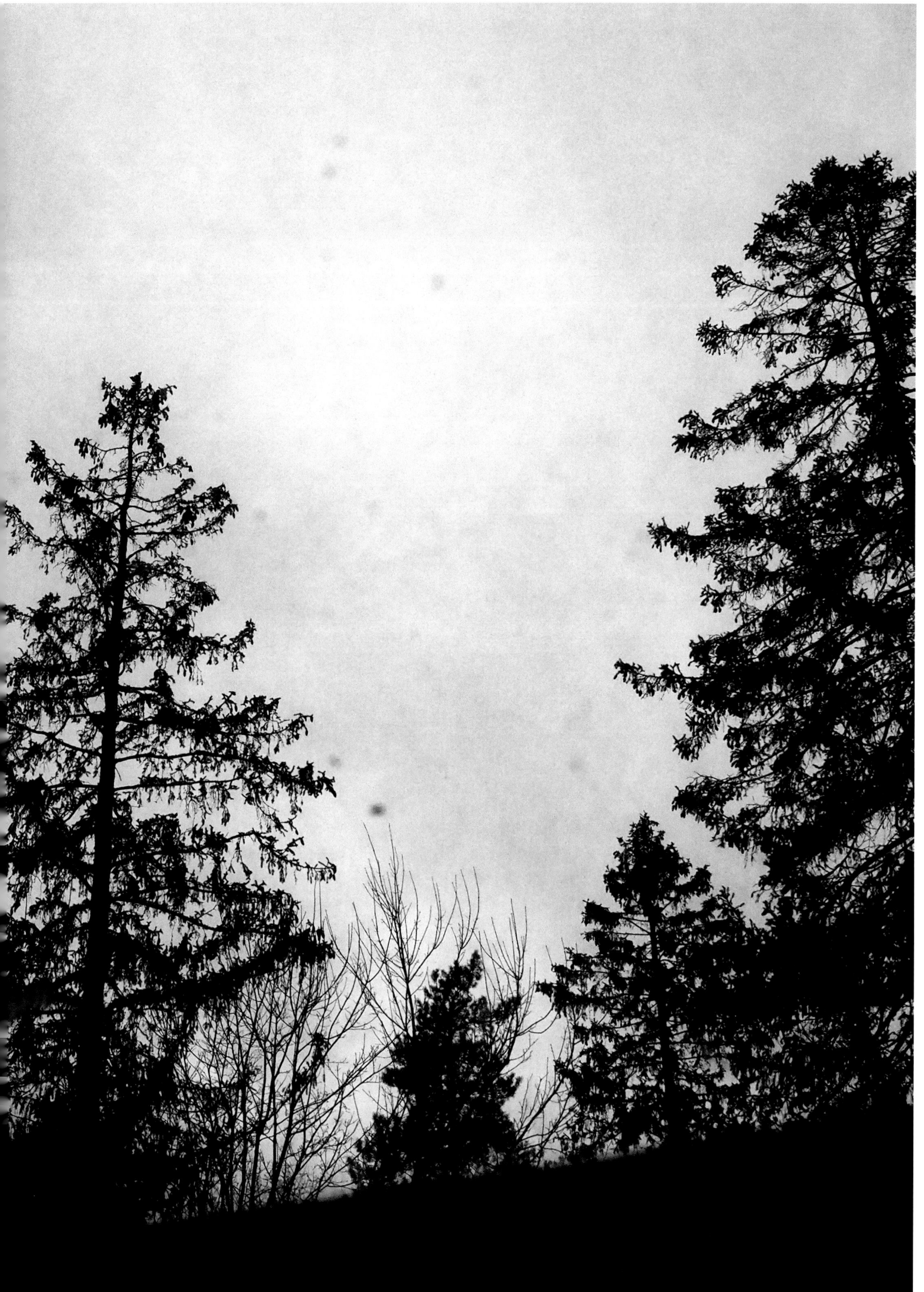

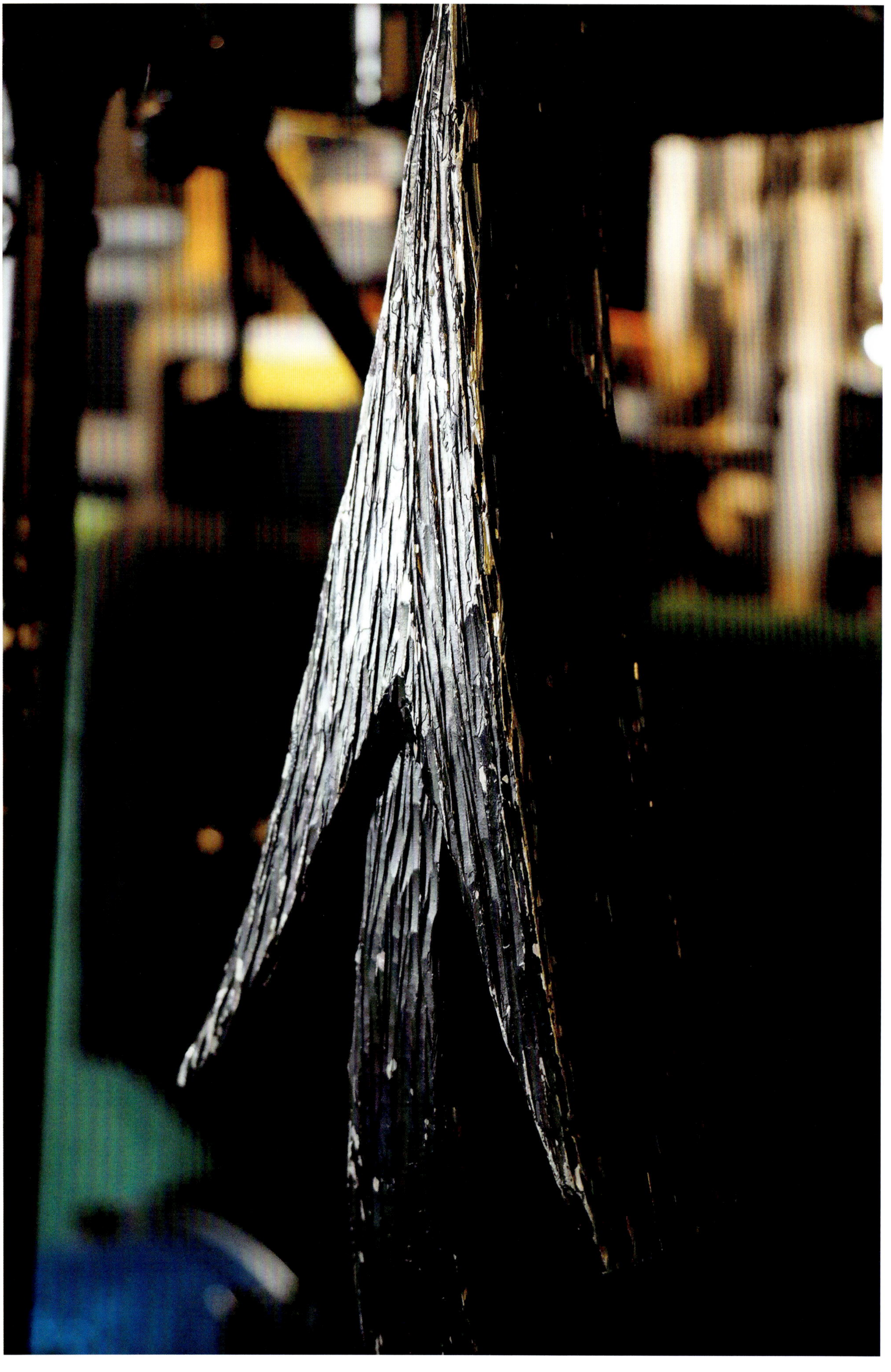

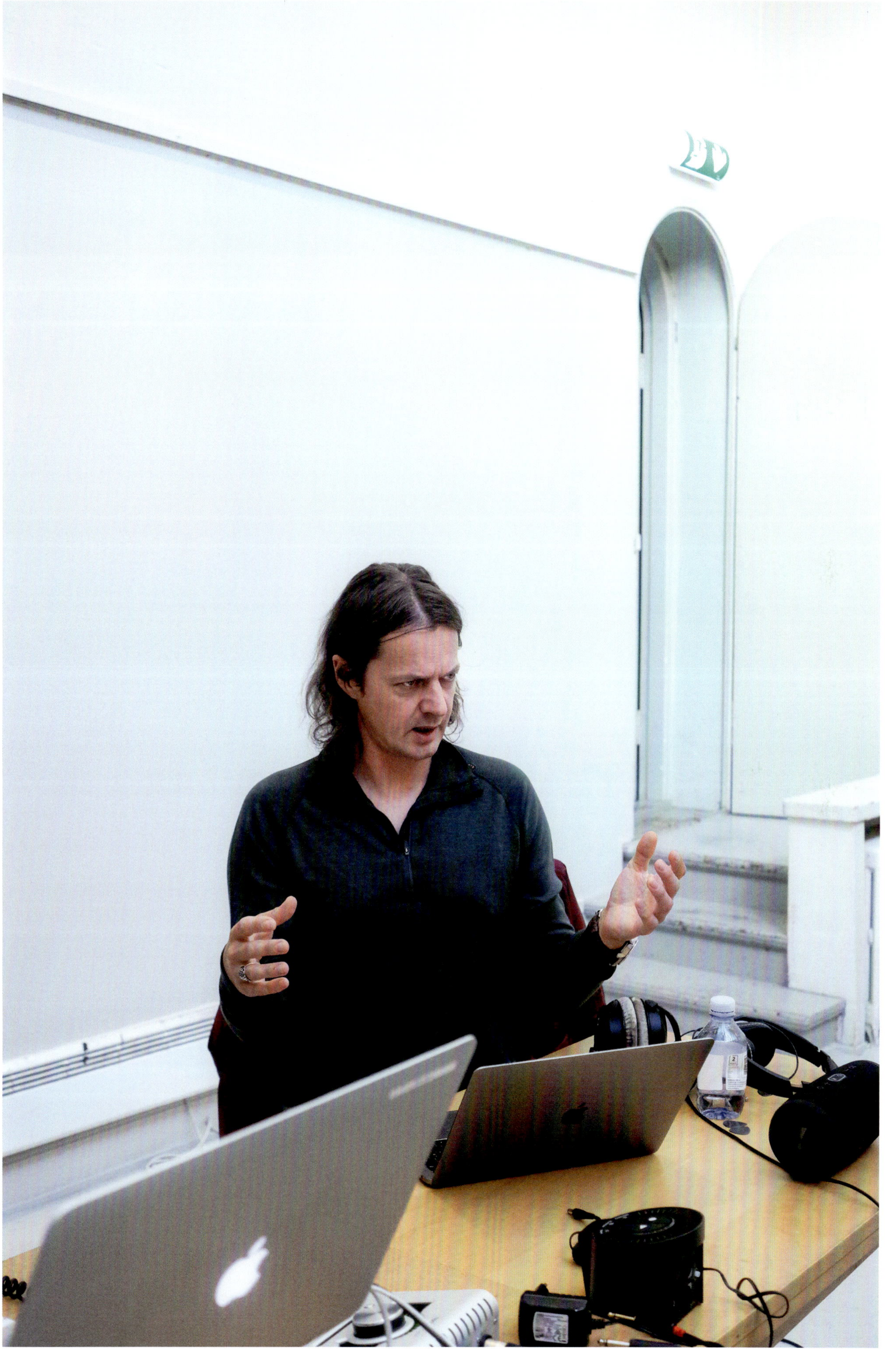

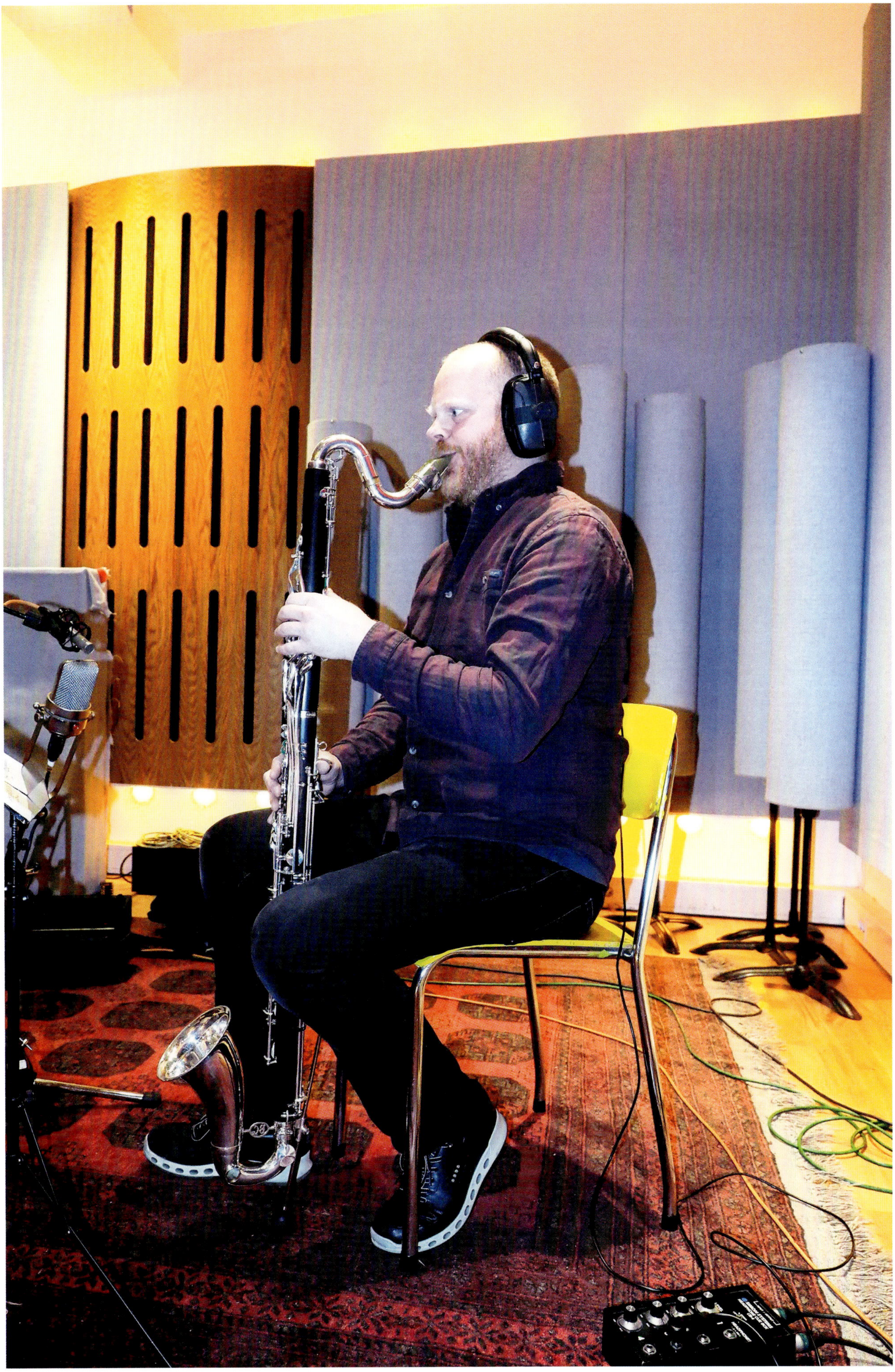

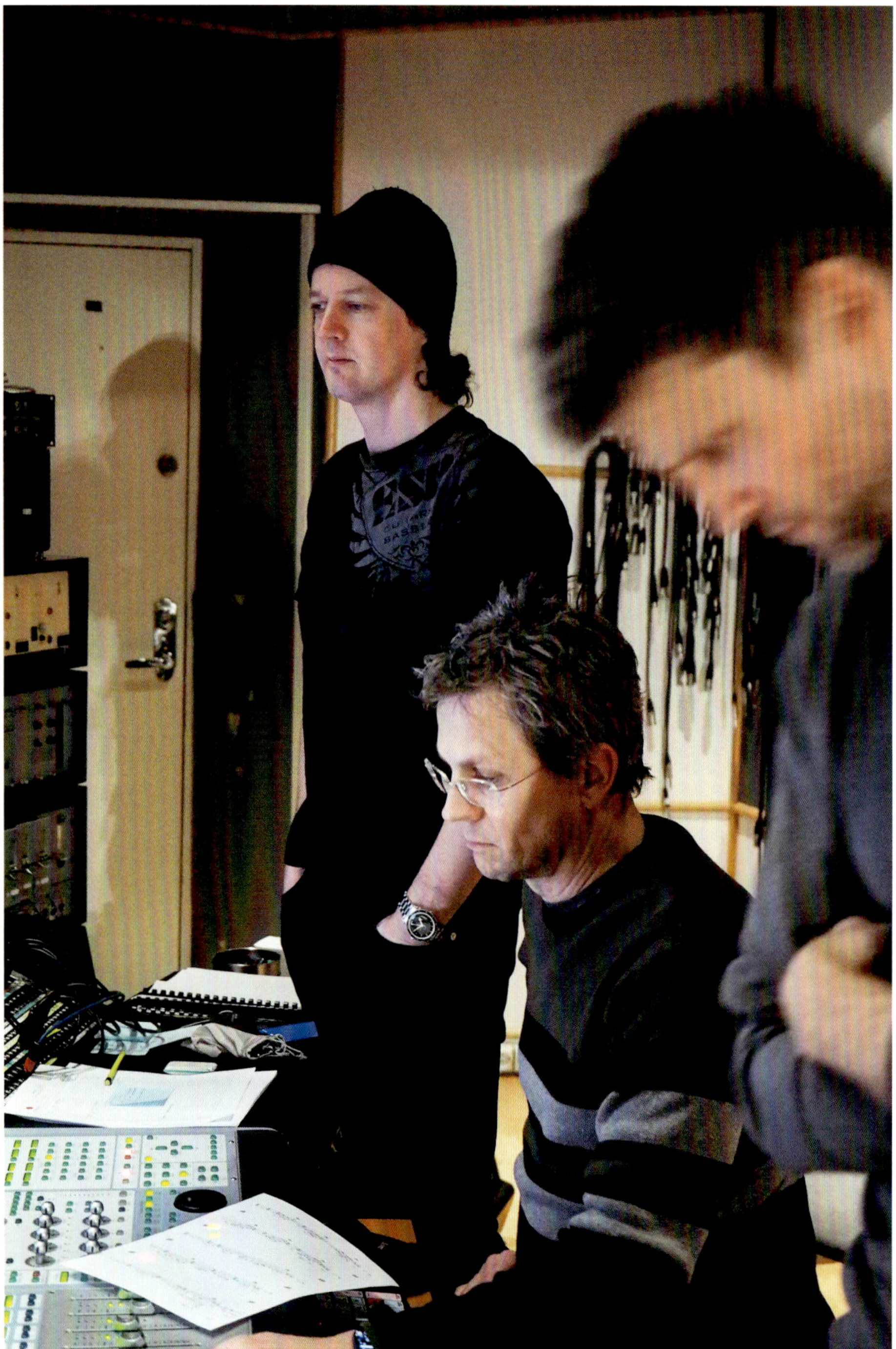

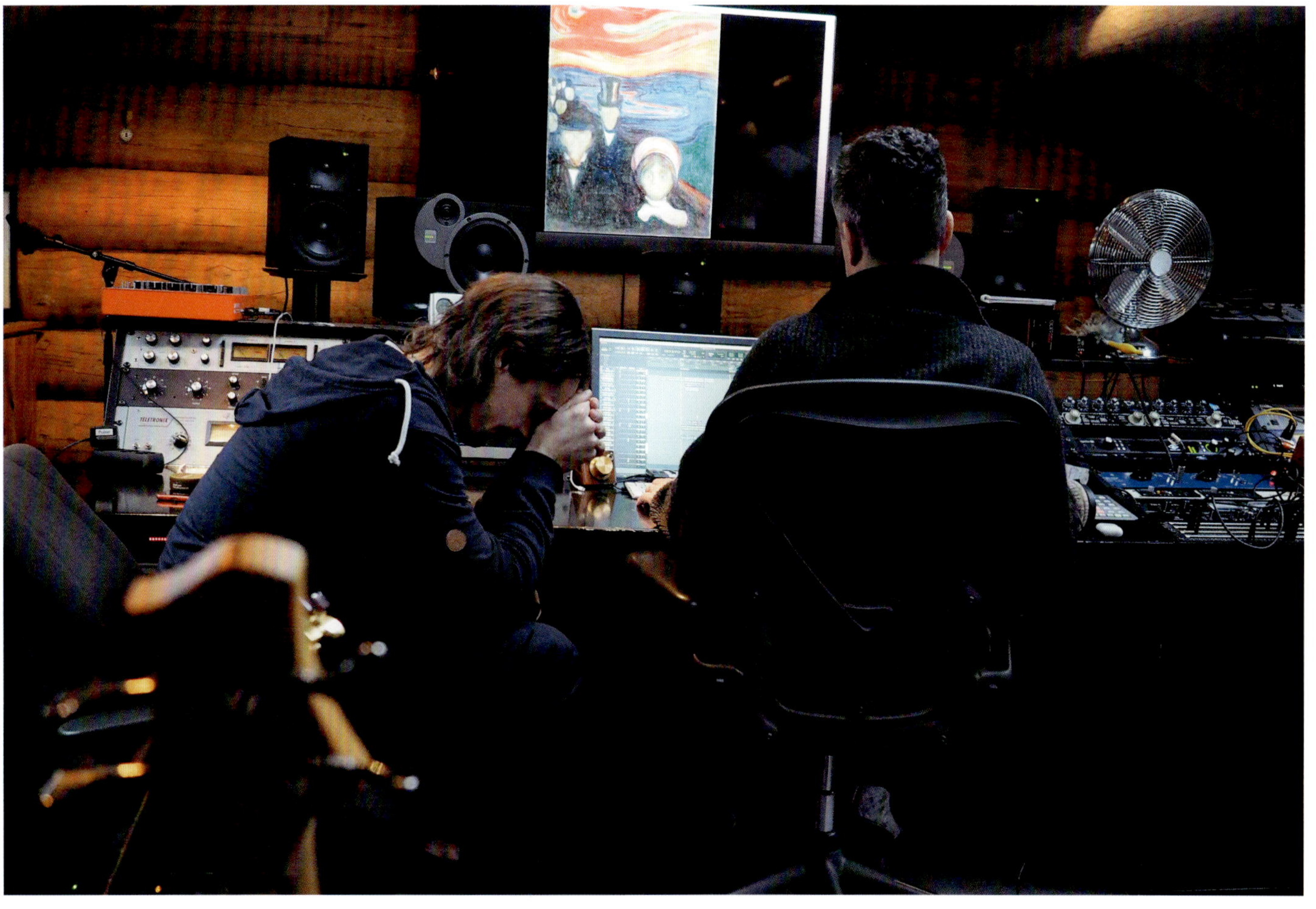

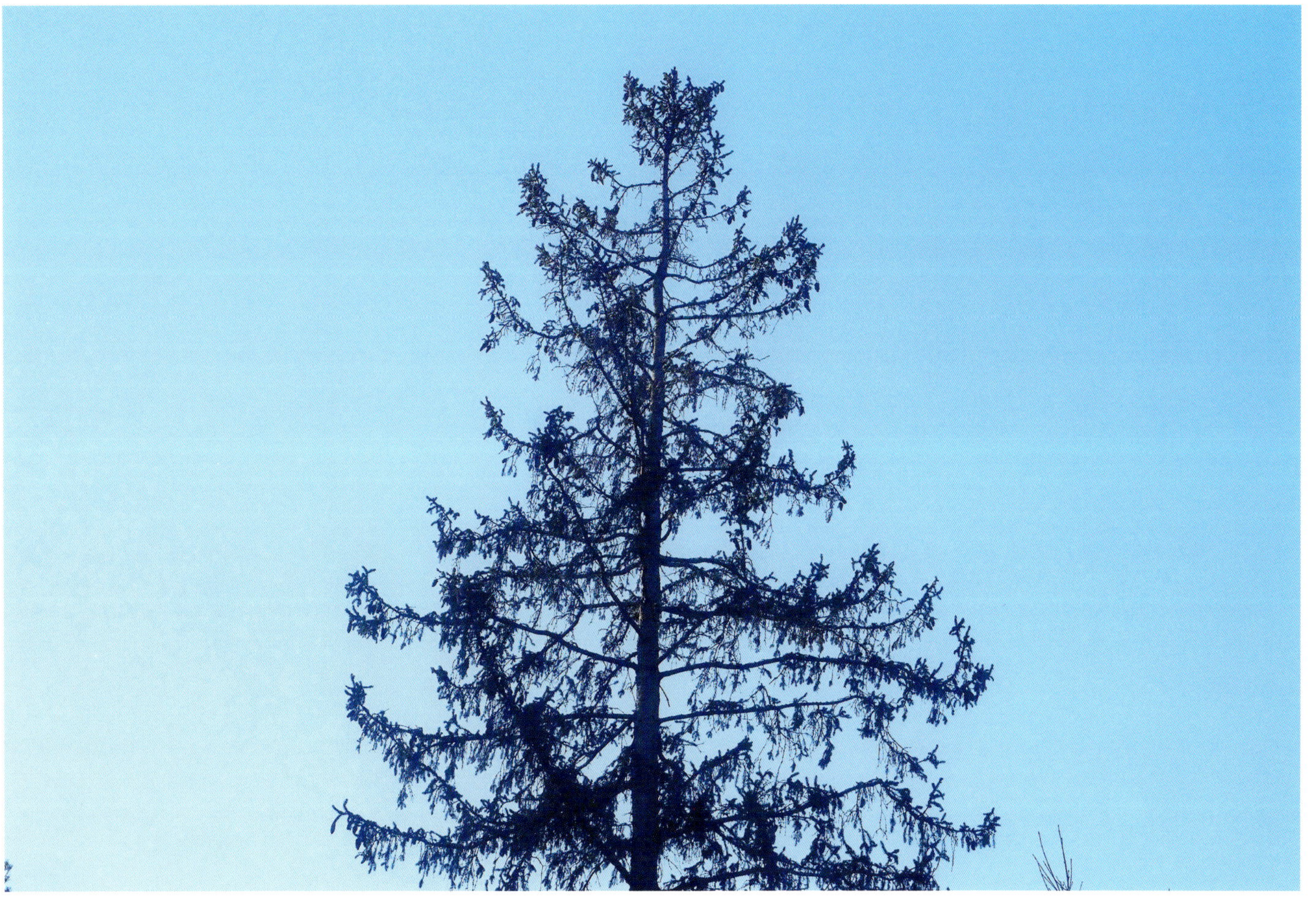

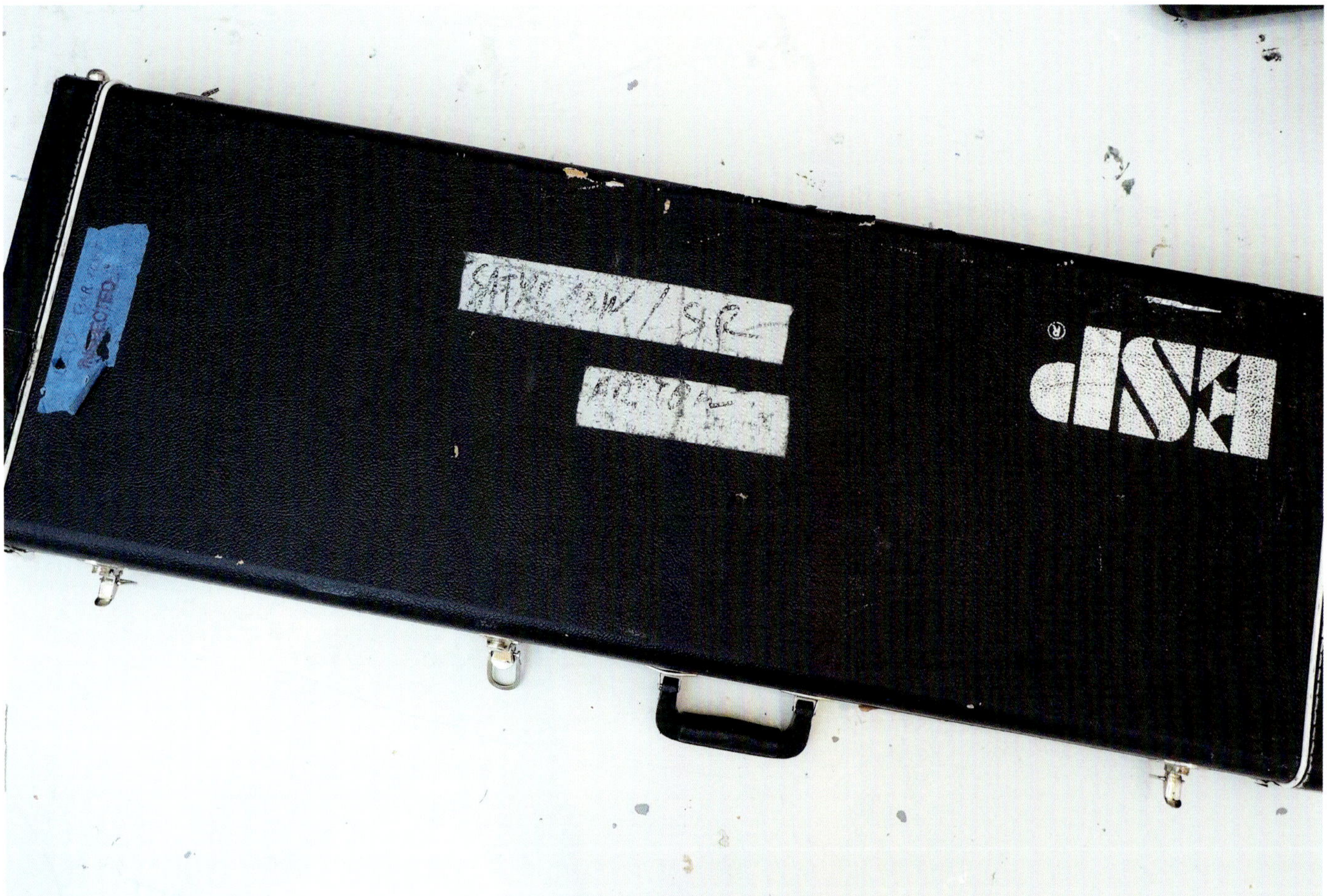

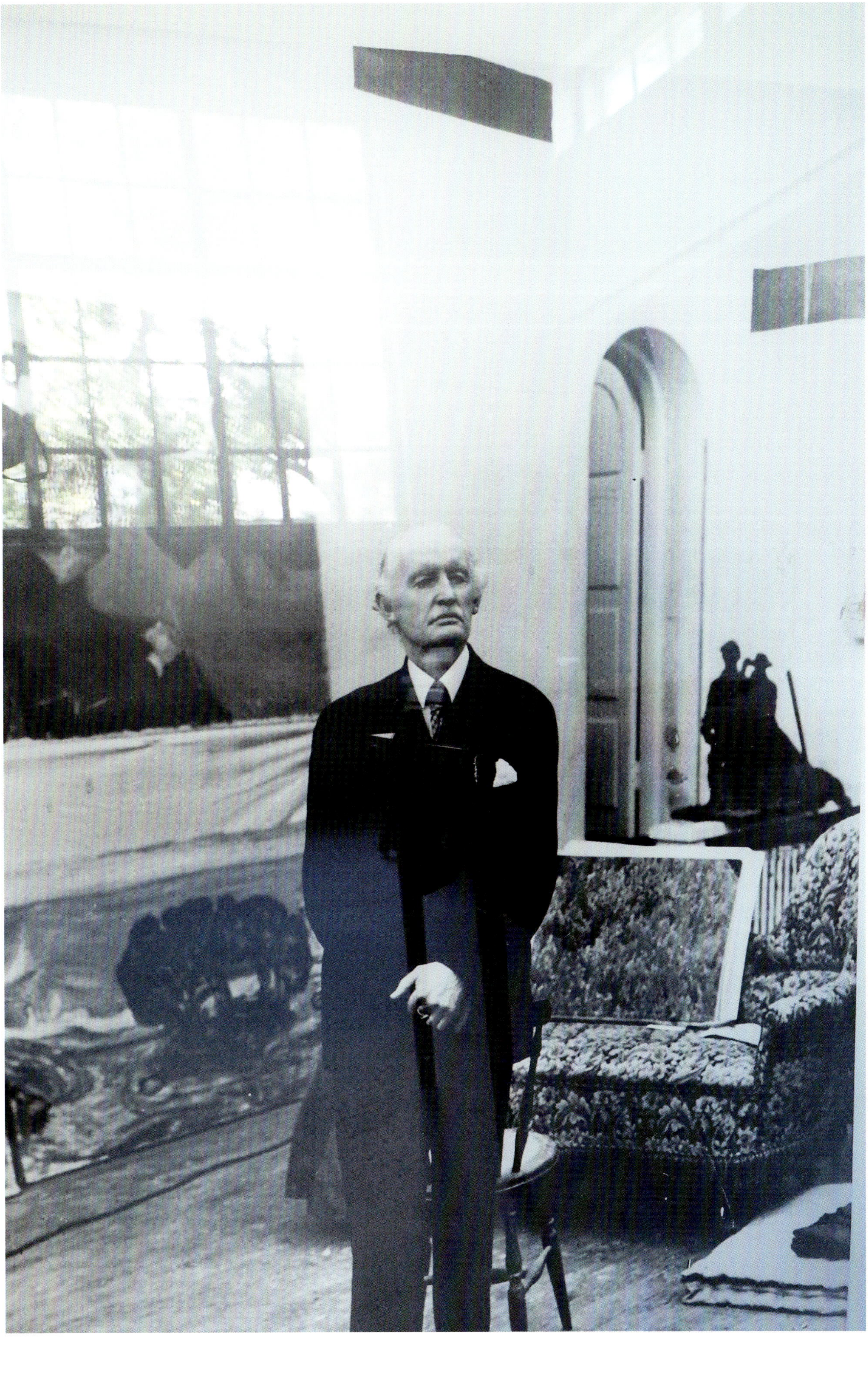

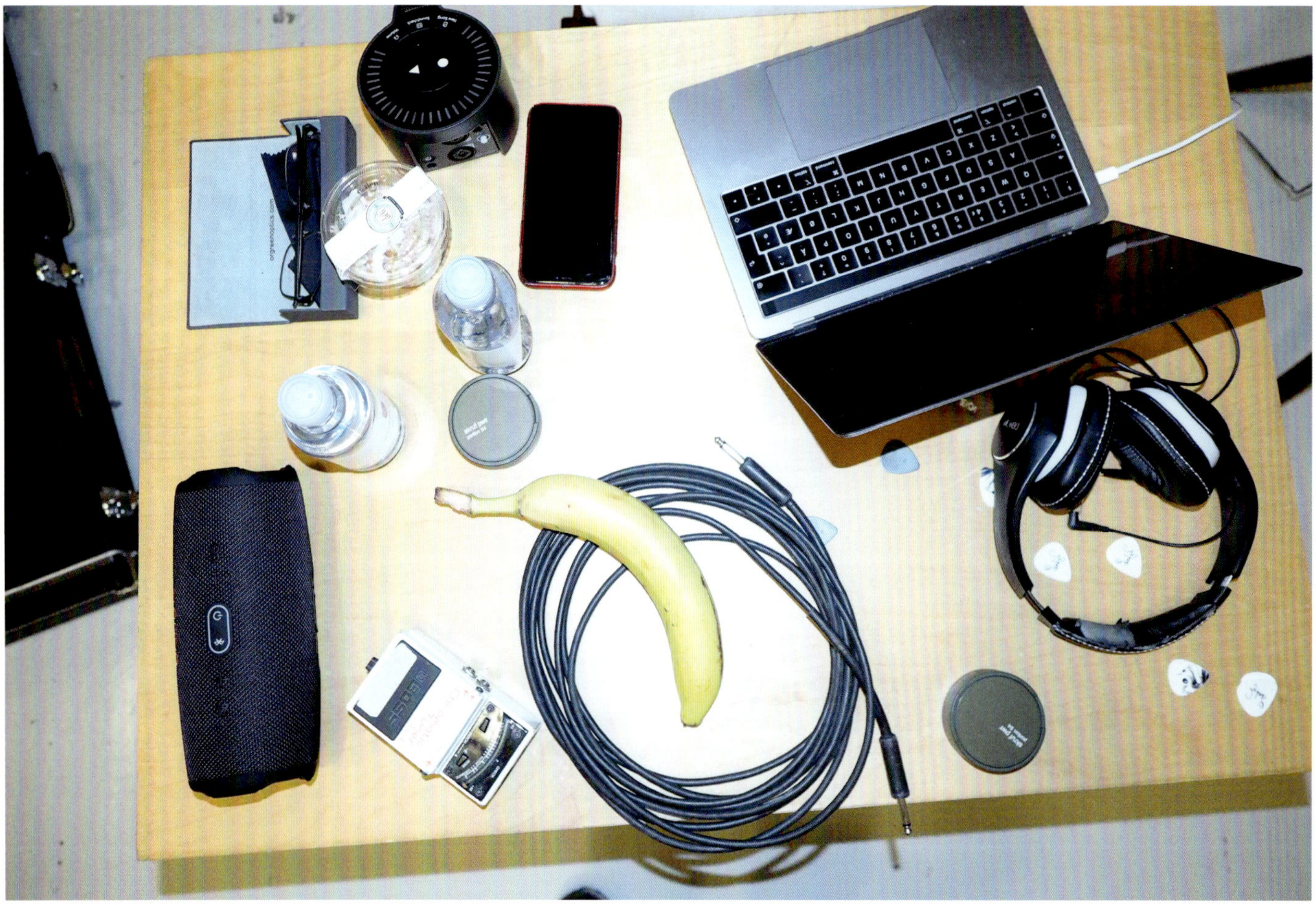

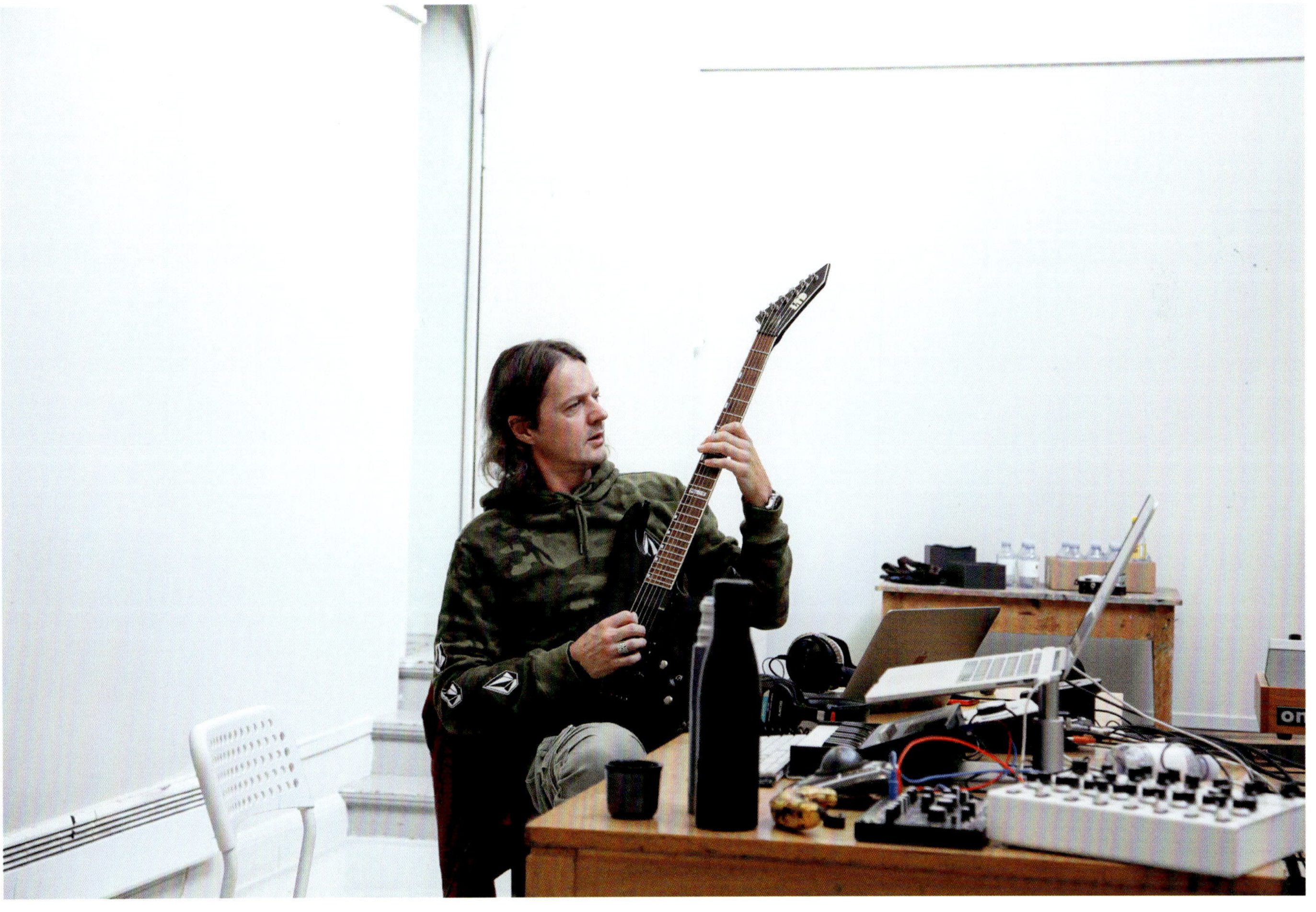

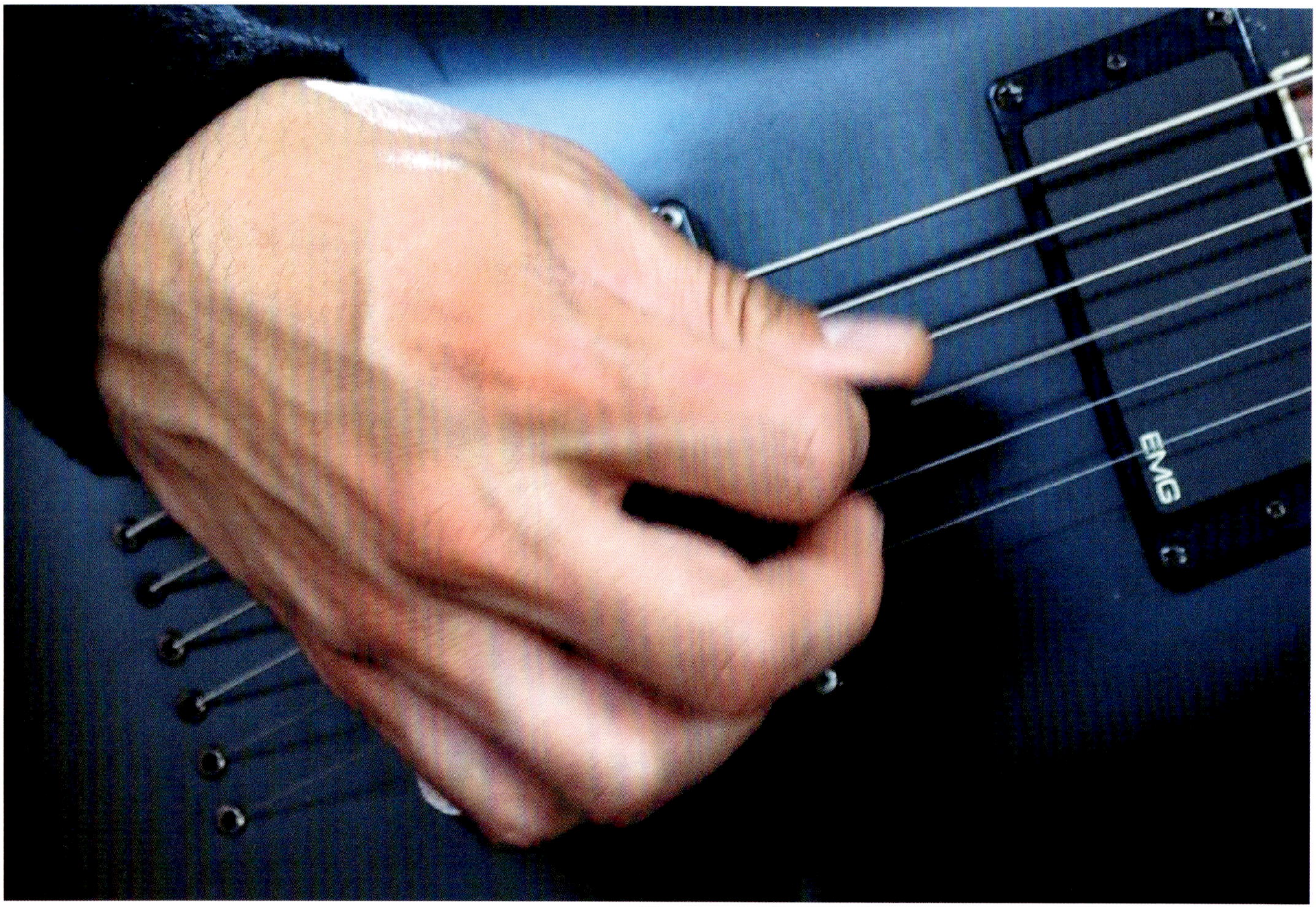
EMG

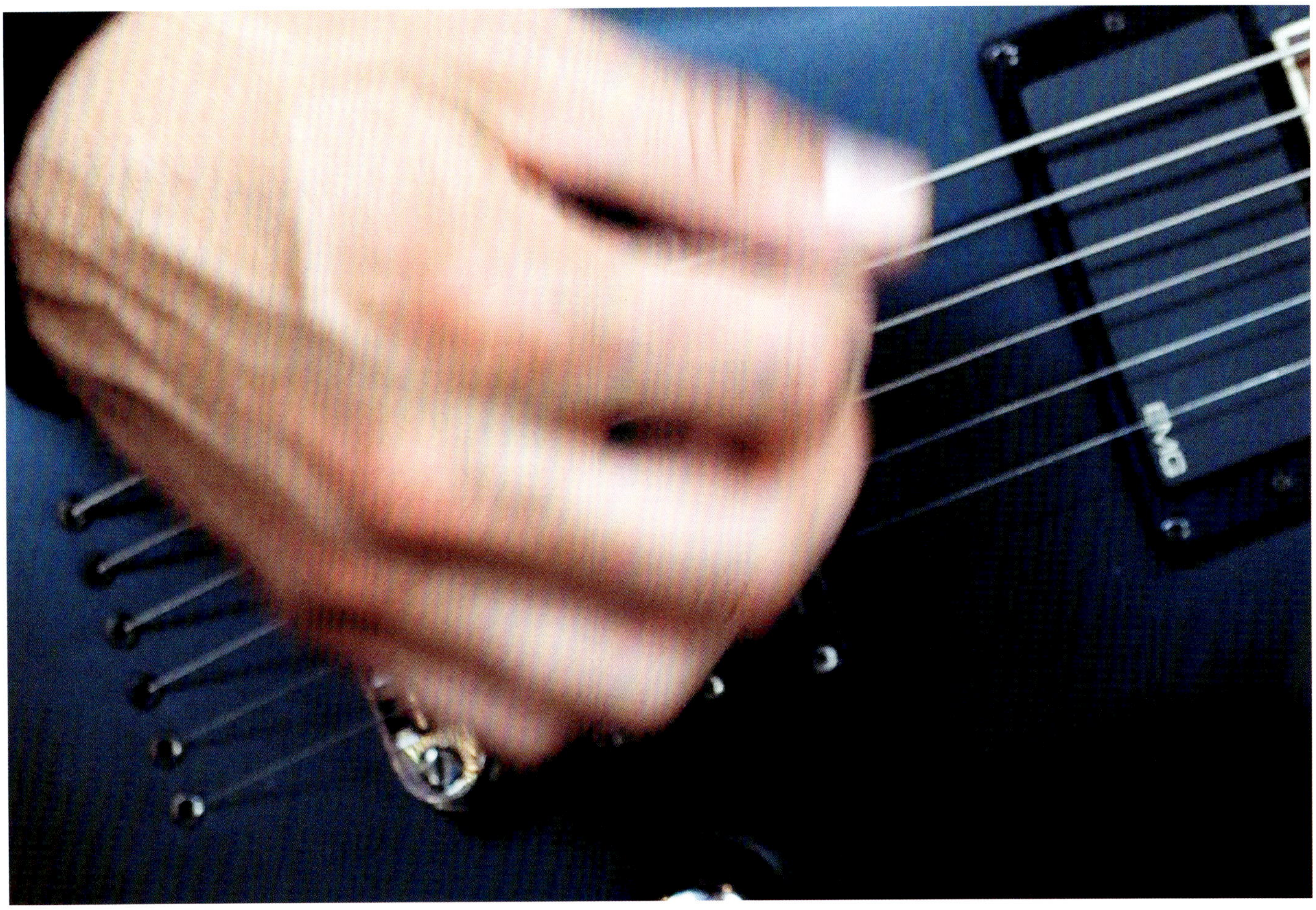

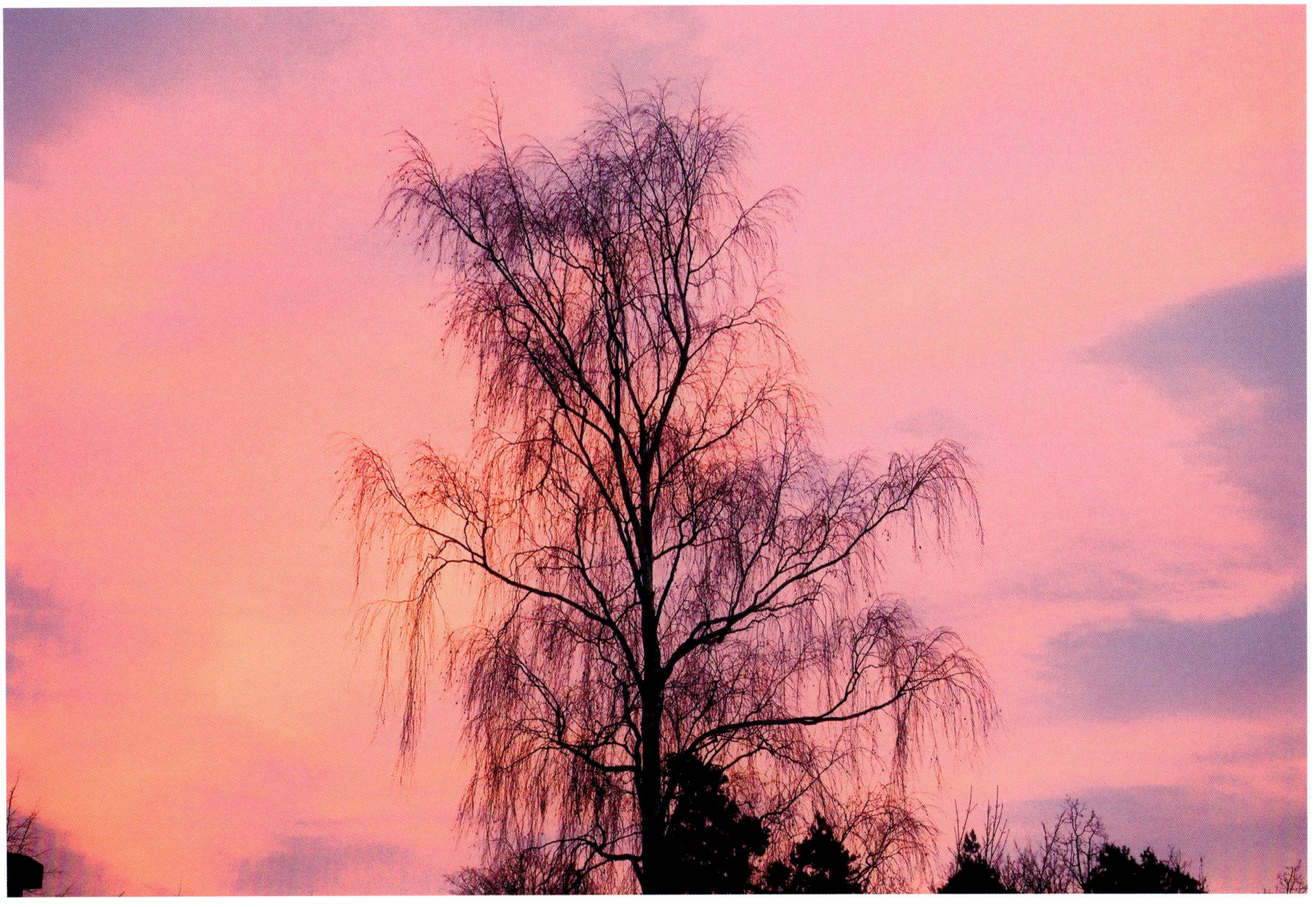

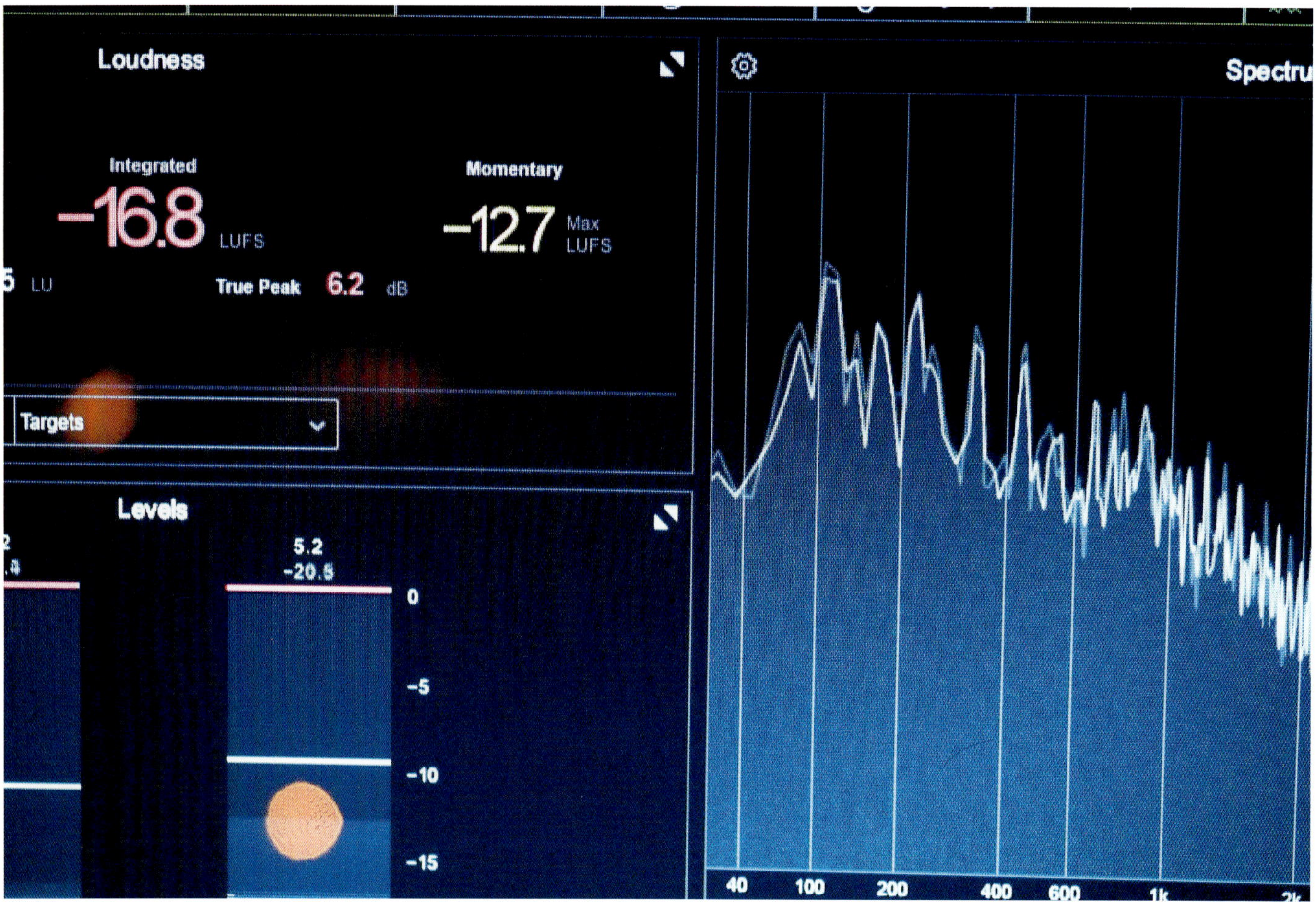
Loudness
Integrated
-16.8 LUFS
Momentary
-12.7 Max LUFS
LU
True Peak 6.2 dB
Targets
Levels
5.2
-20.5
0
-5
-10
-15
40
100
200
400
600
1k

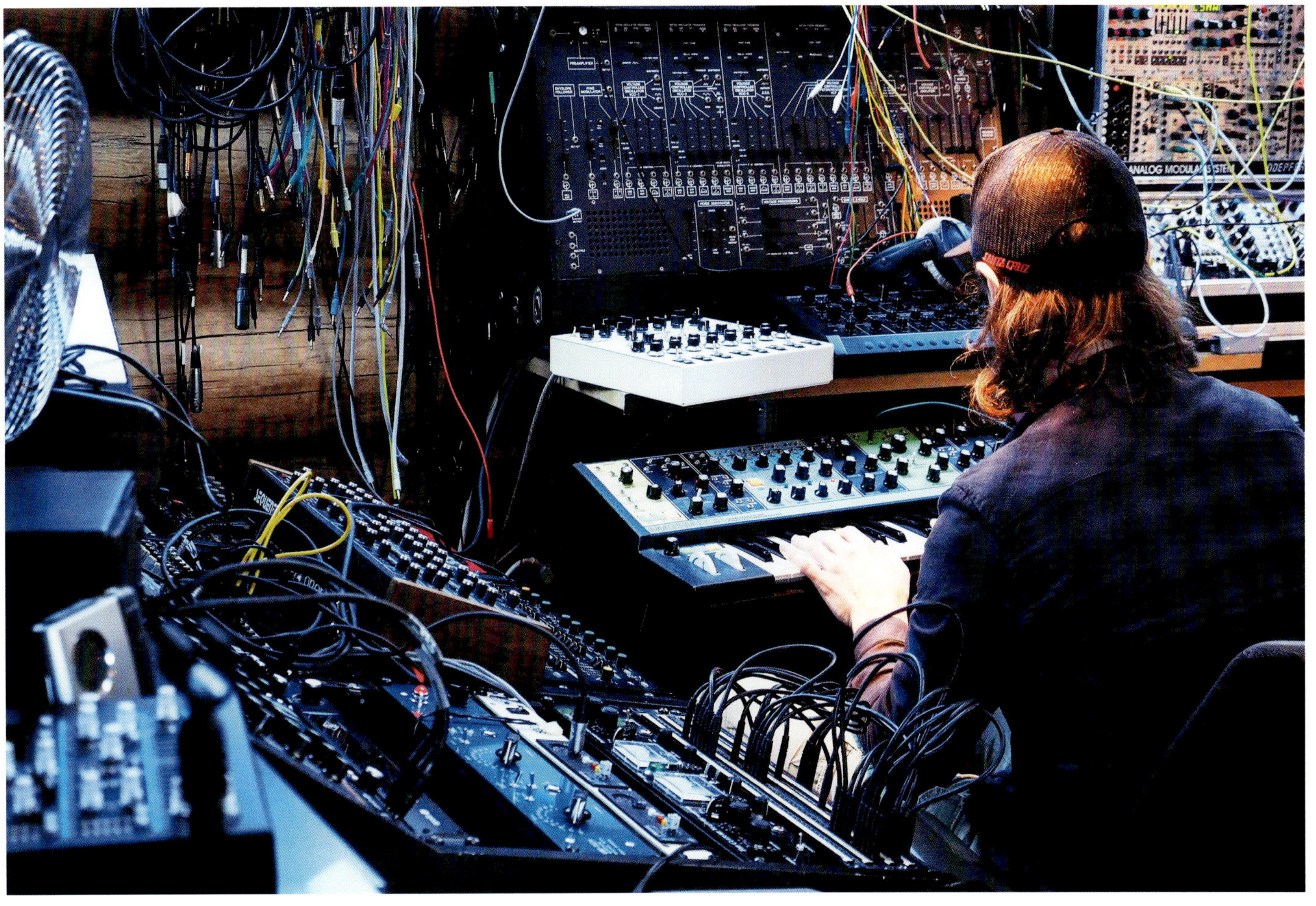

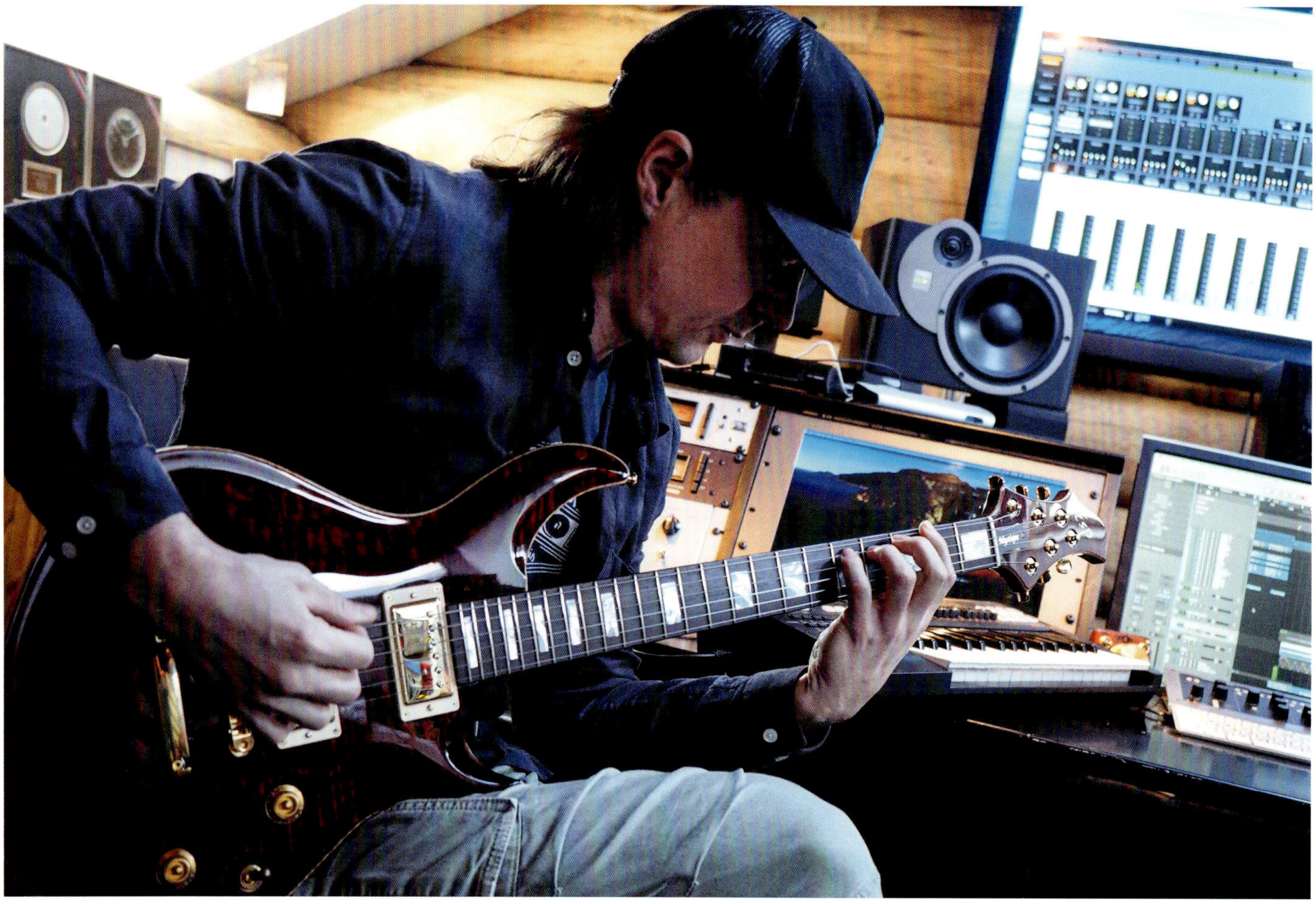

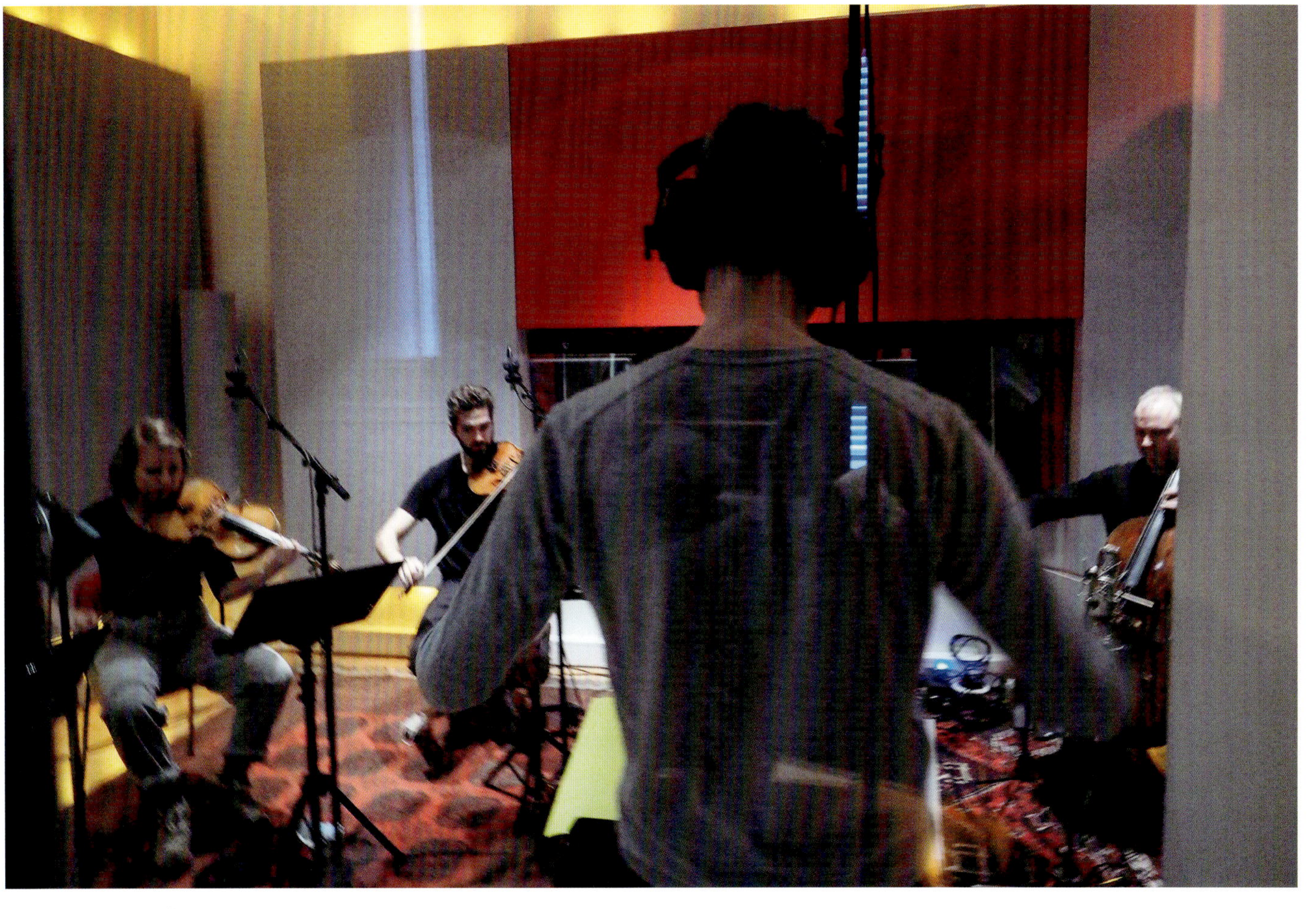

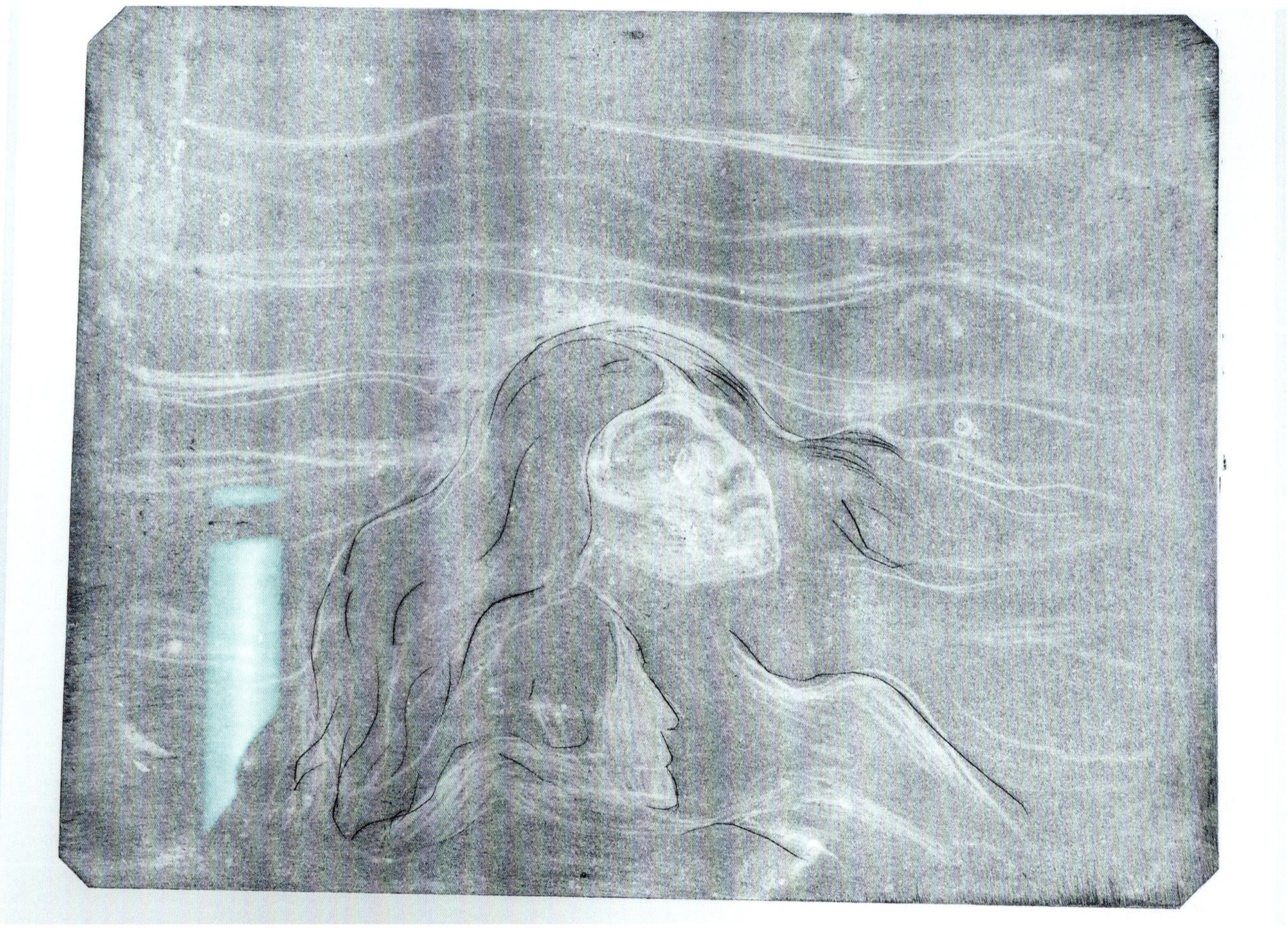

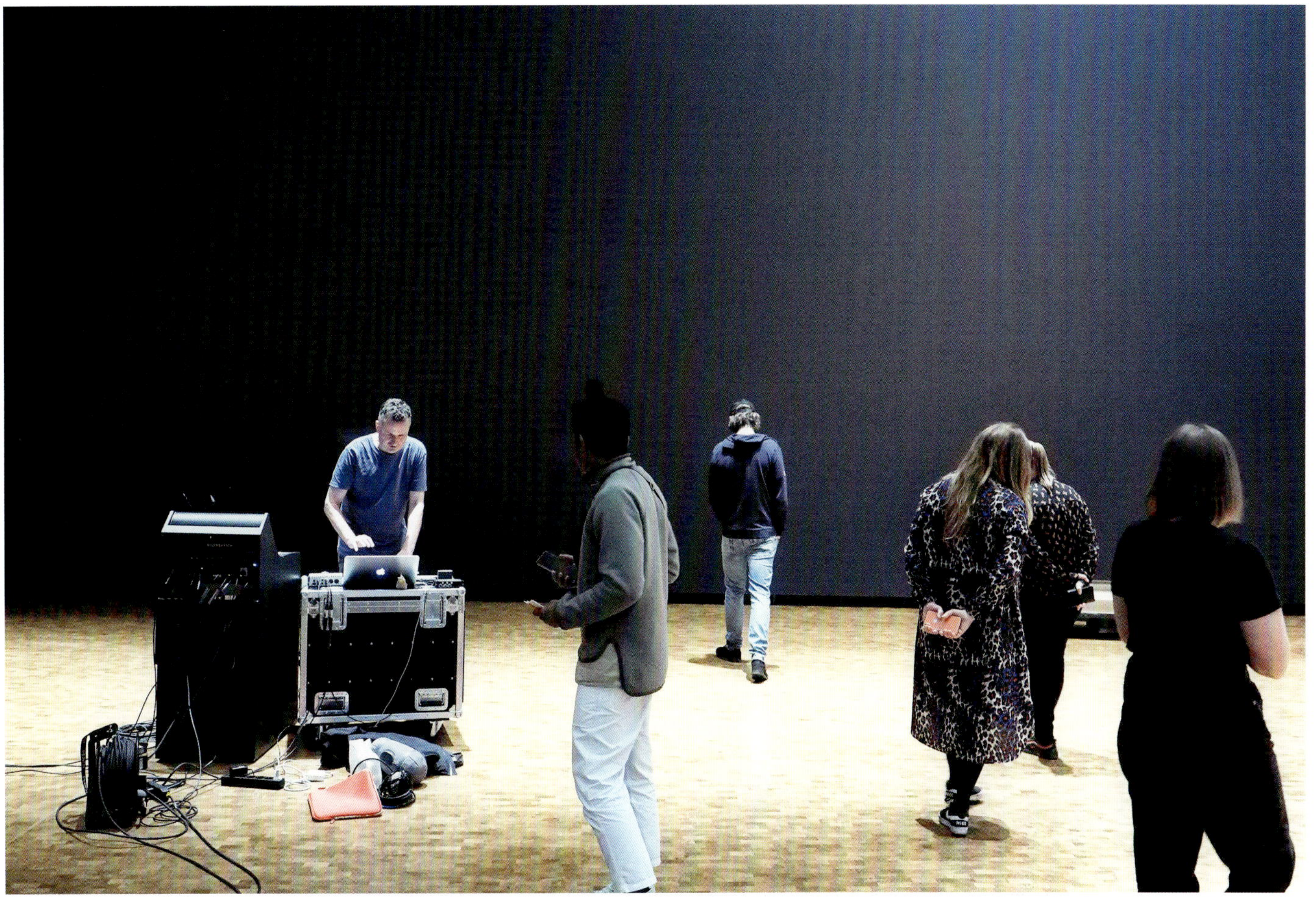

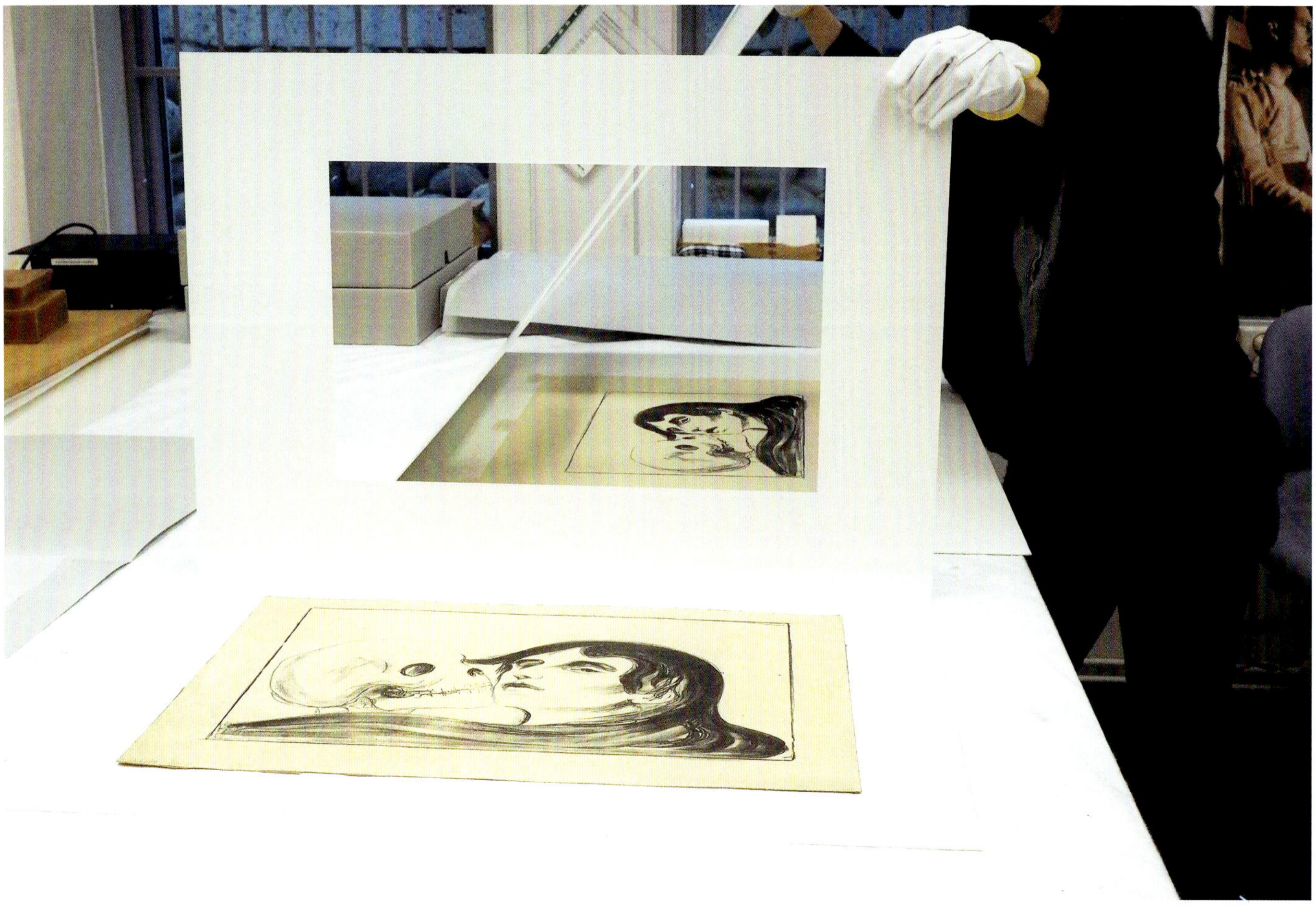

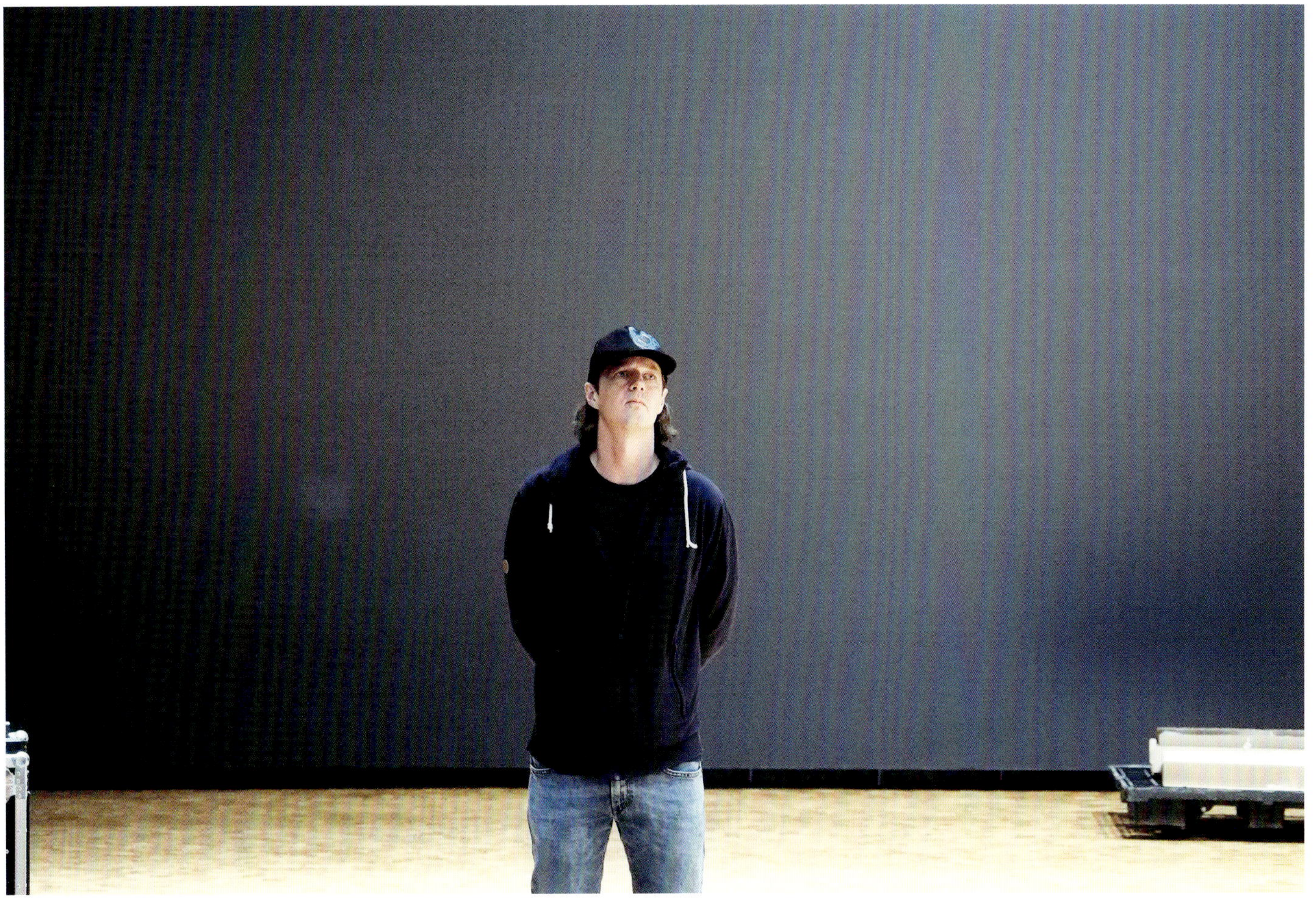

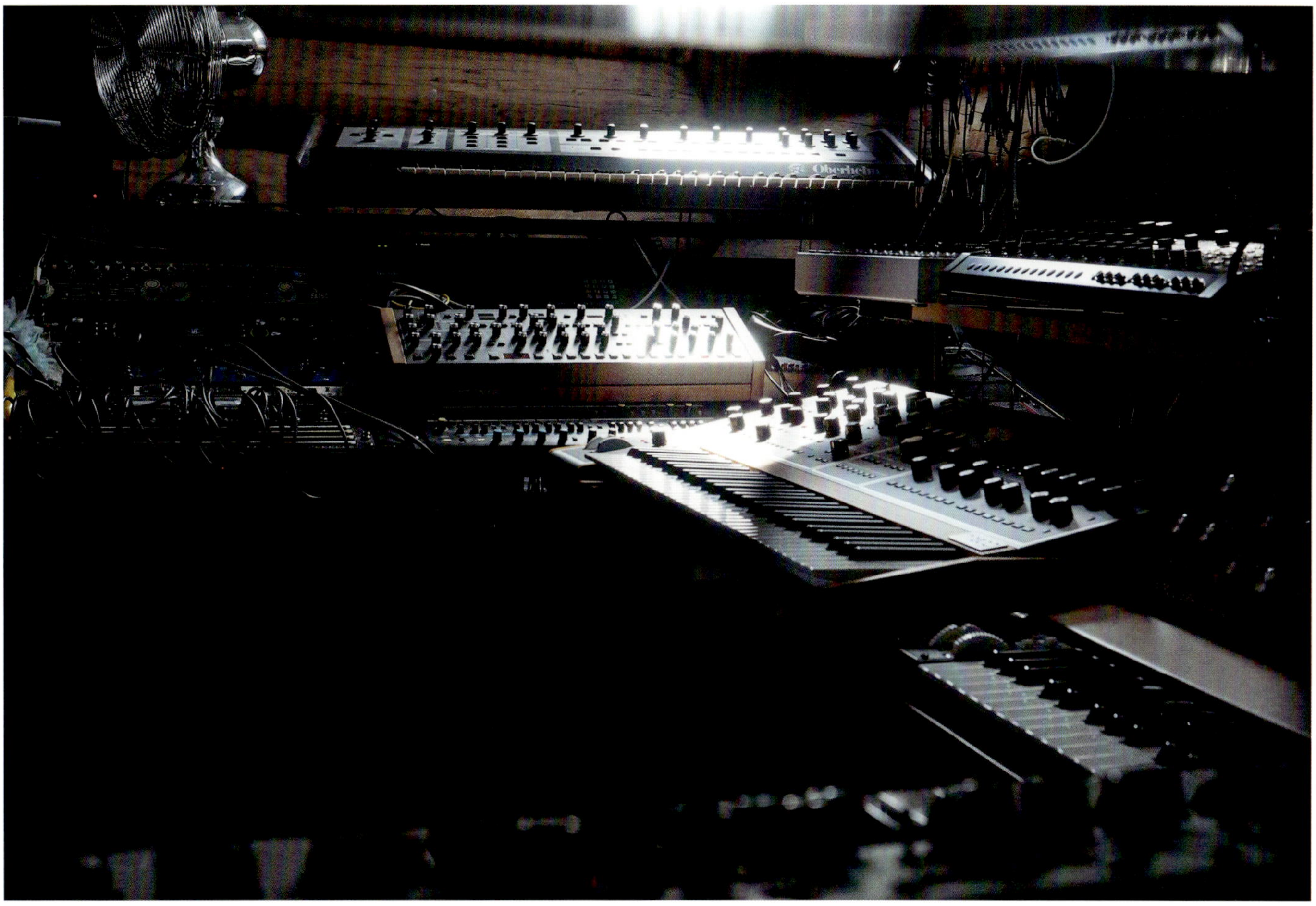
Oberheim

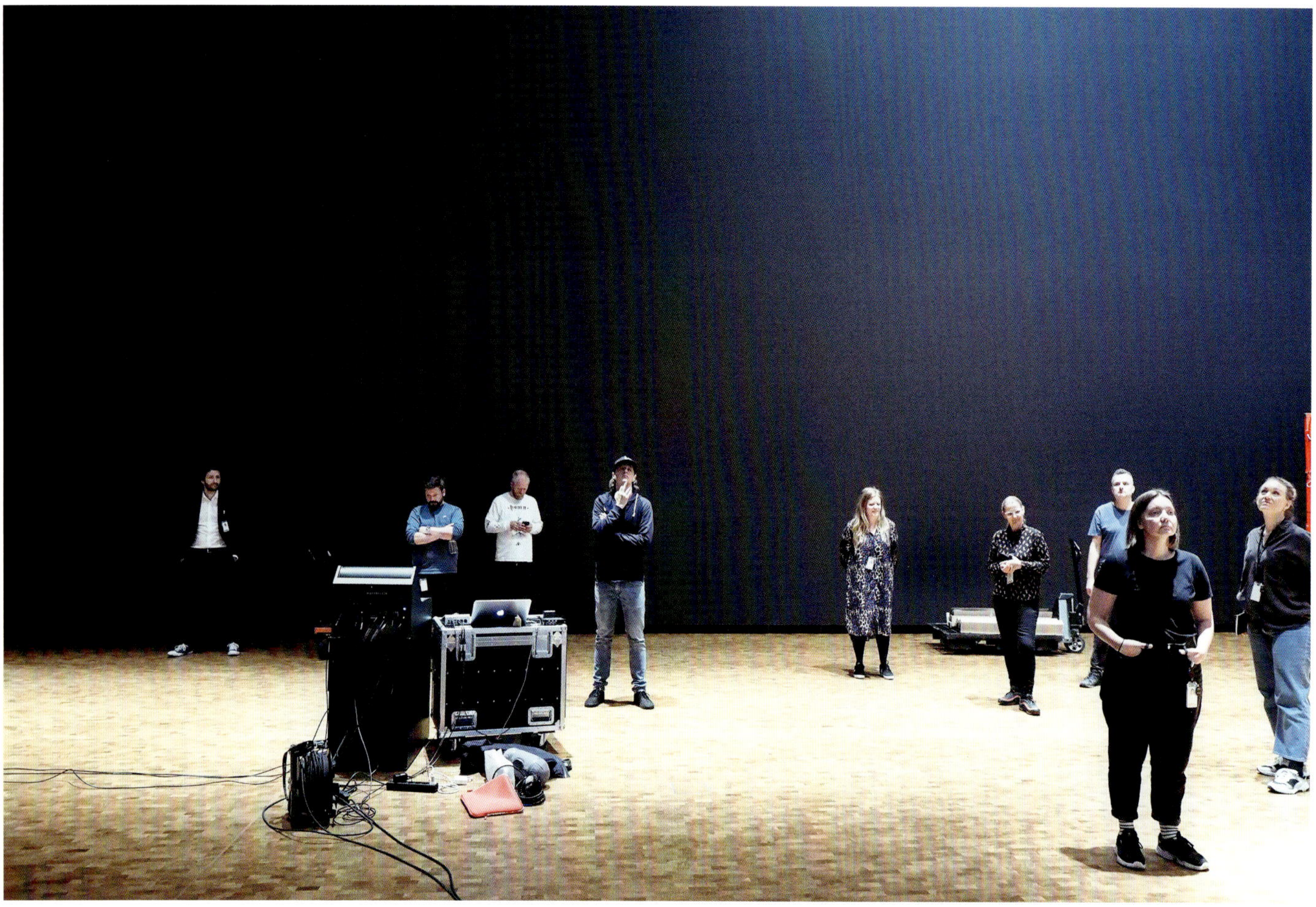

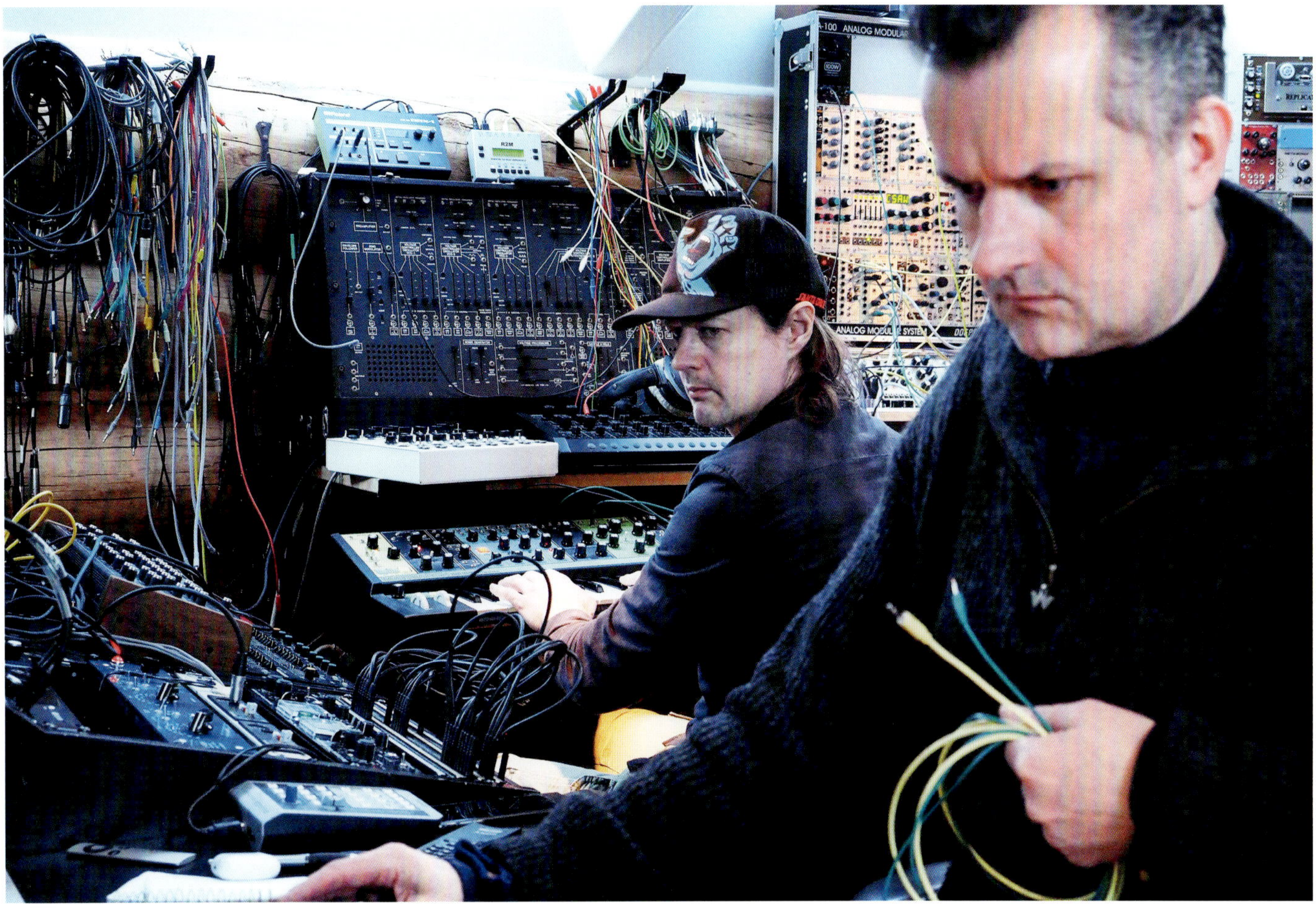
ANALOG MODULAR SYSTEM

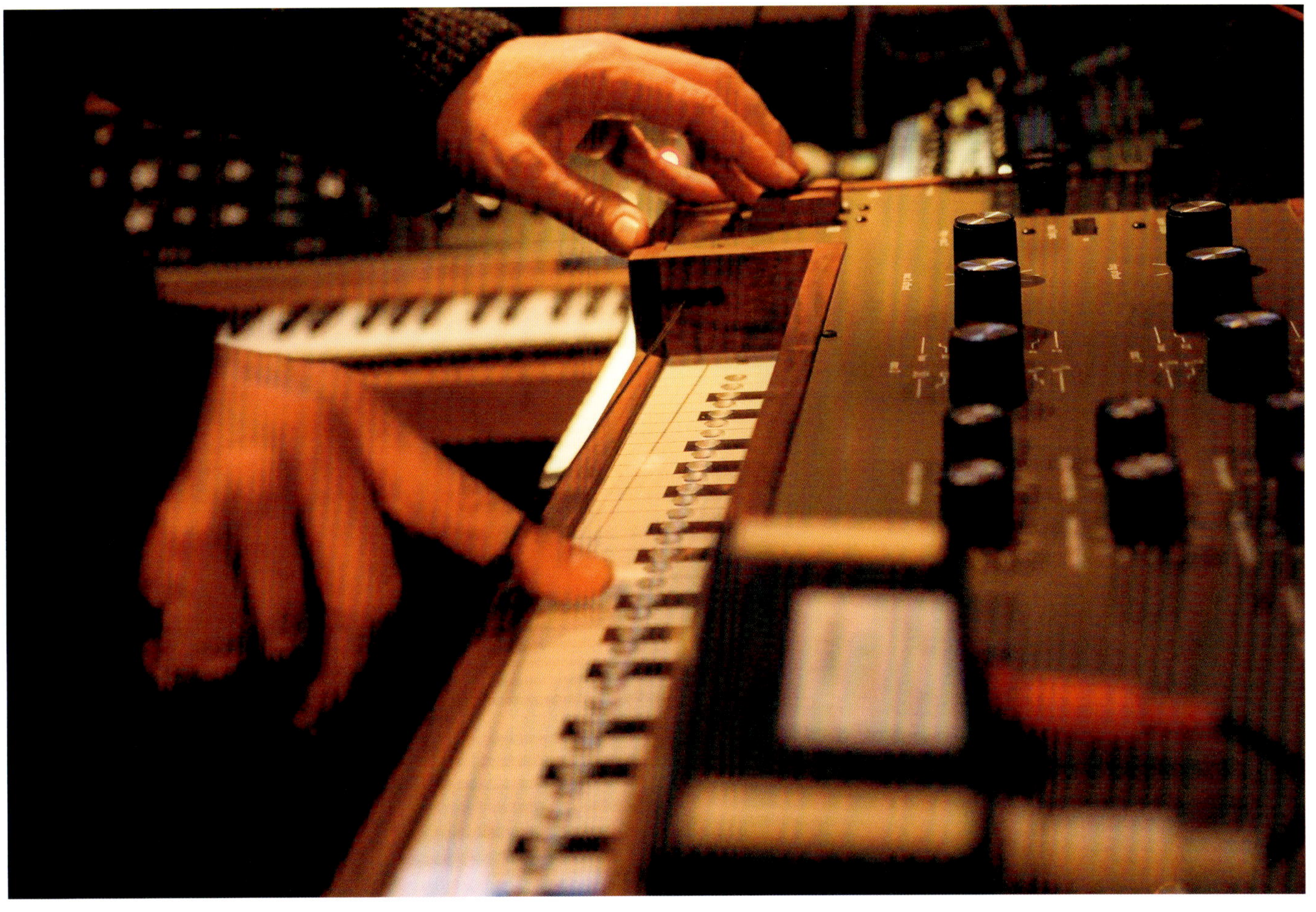

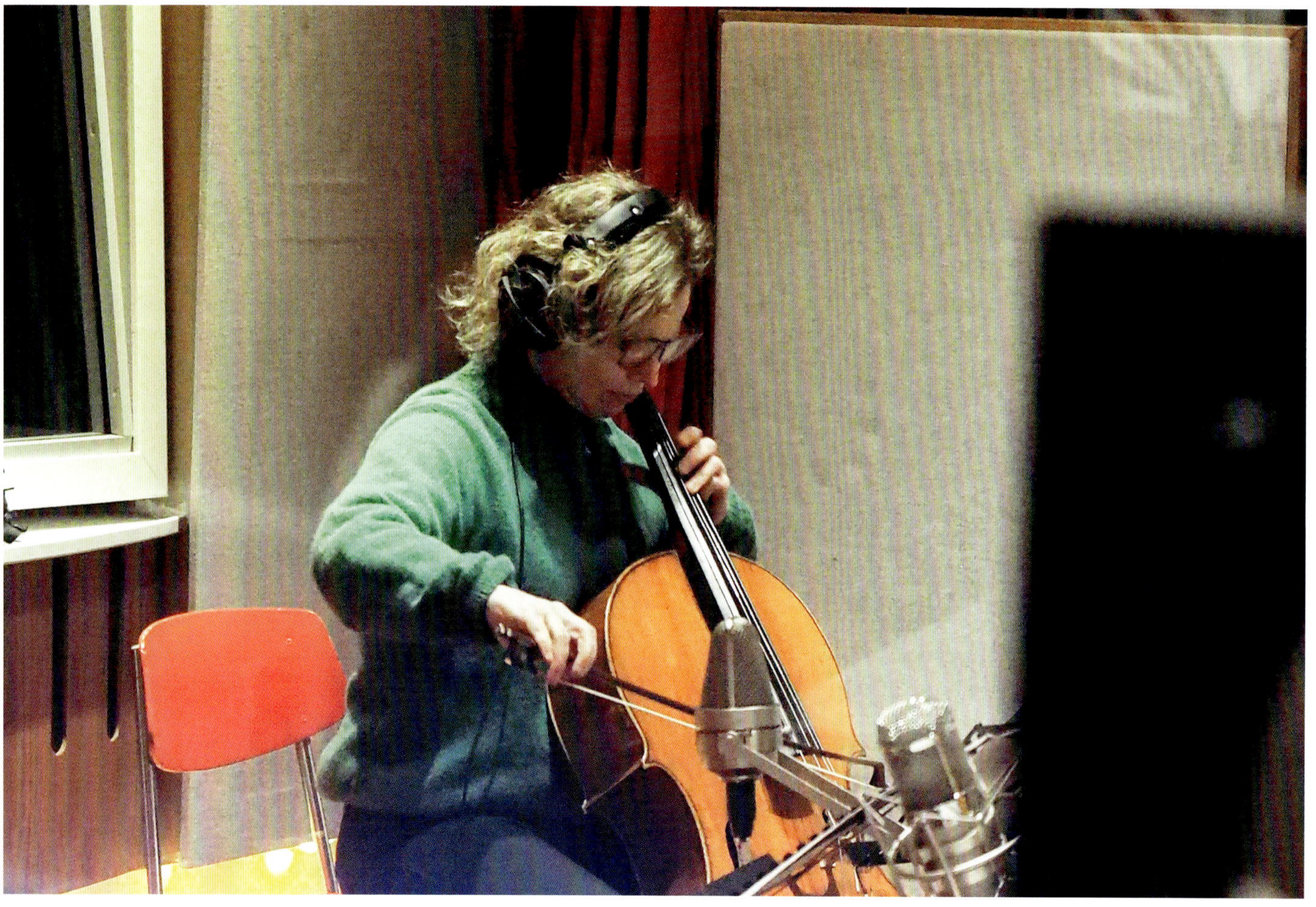

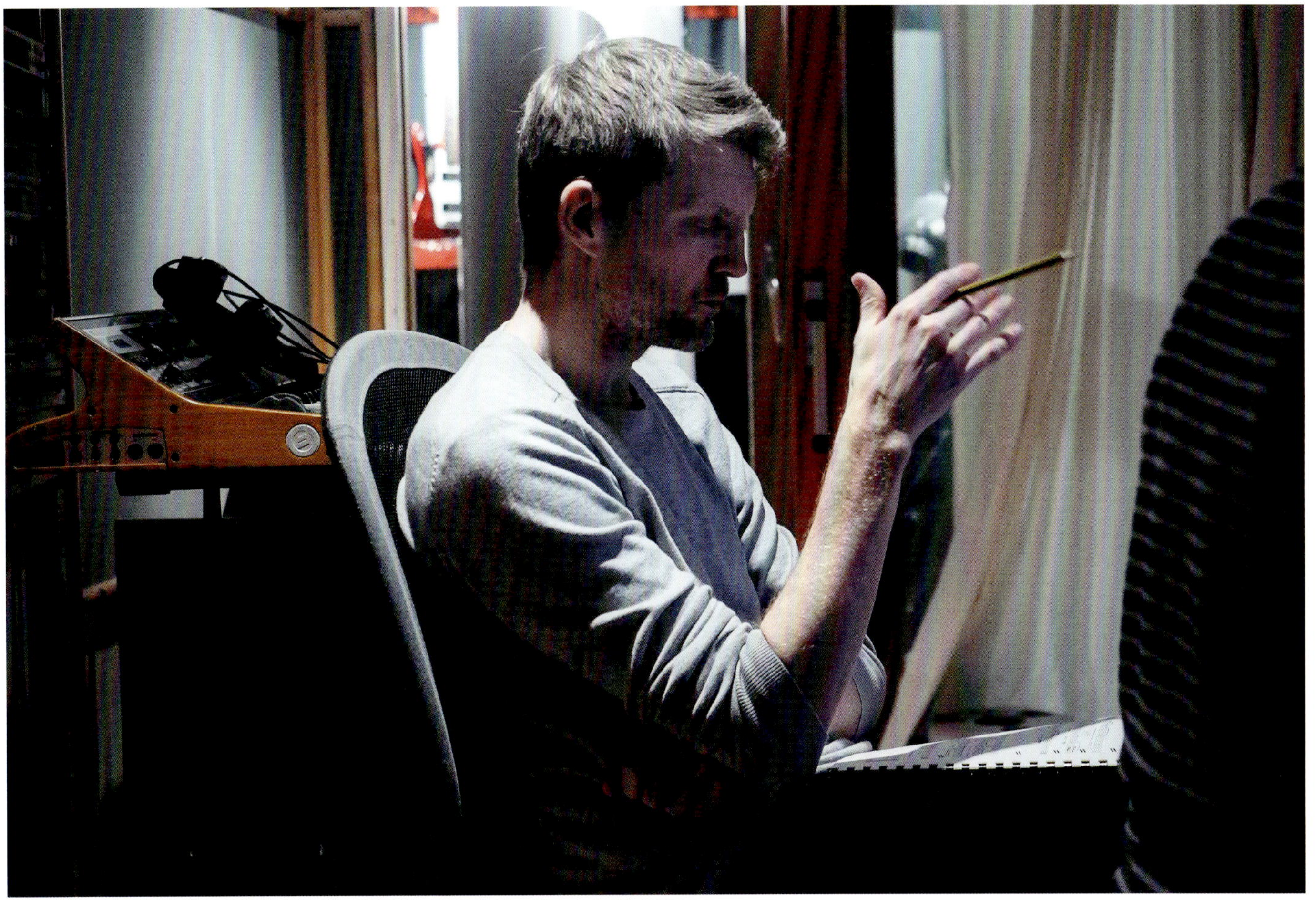

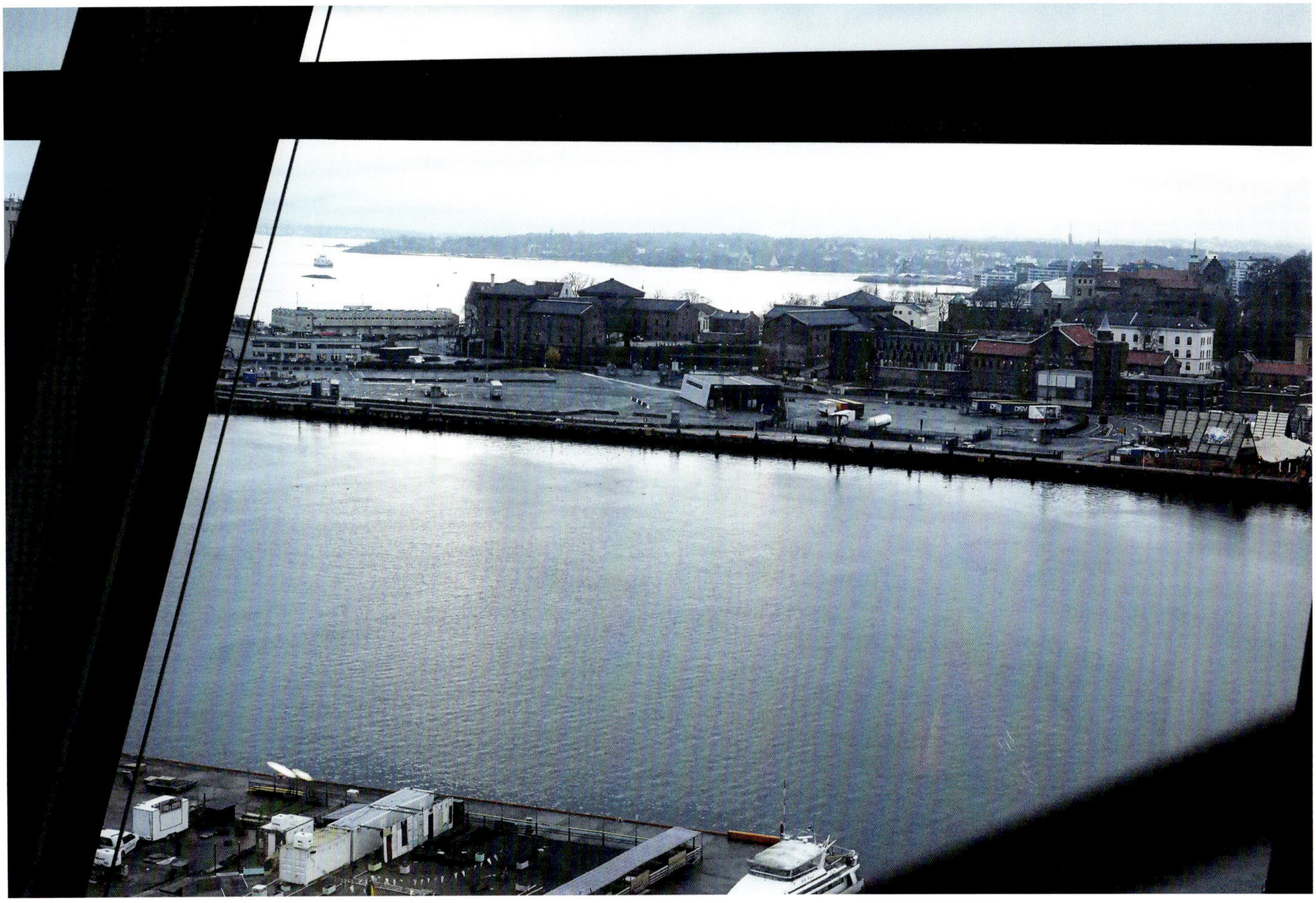

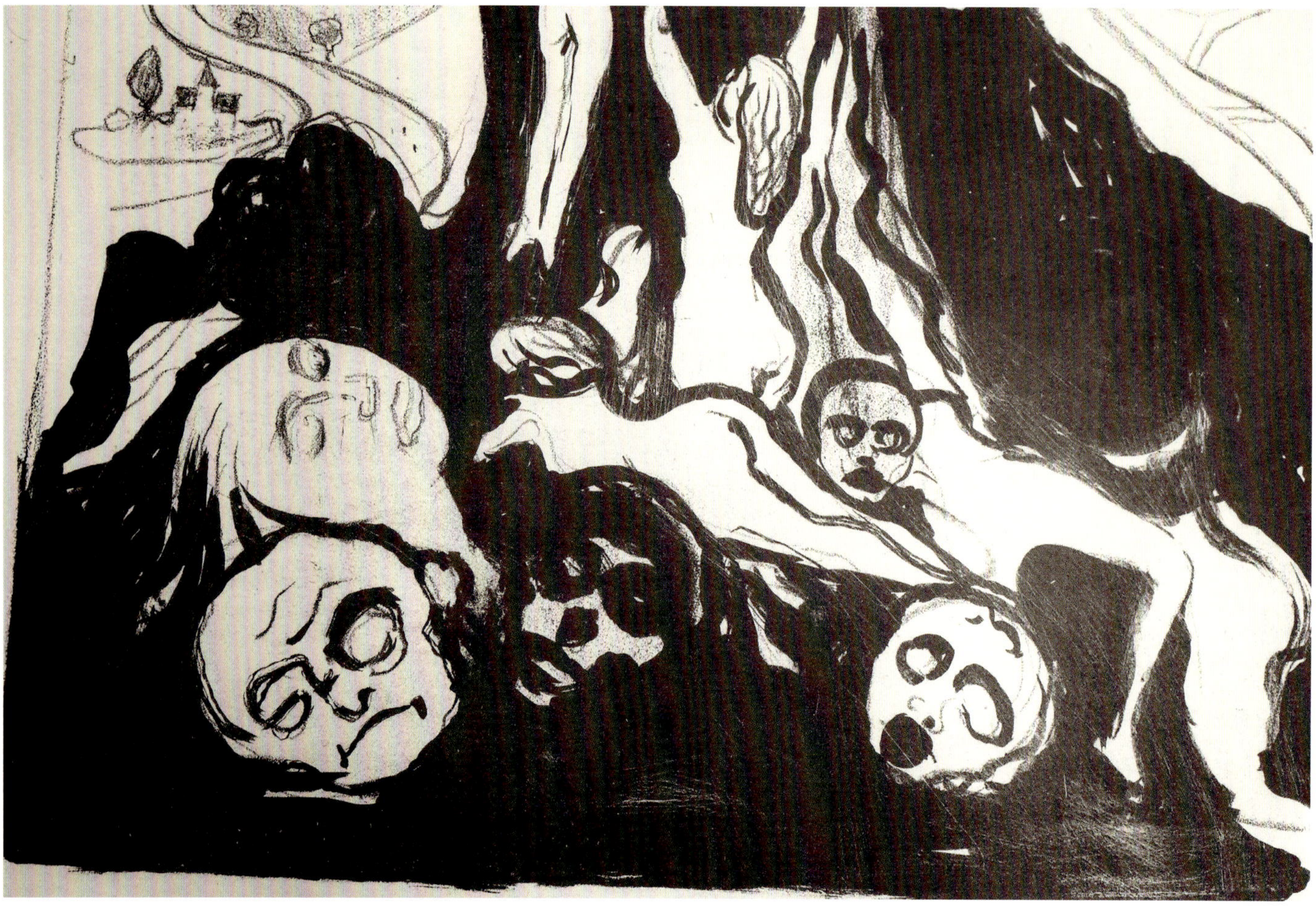

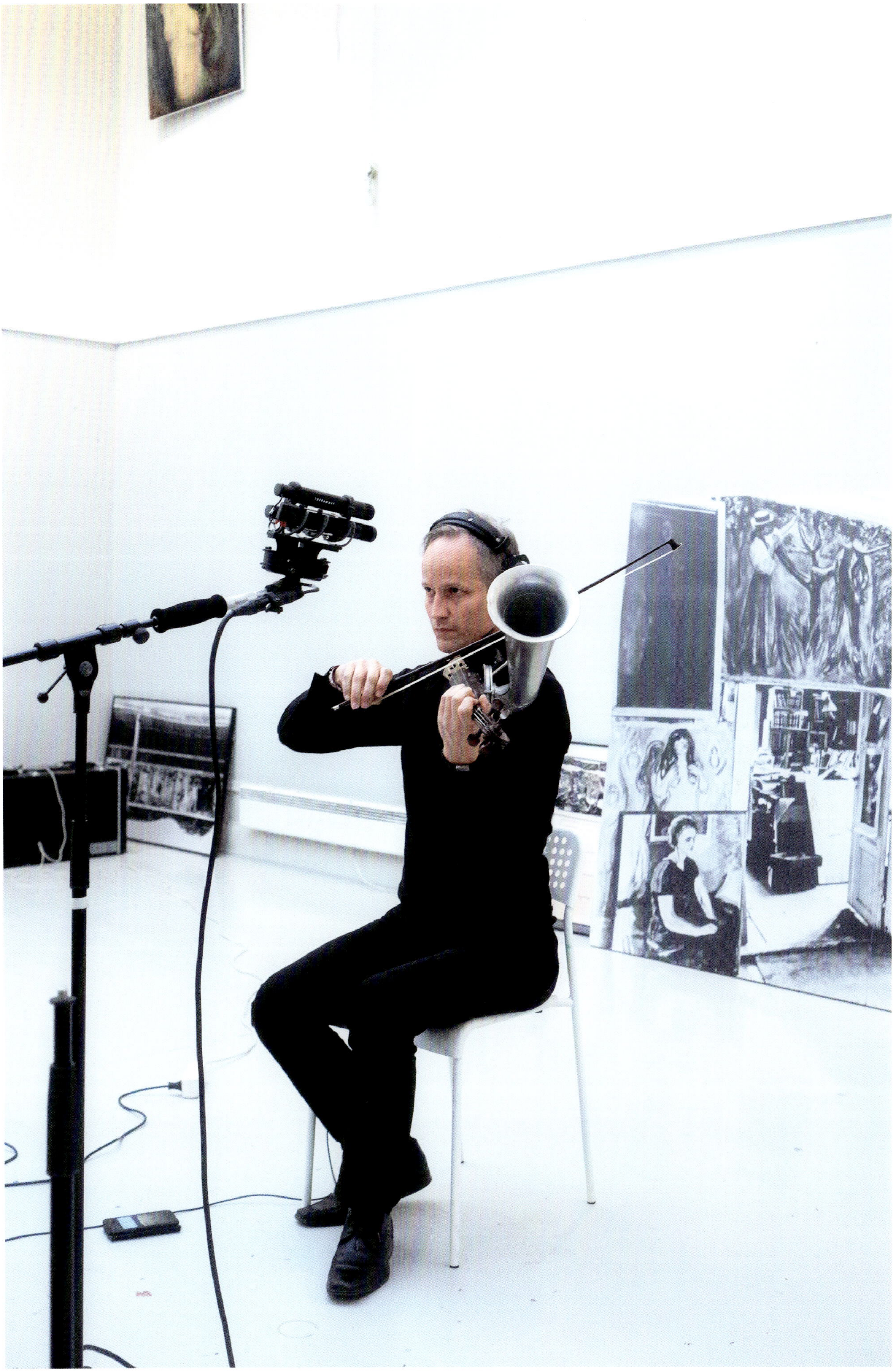

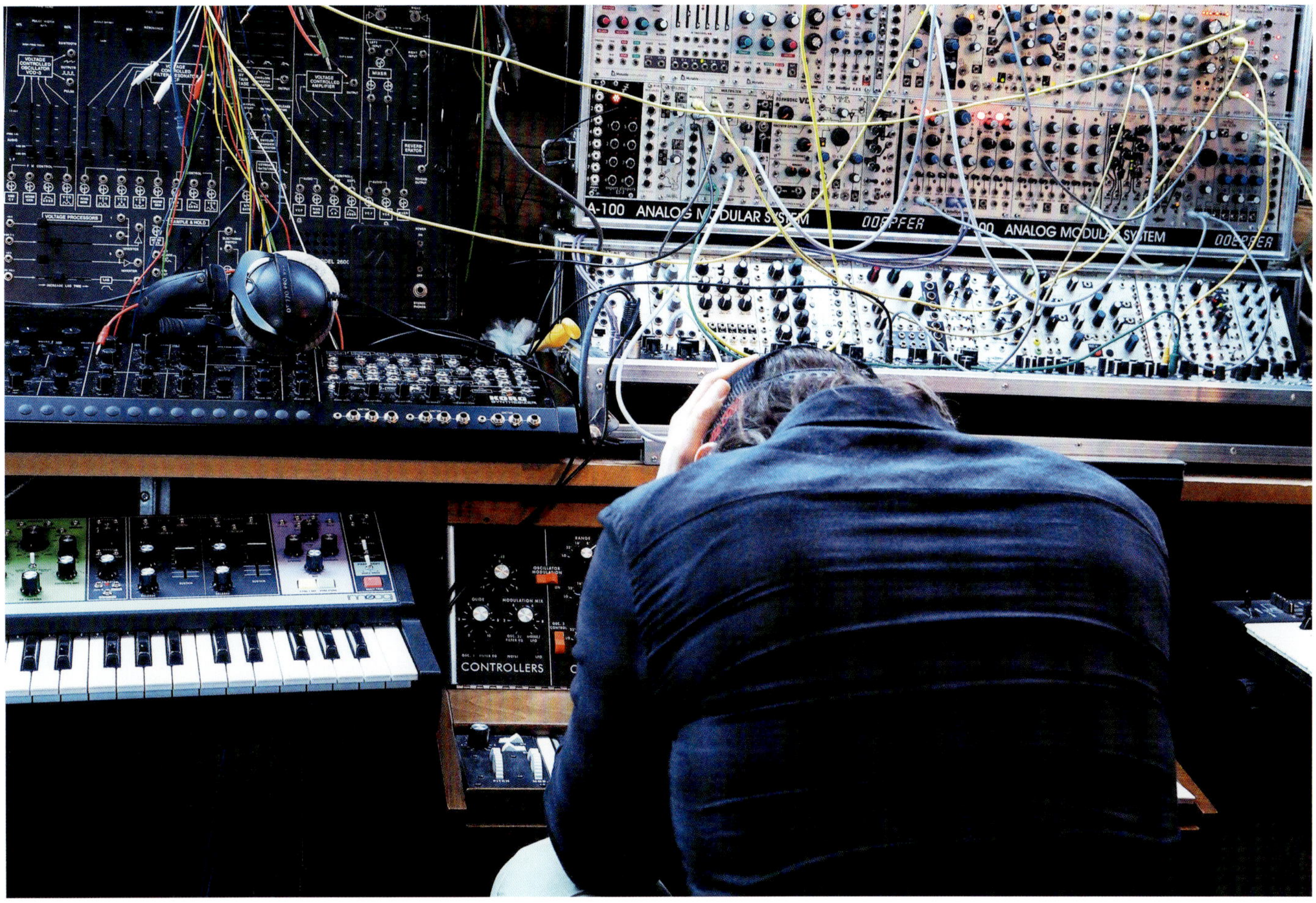
A-100 ANALOG MODULAR SYSTEM
DOEPFER
CONTROLLERS

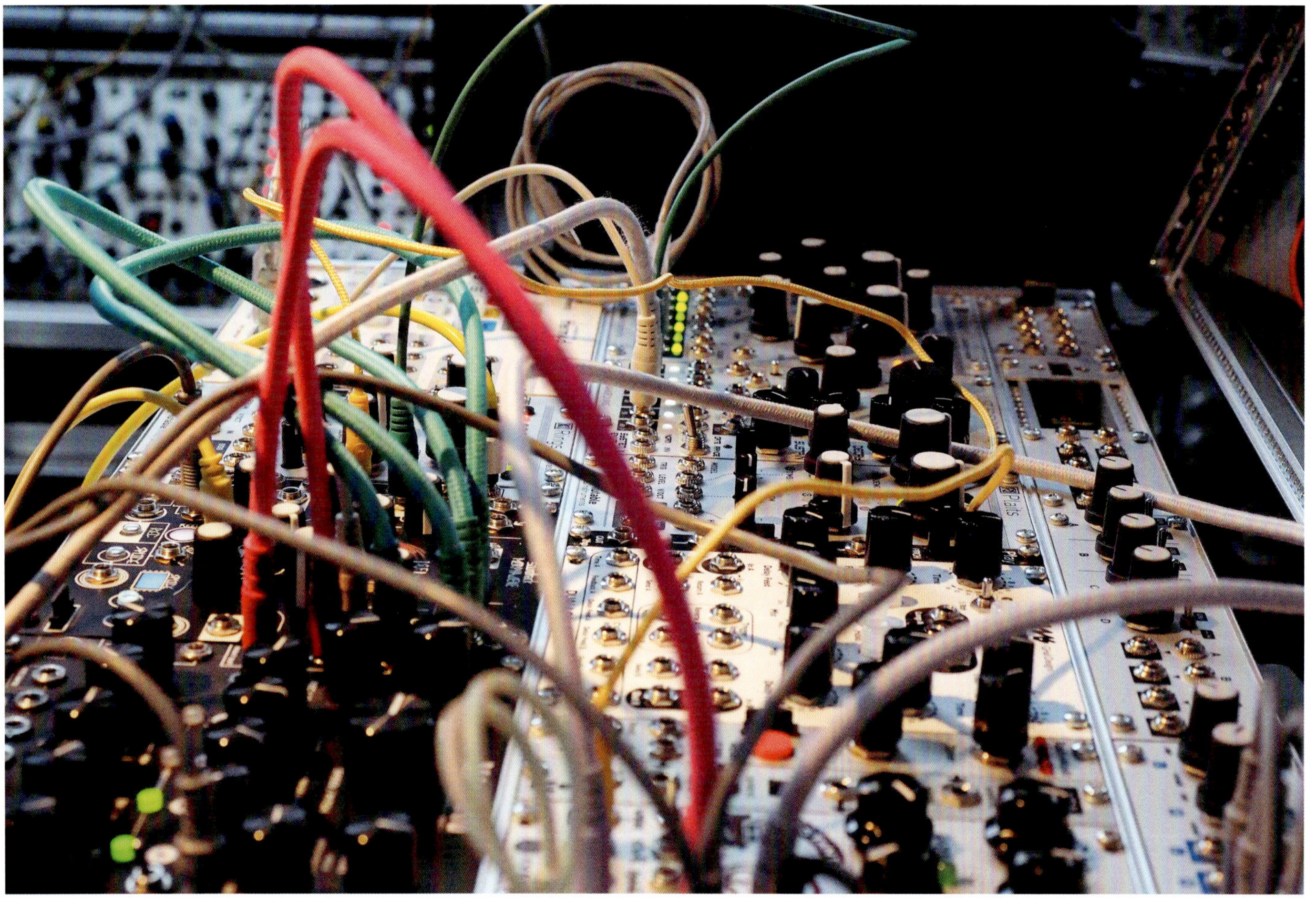

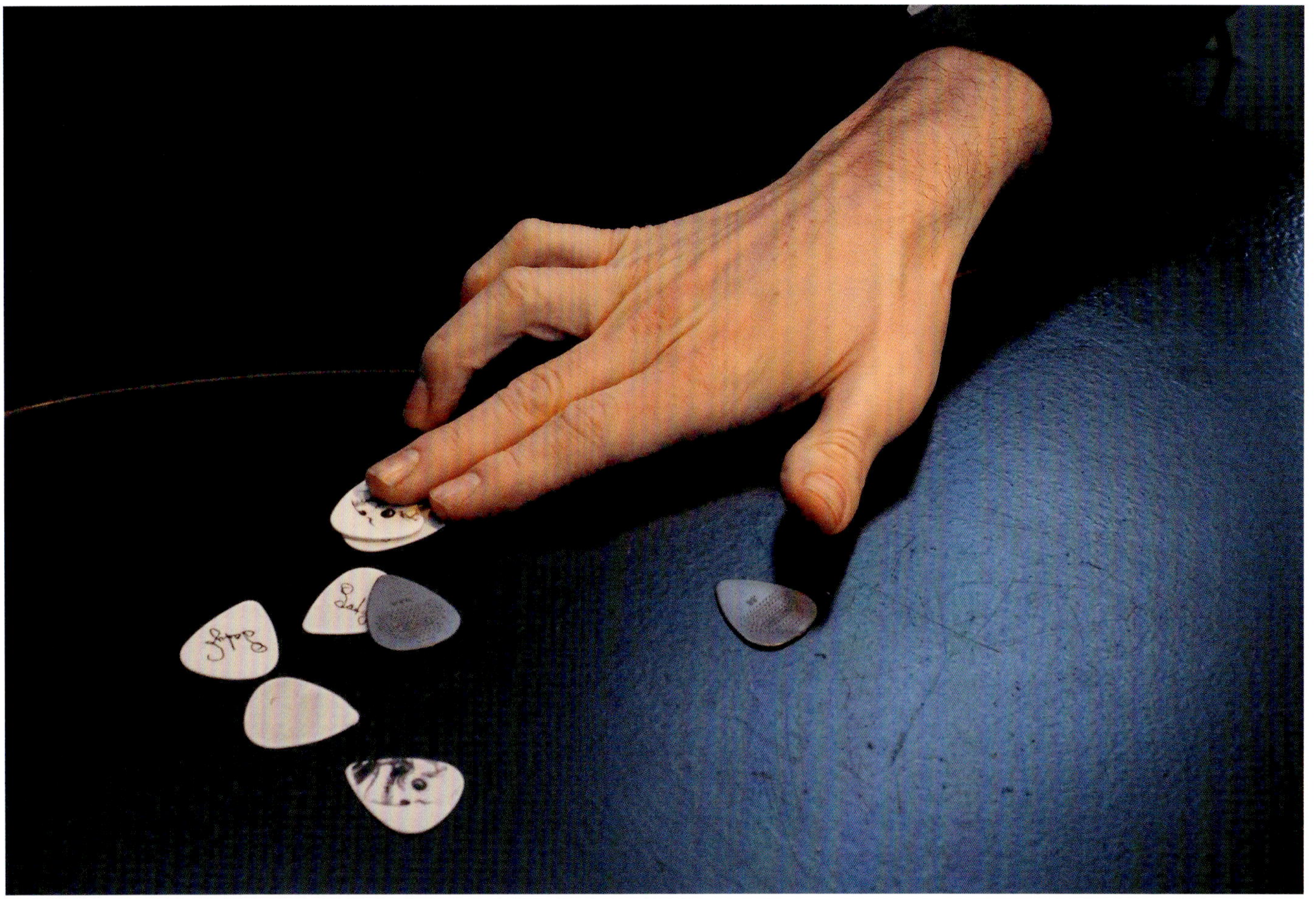

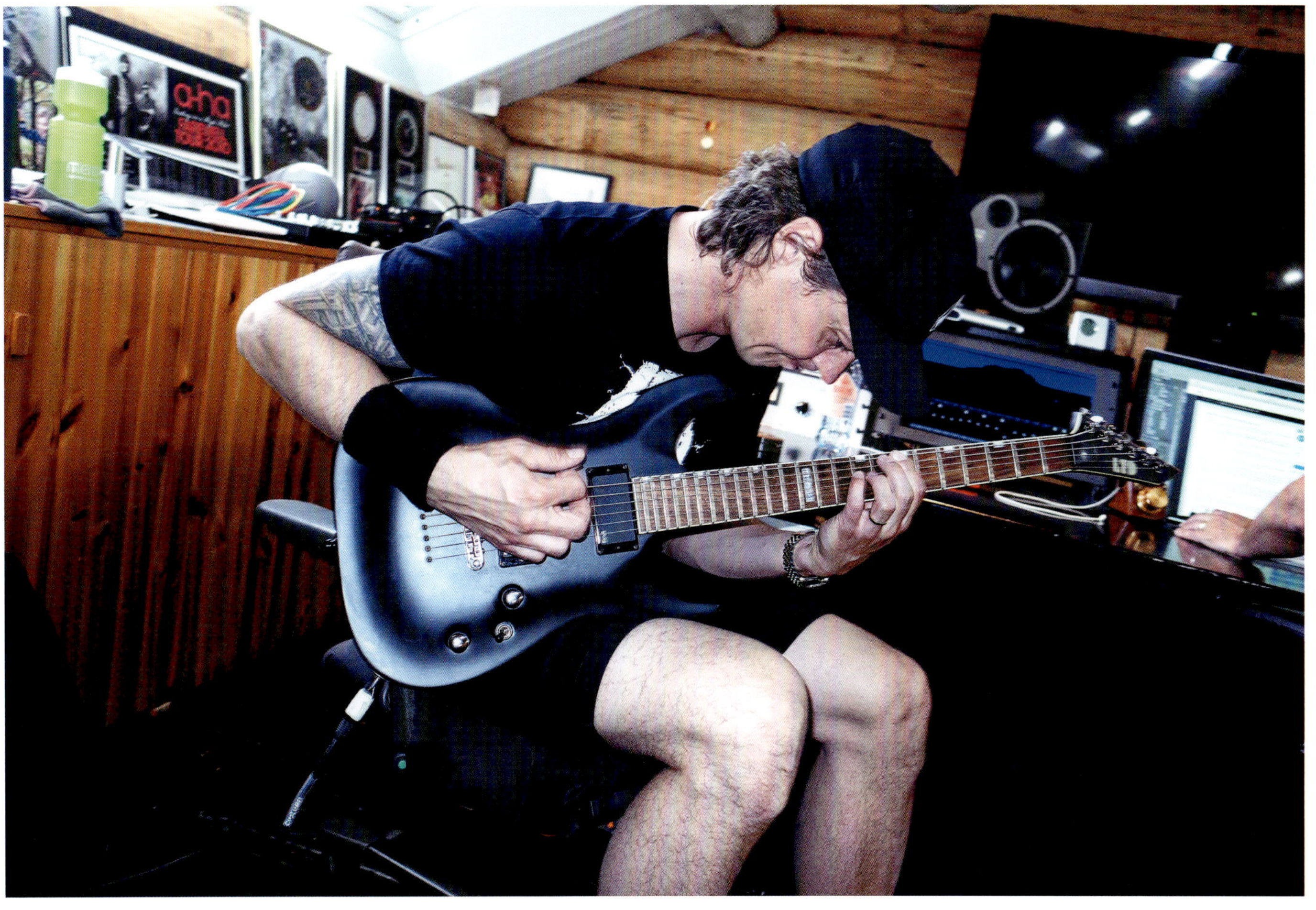
a-ha

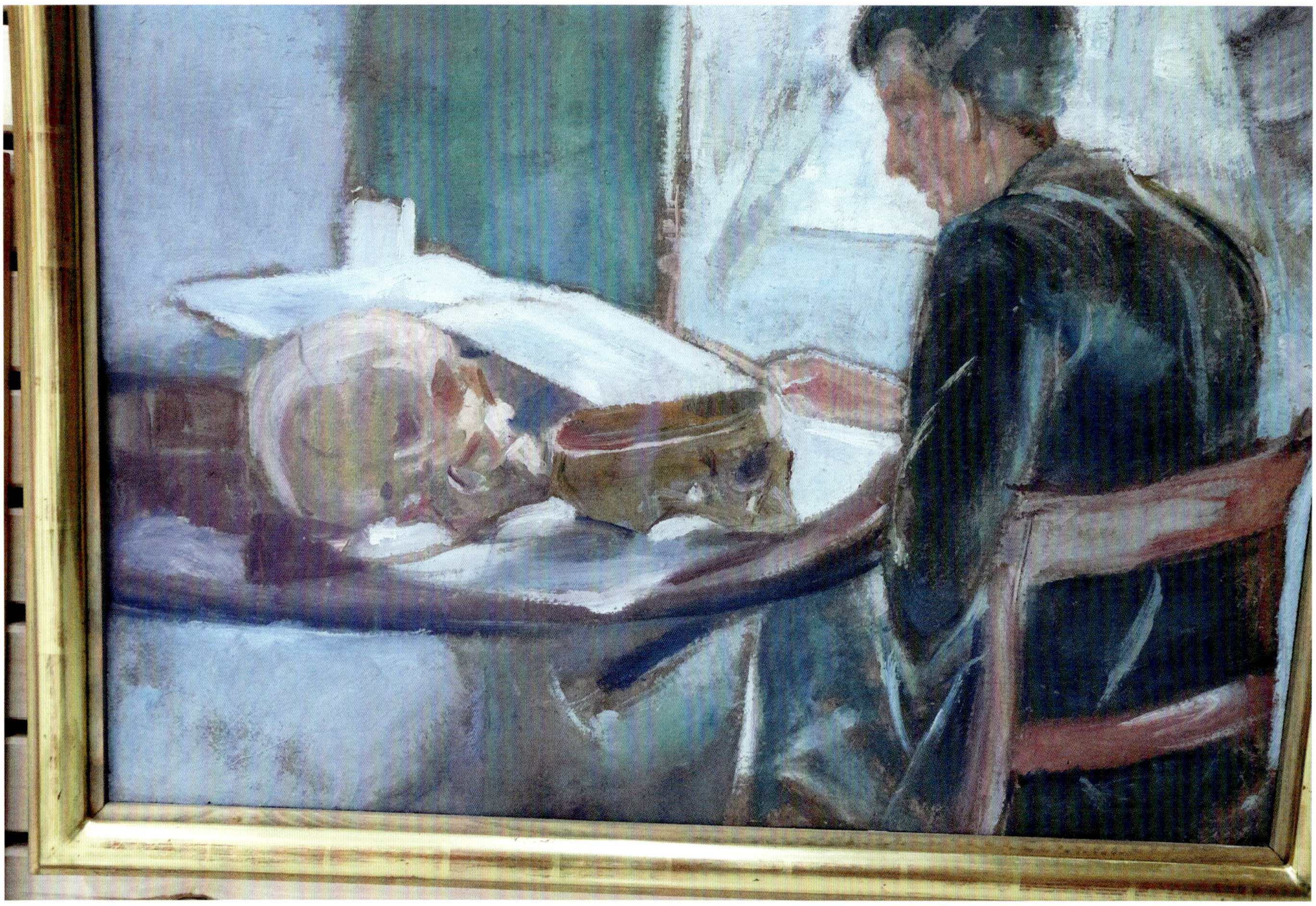

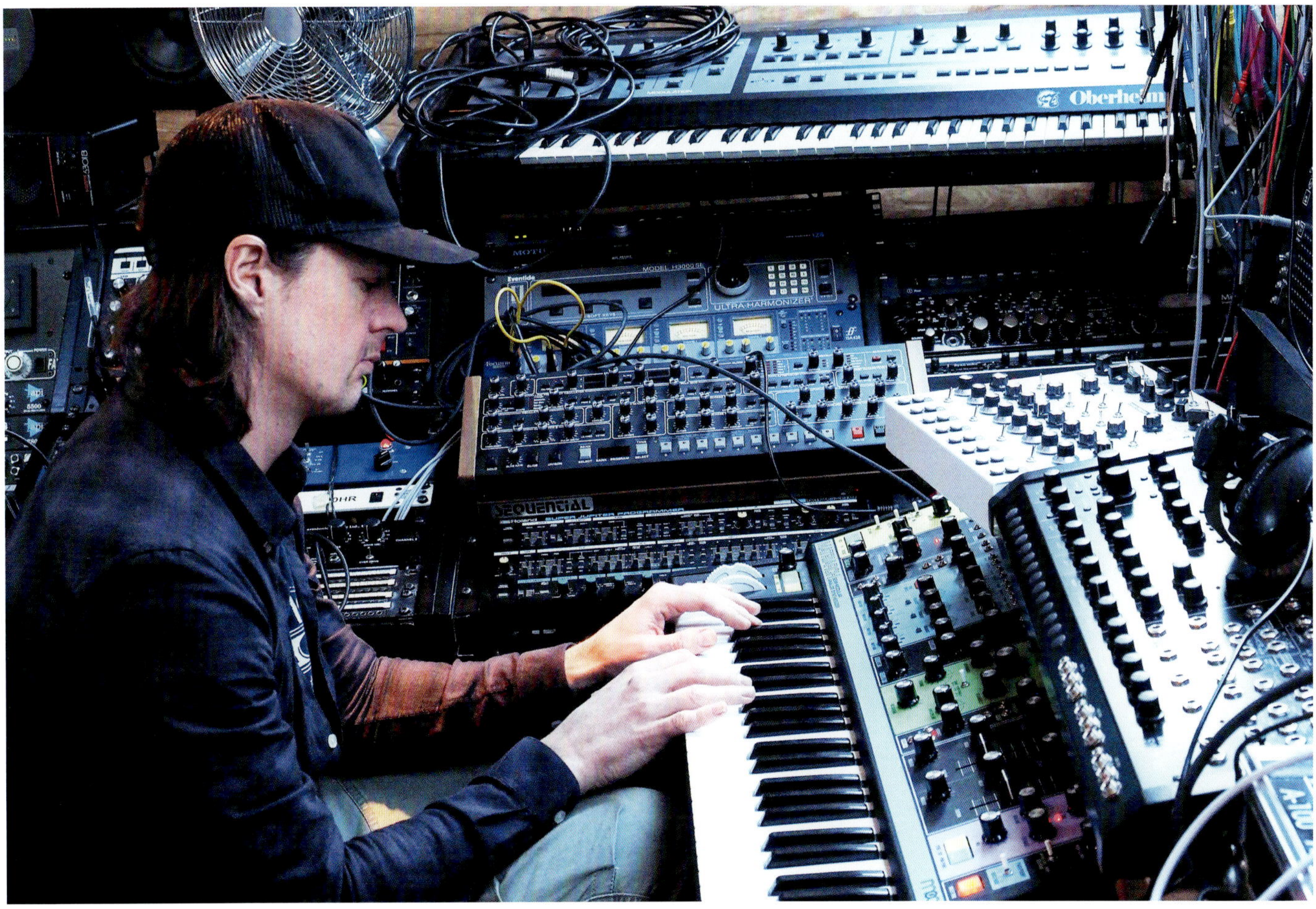
Oberheim
Eventide
ULTRA-HARMONIZER
SEQUENTIAL

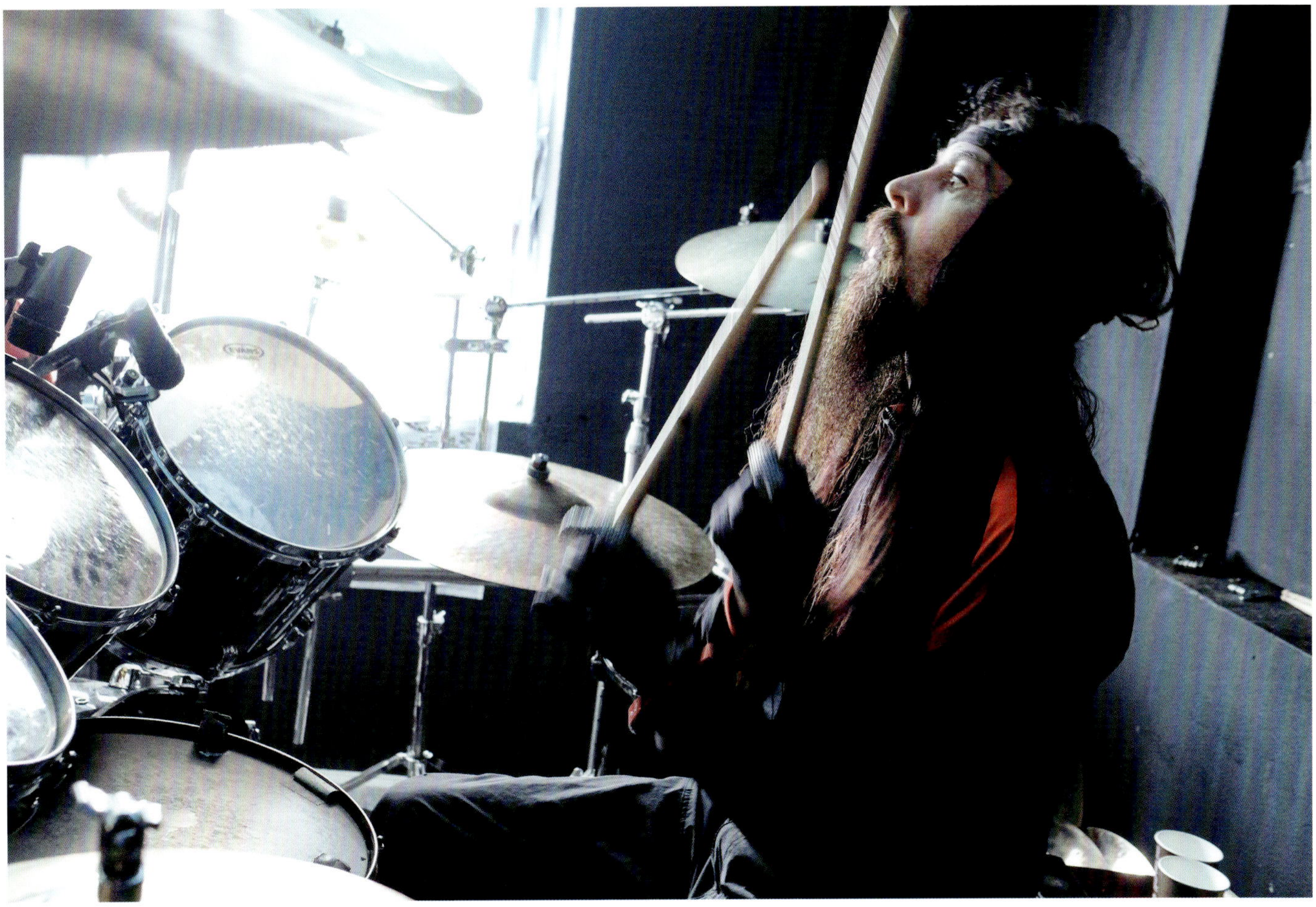

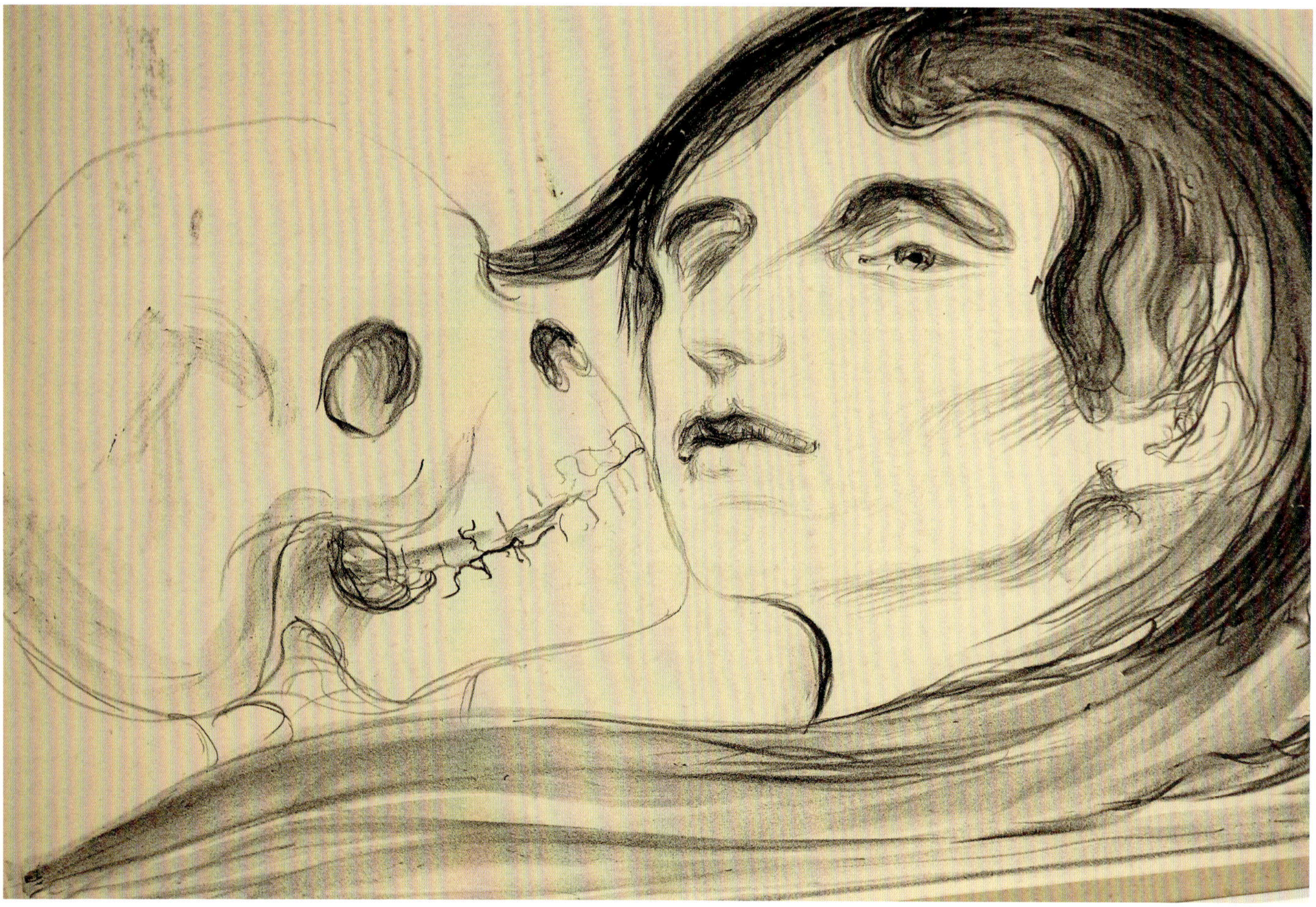

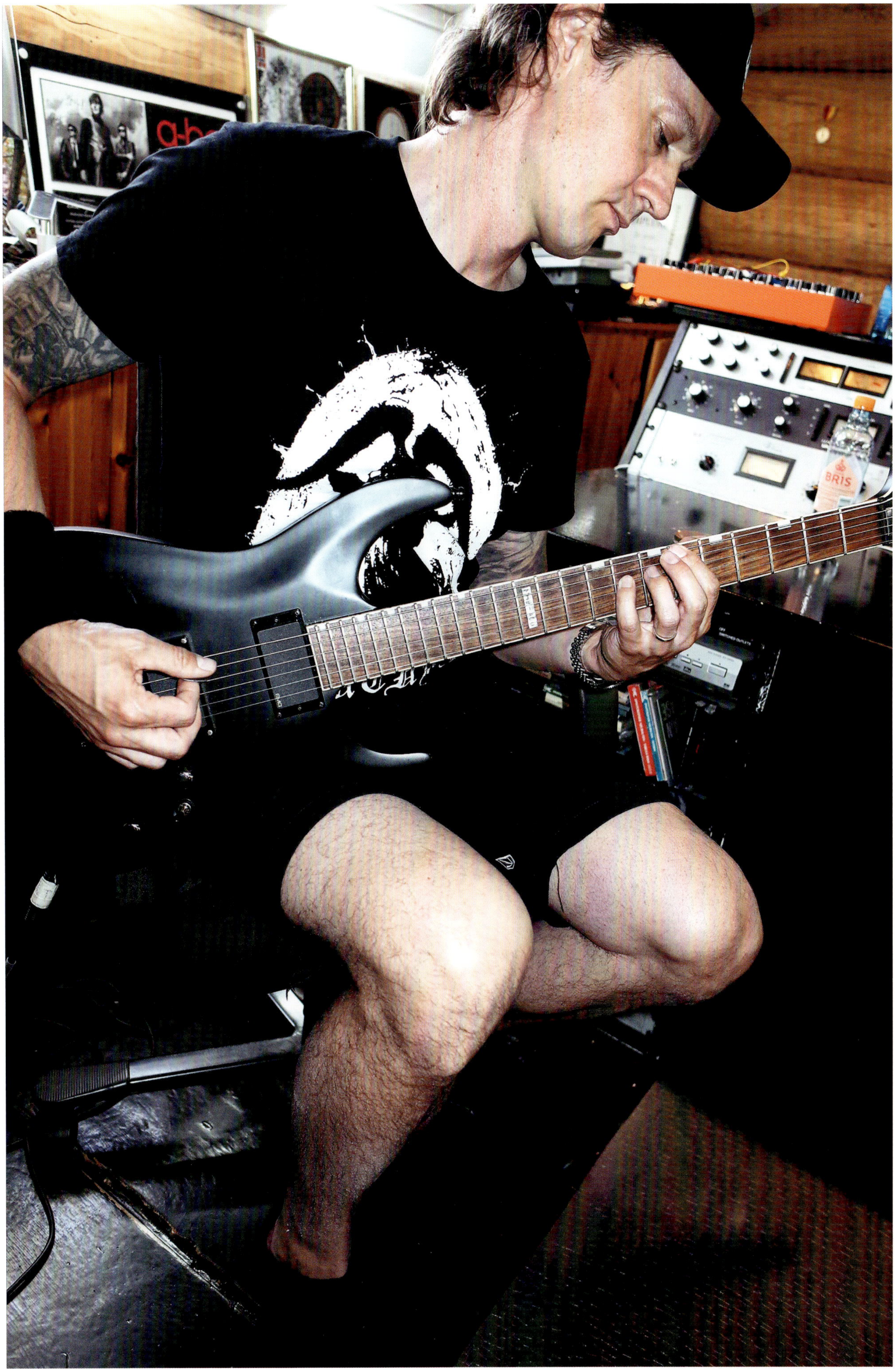

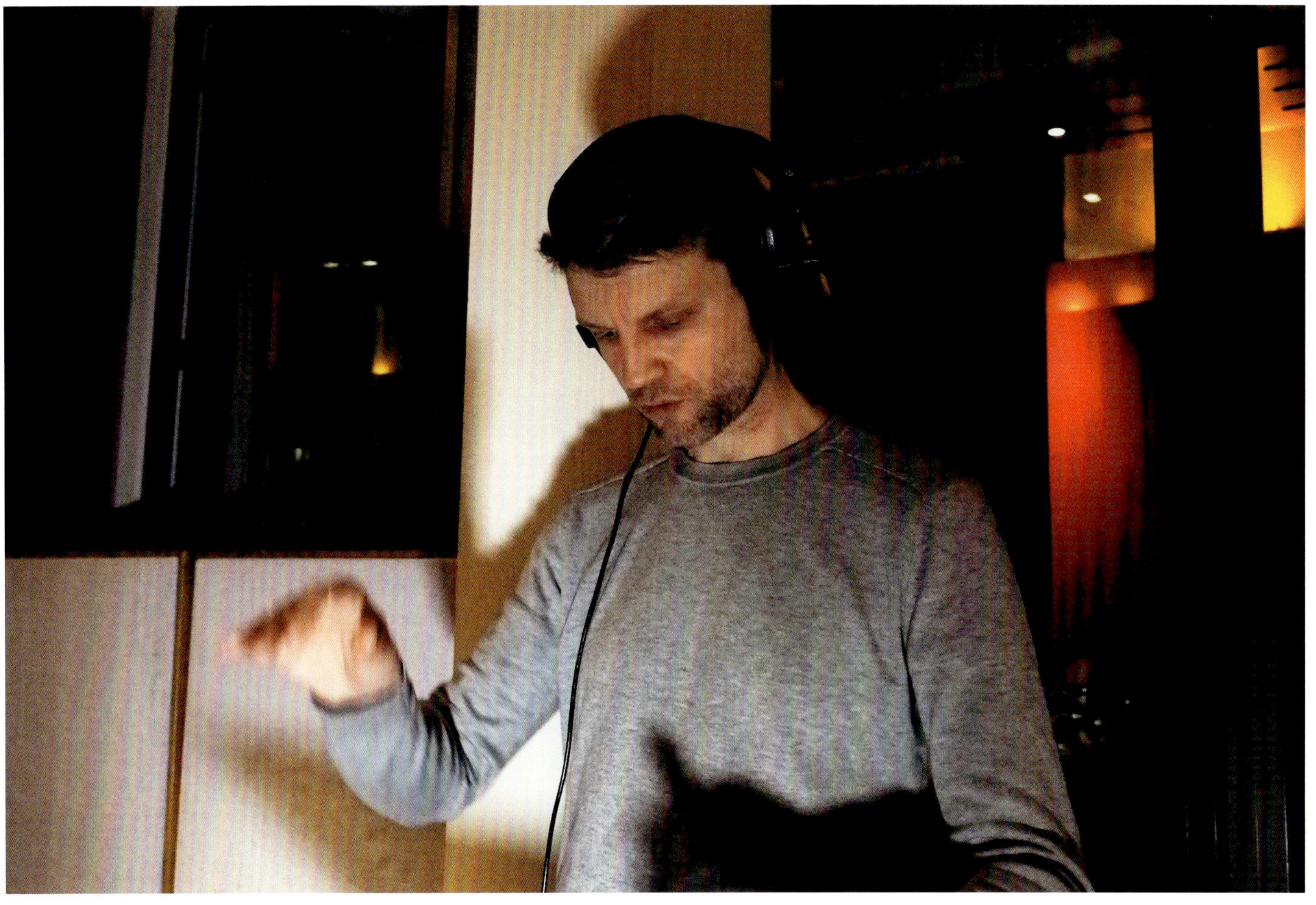

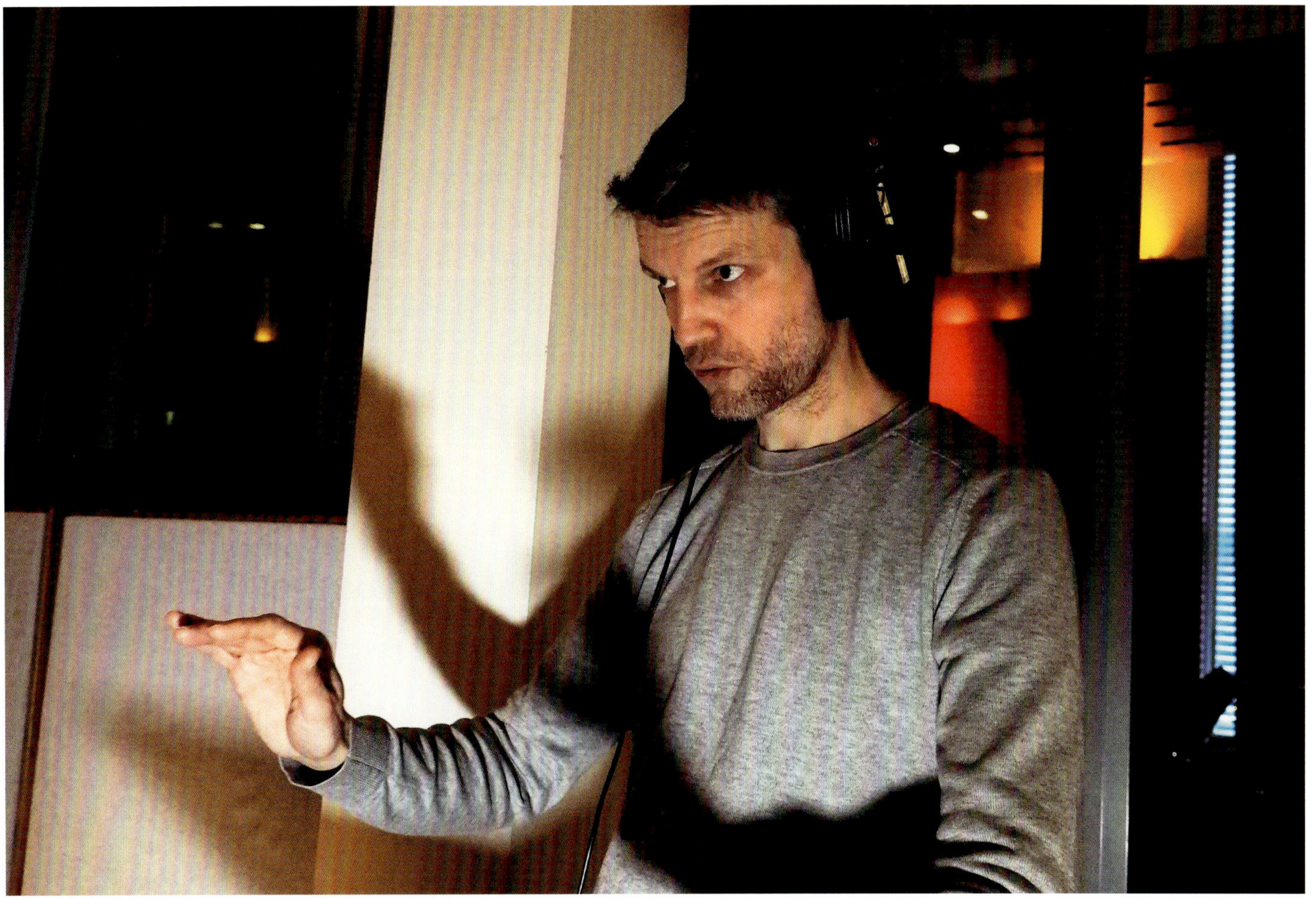

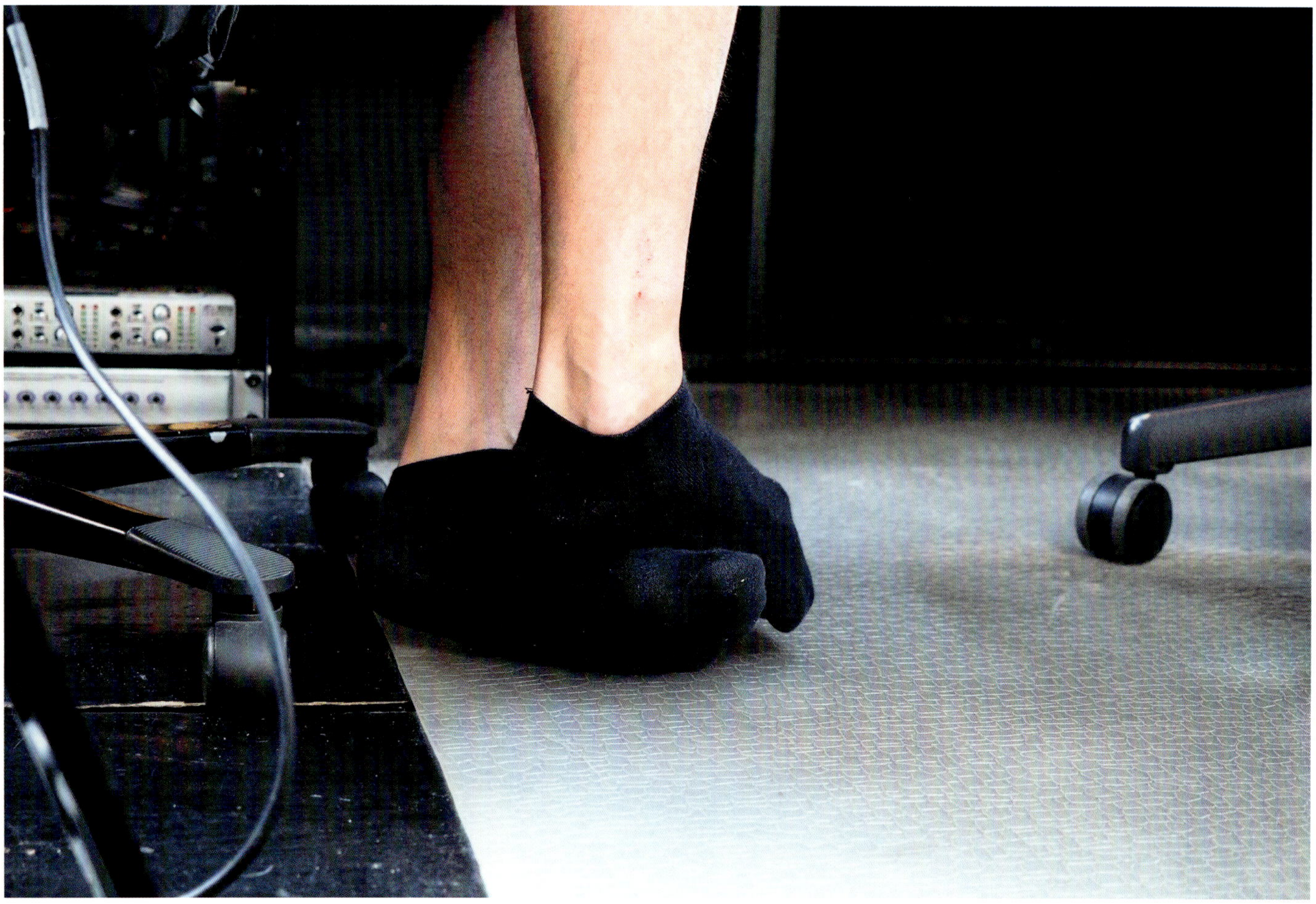

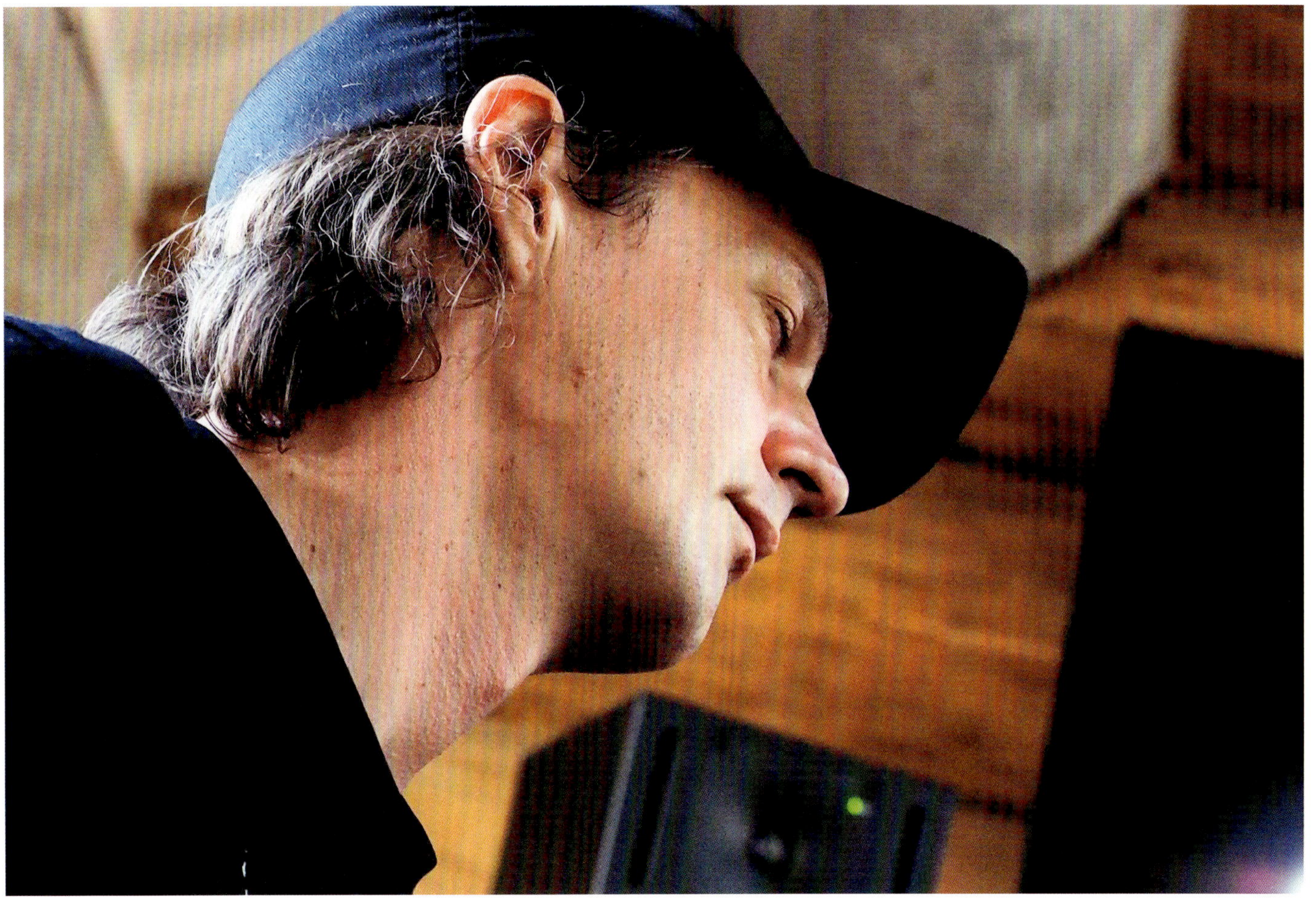

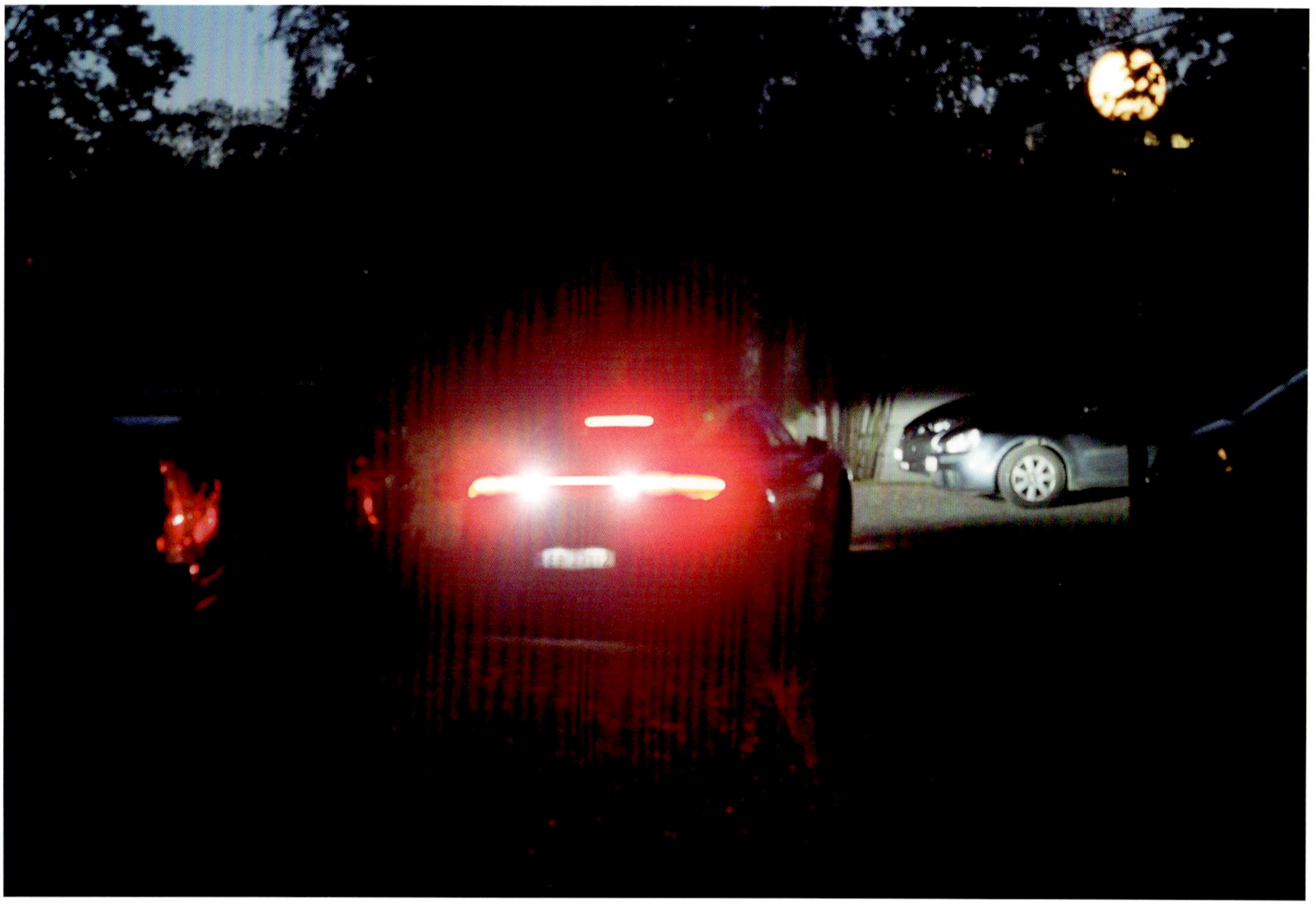

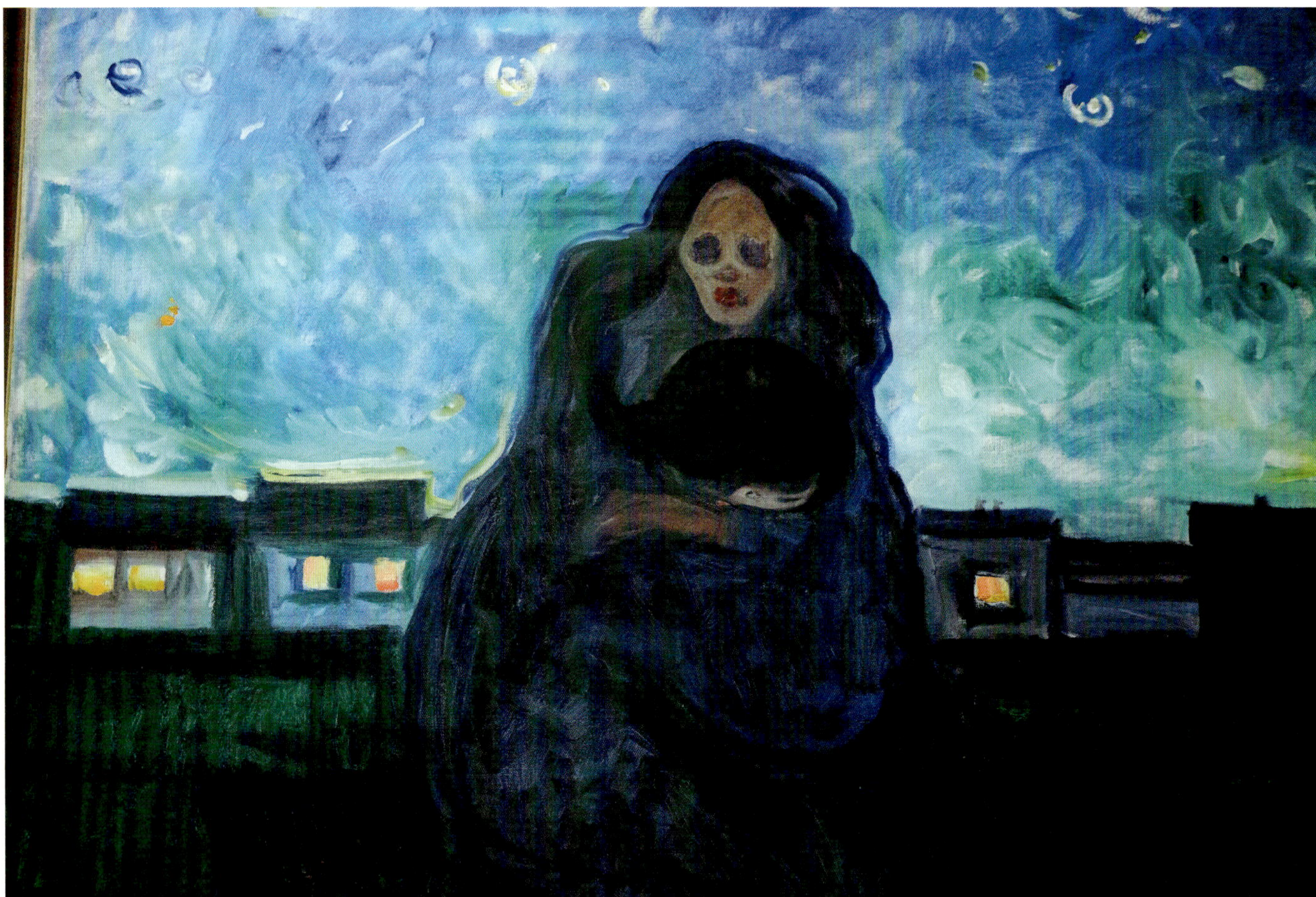

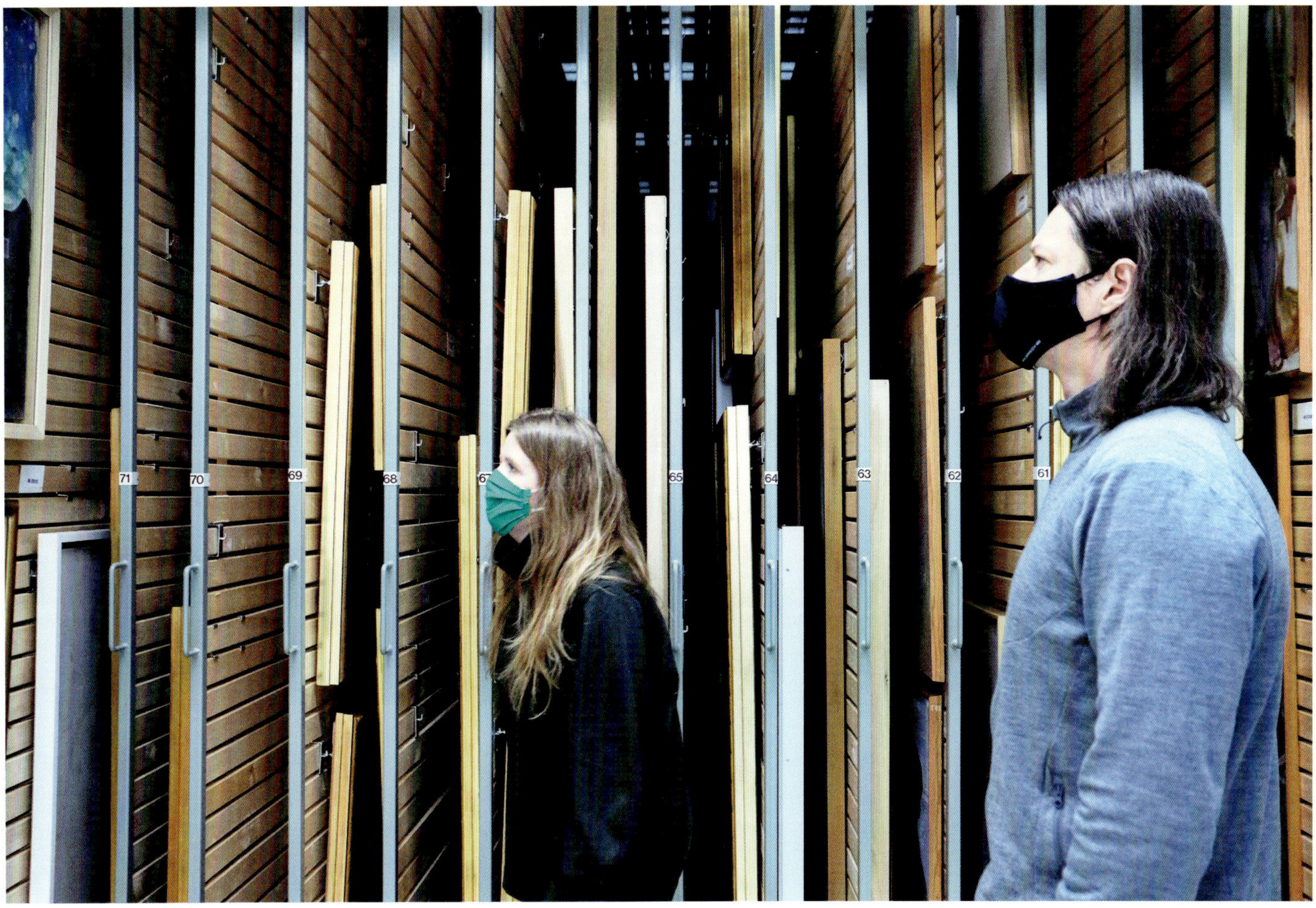
71
70
69
68
67
65
64
63
62
61

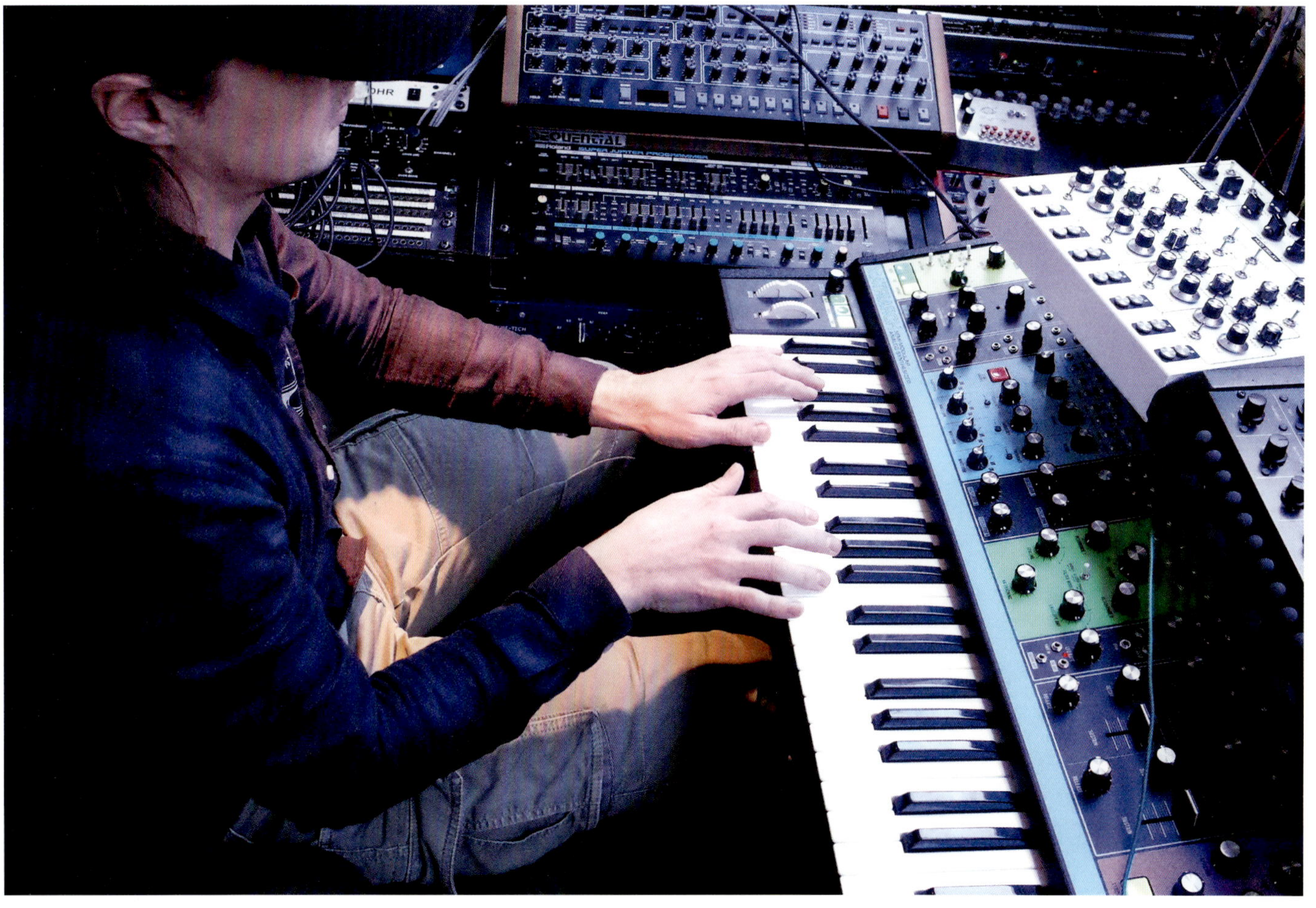

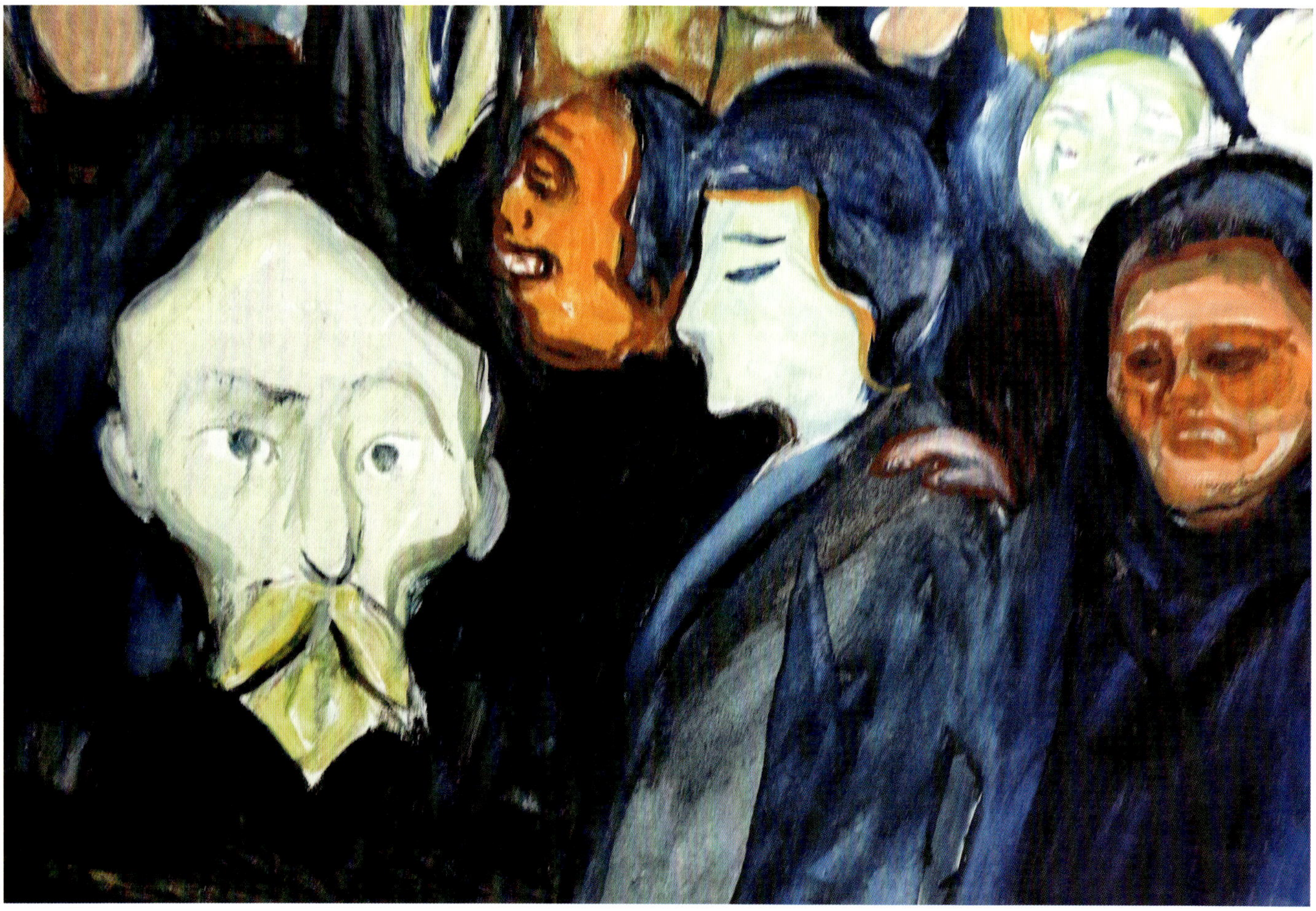

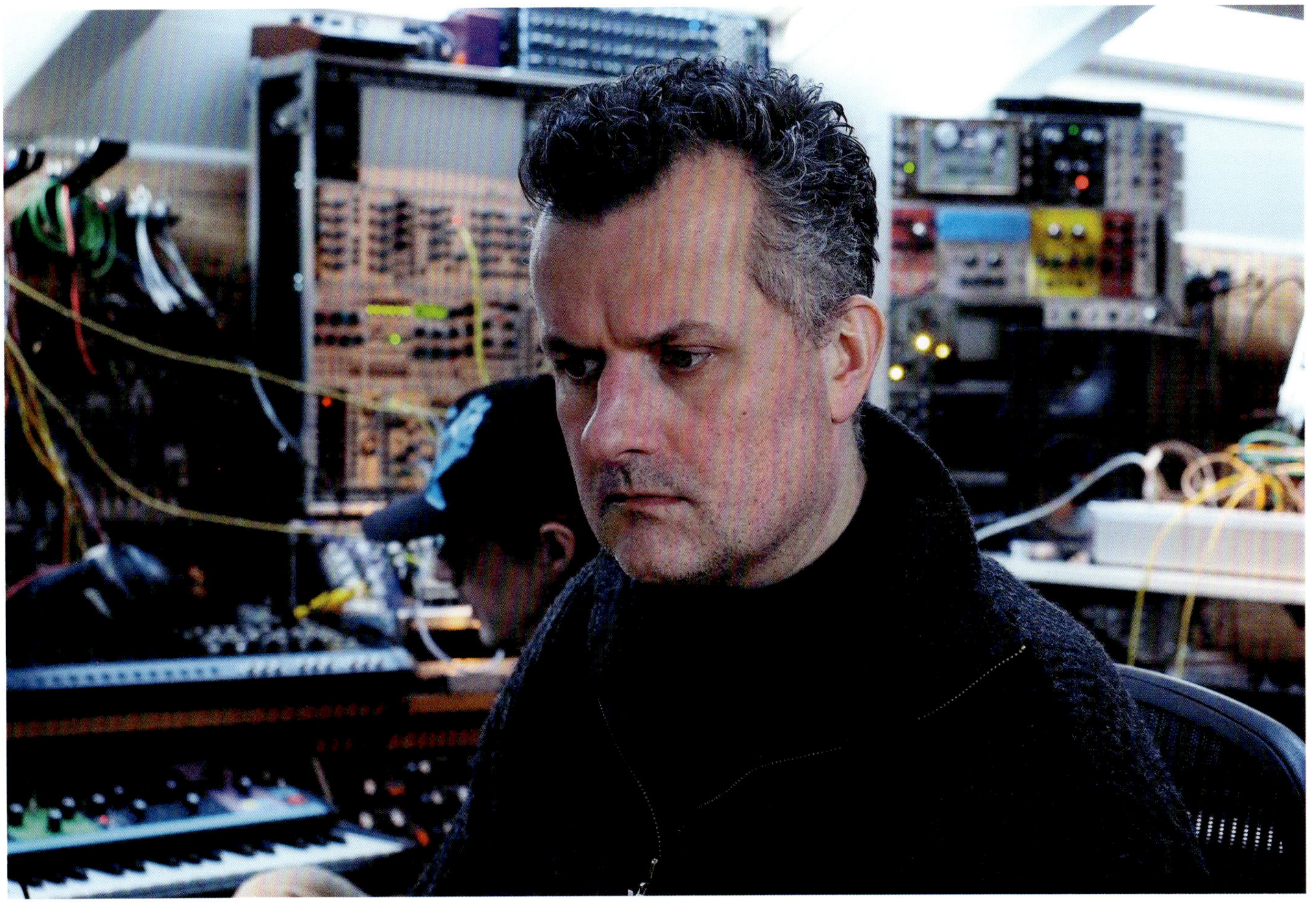

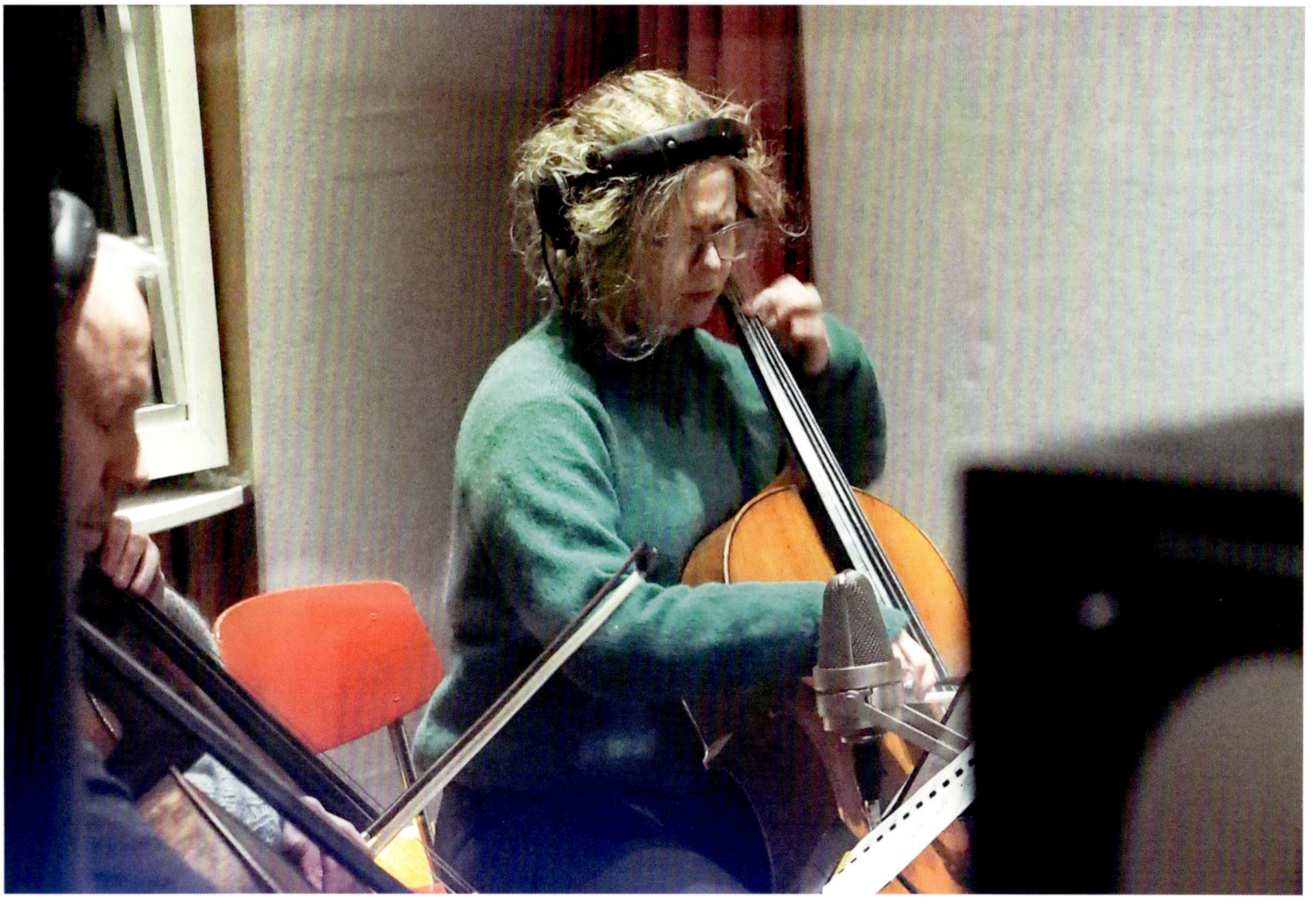

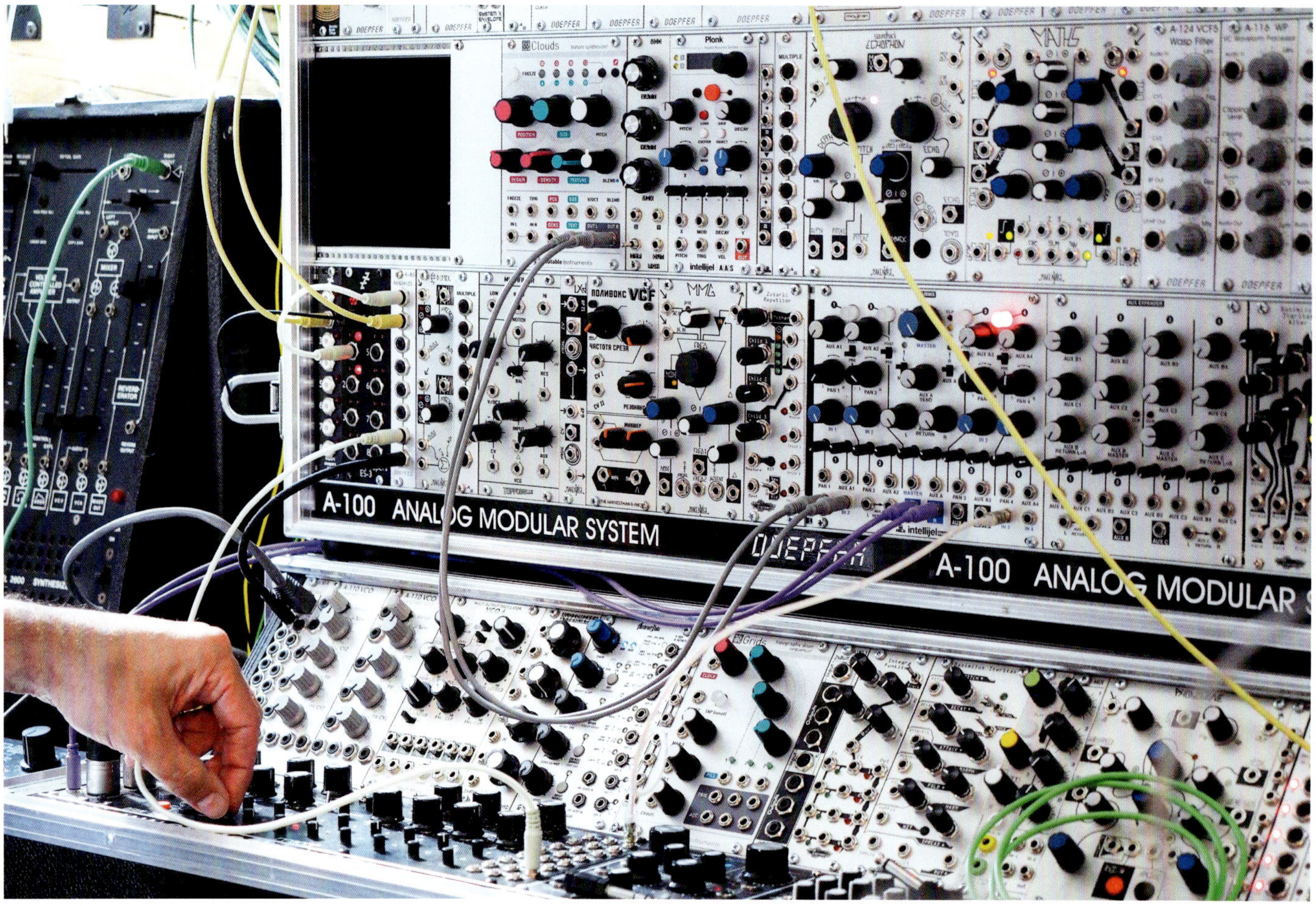
A-100 ANALOG MODULAR SYSTEM
DOEPFER
A-100 ANALOG MODULAR
MATHS
Plonk
Clouds
intellijel

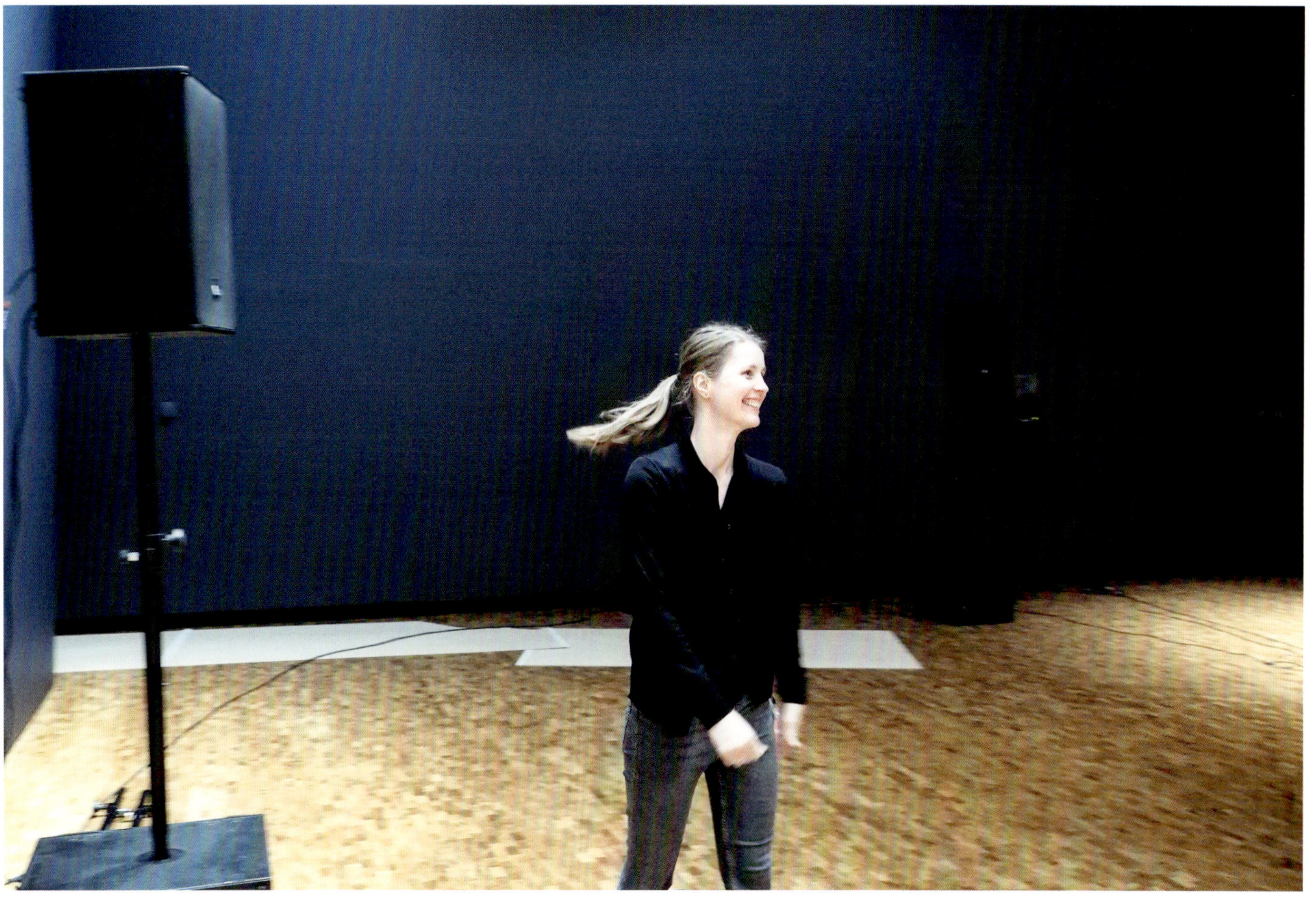

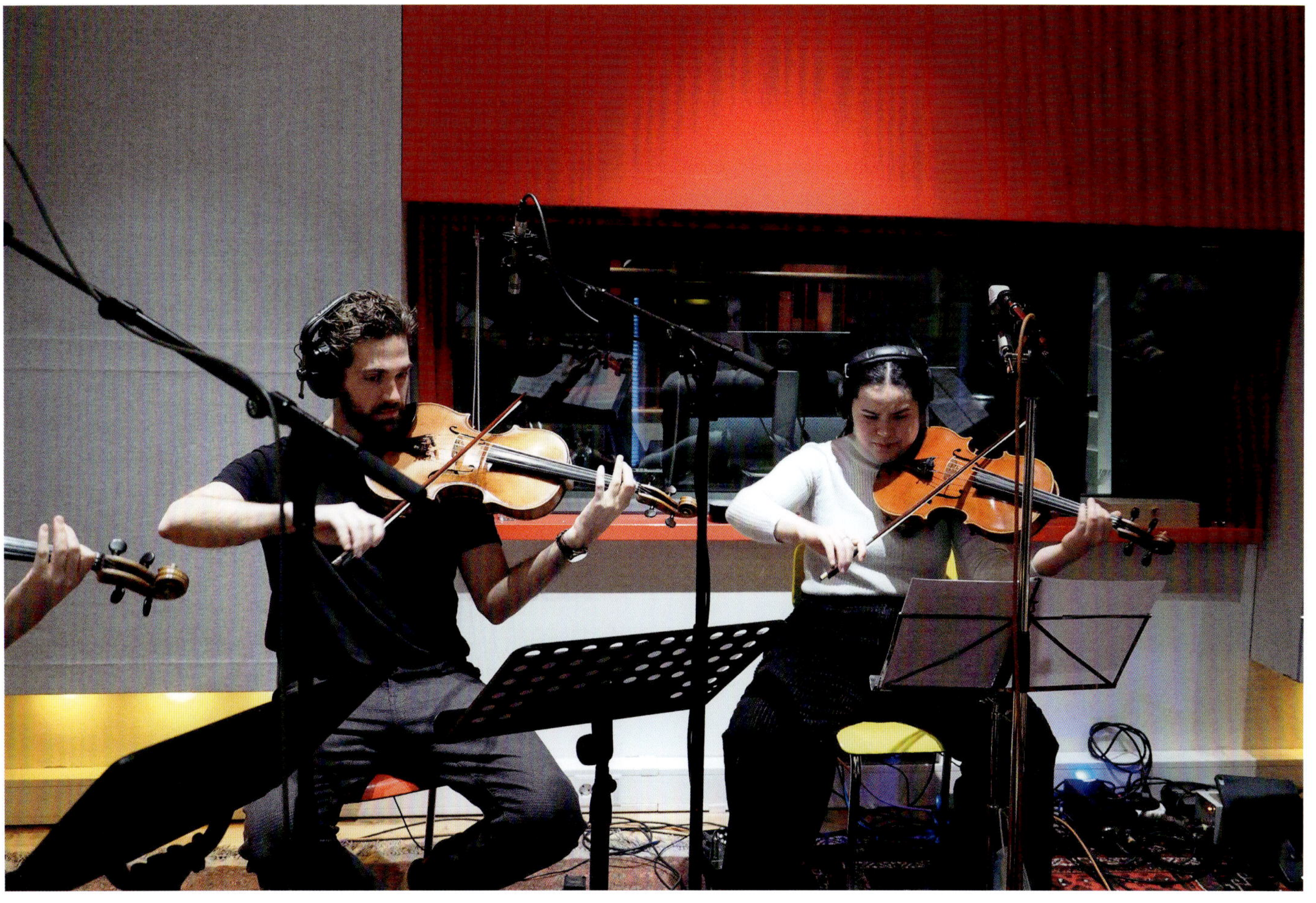

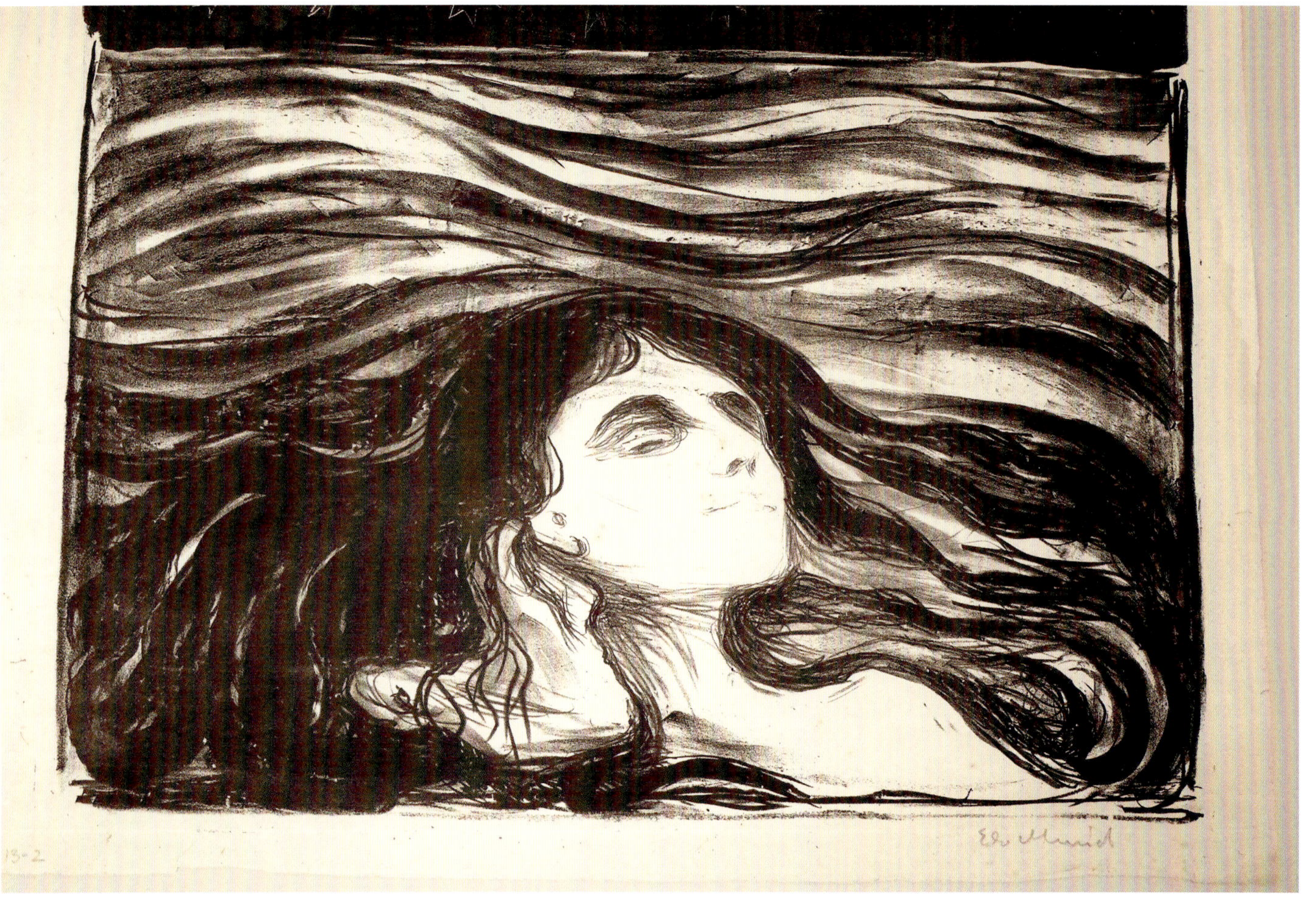

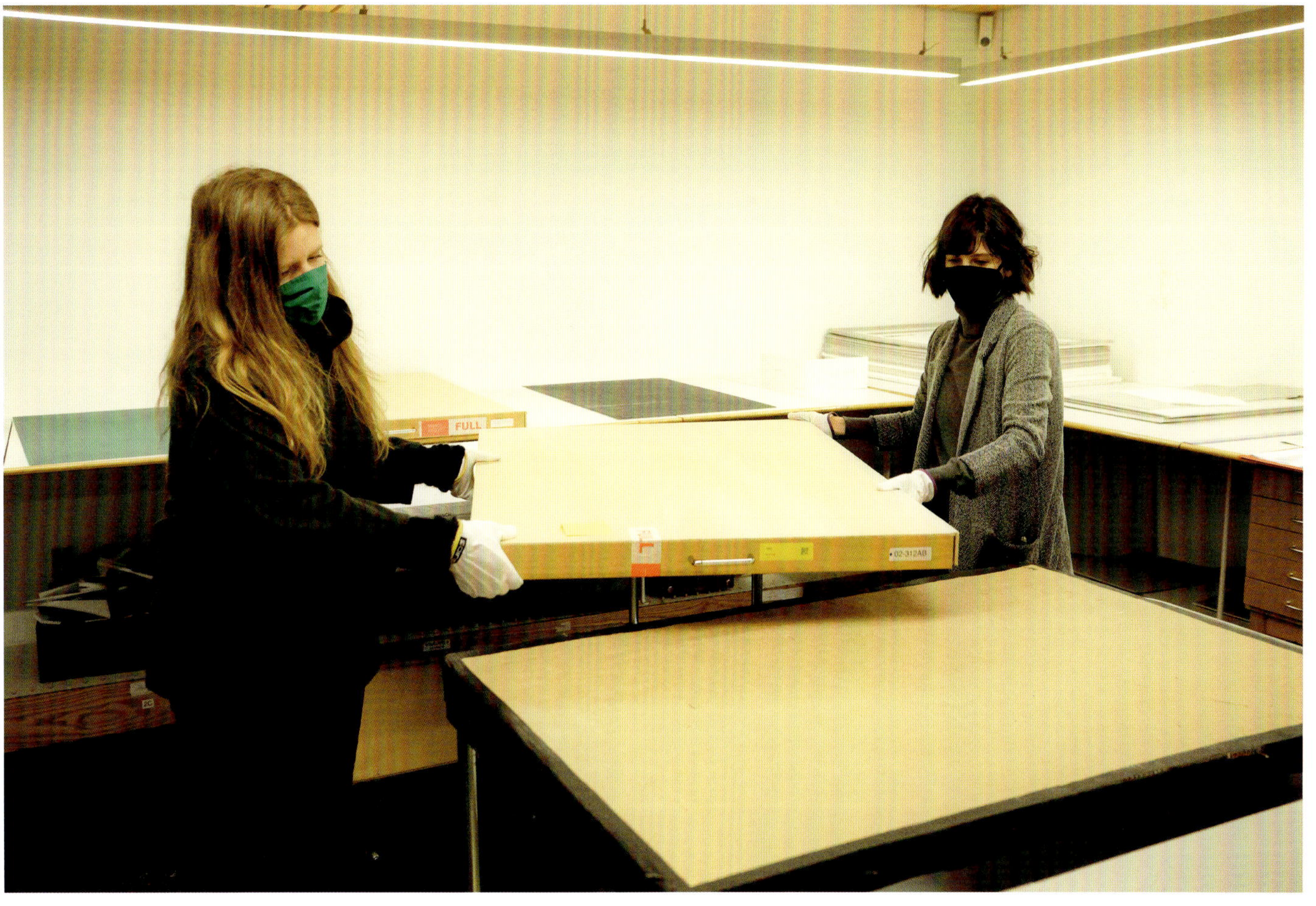
FULL

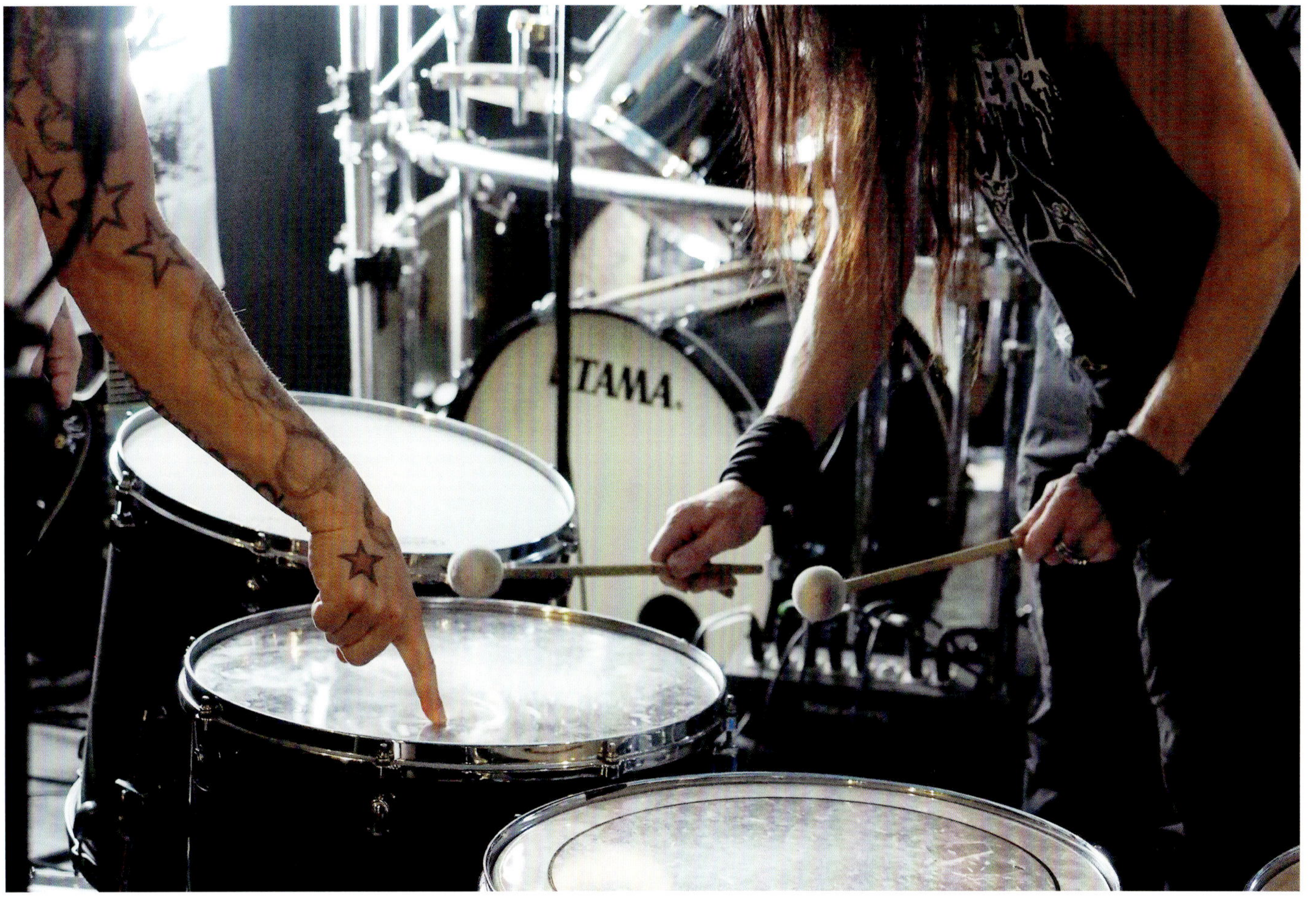
TAMA

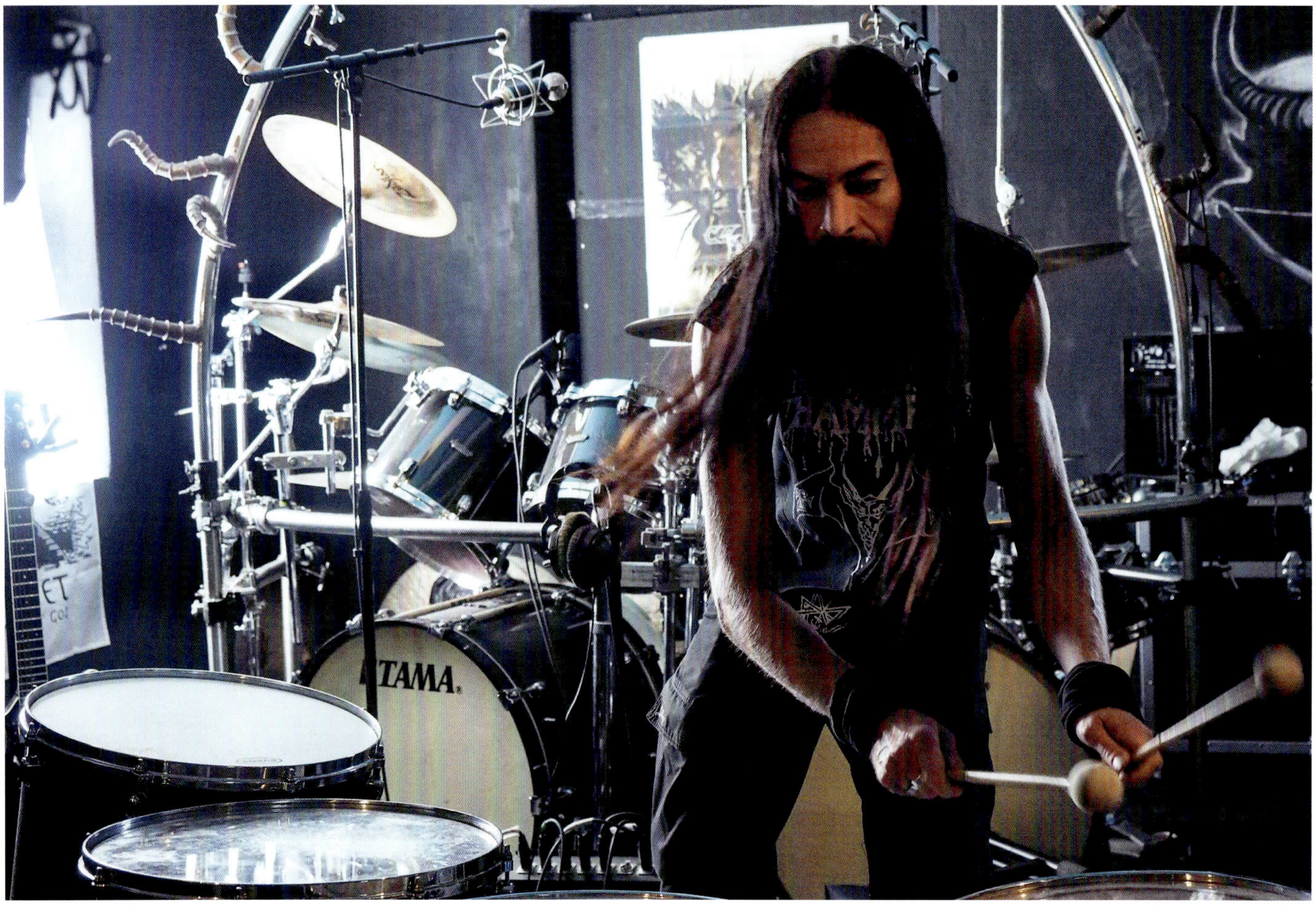
TAMA

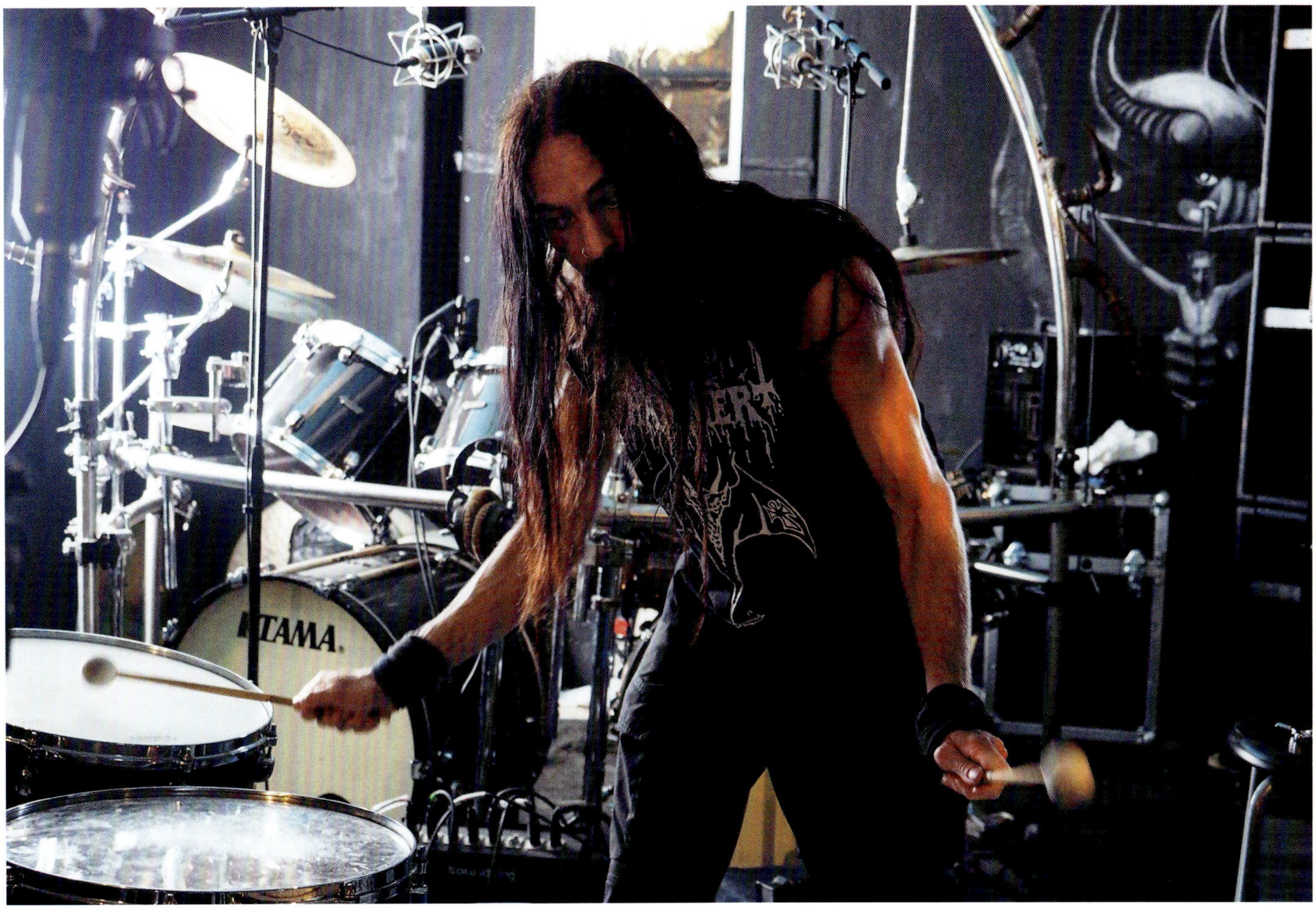
TAMA

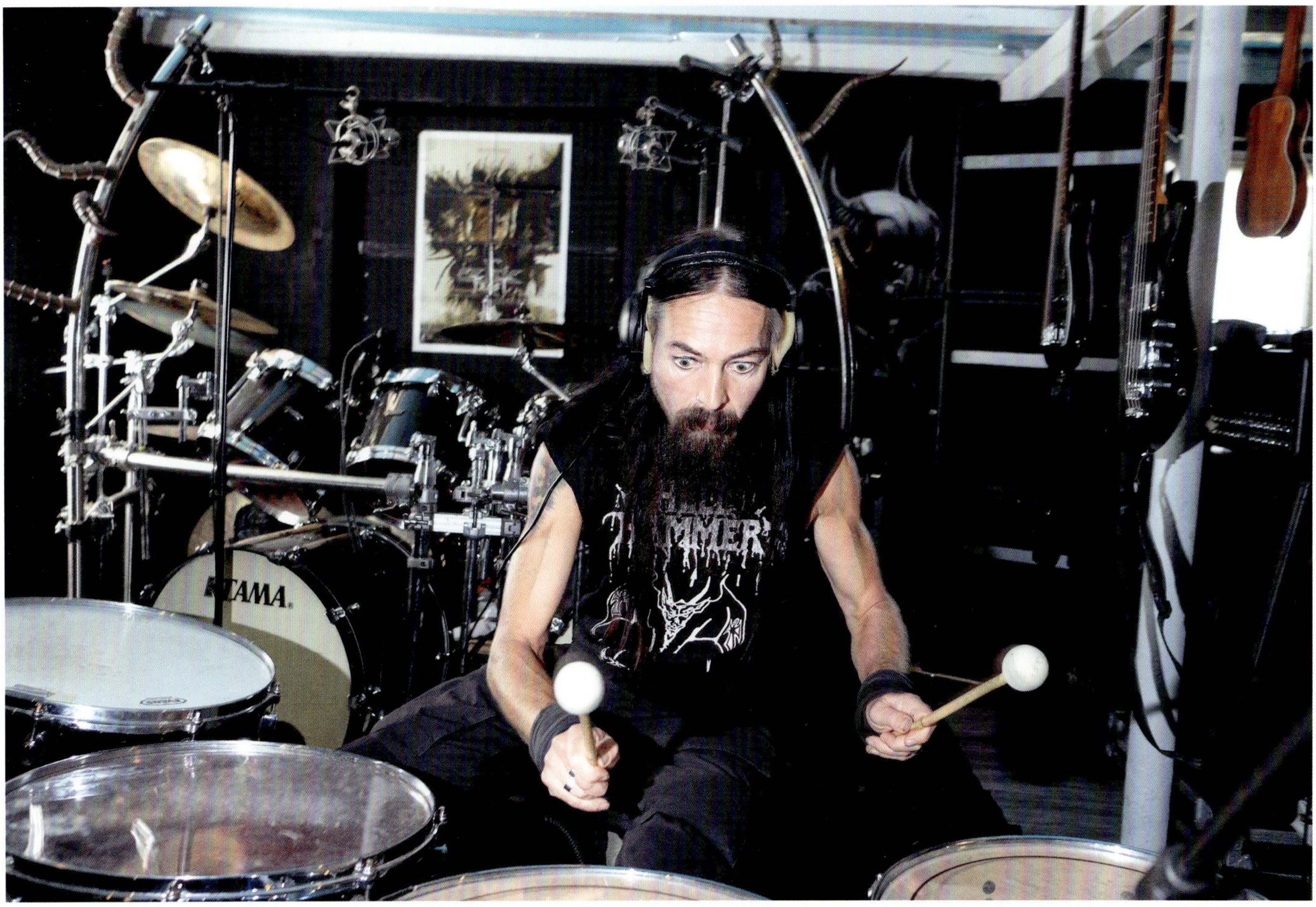
TAMA

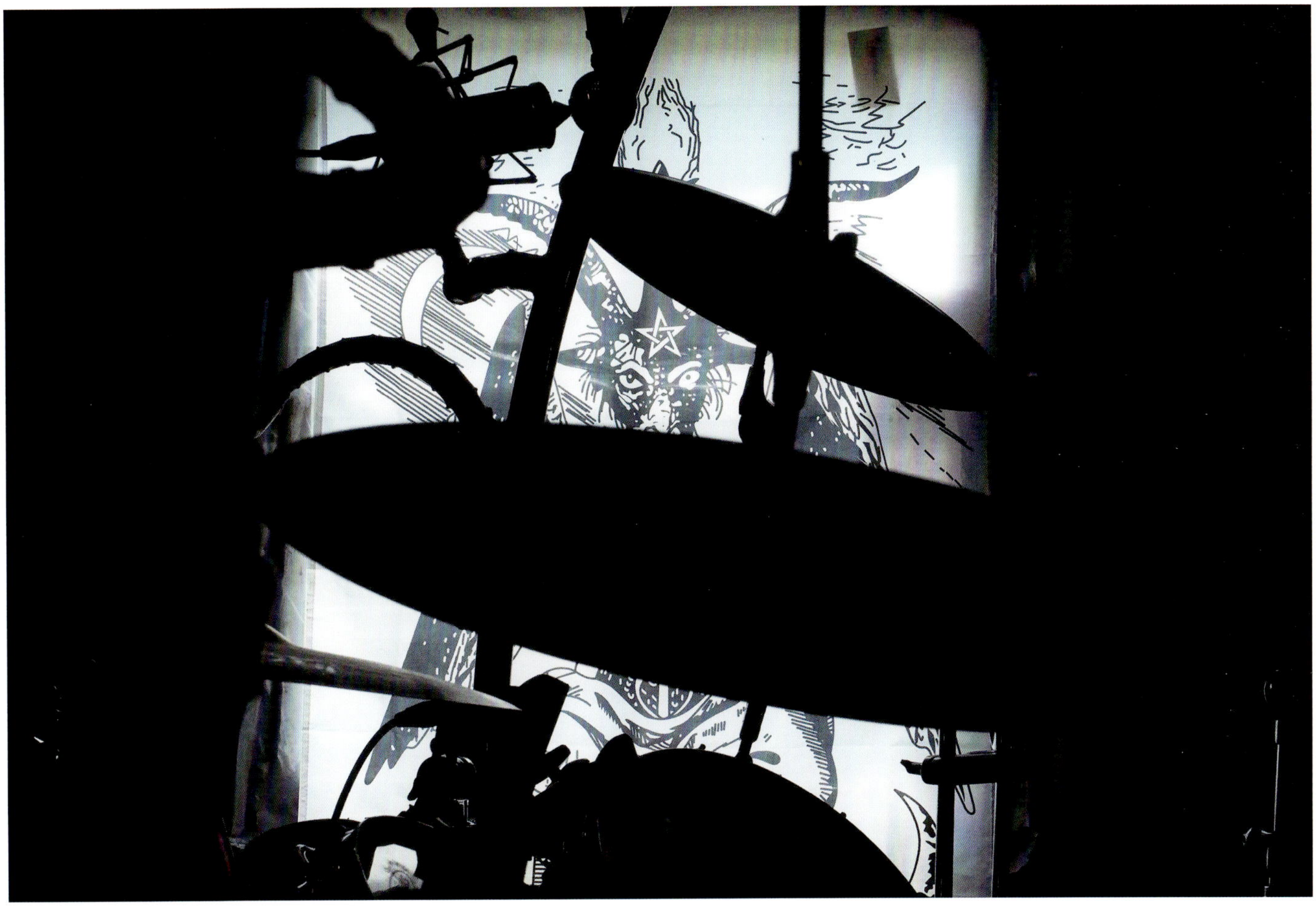

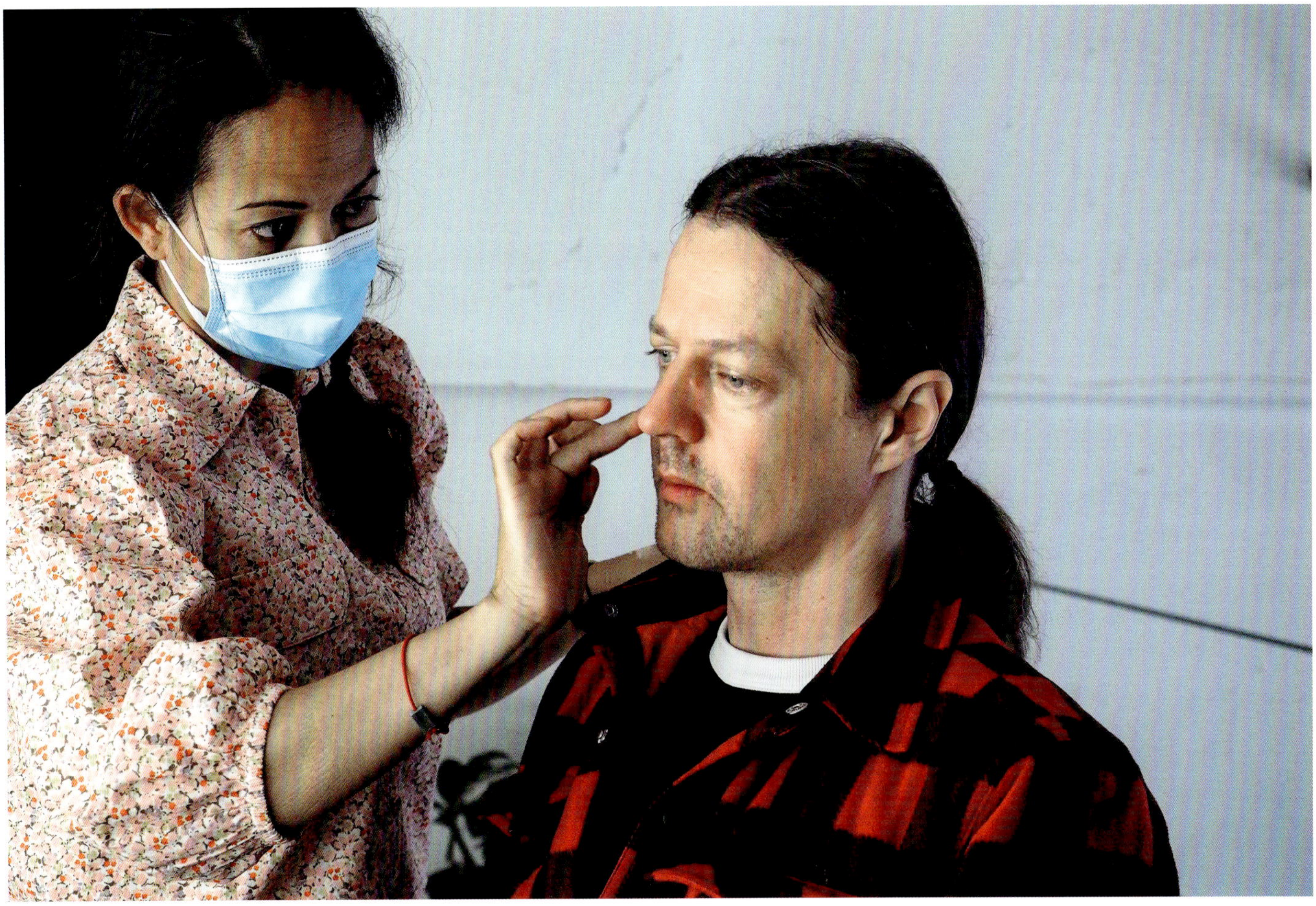

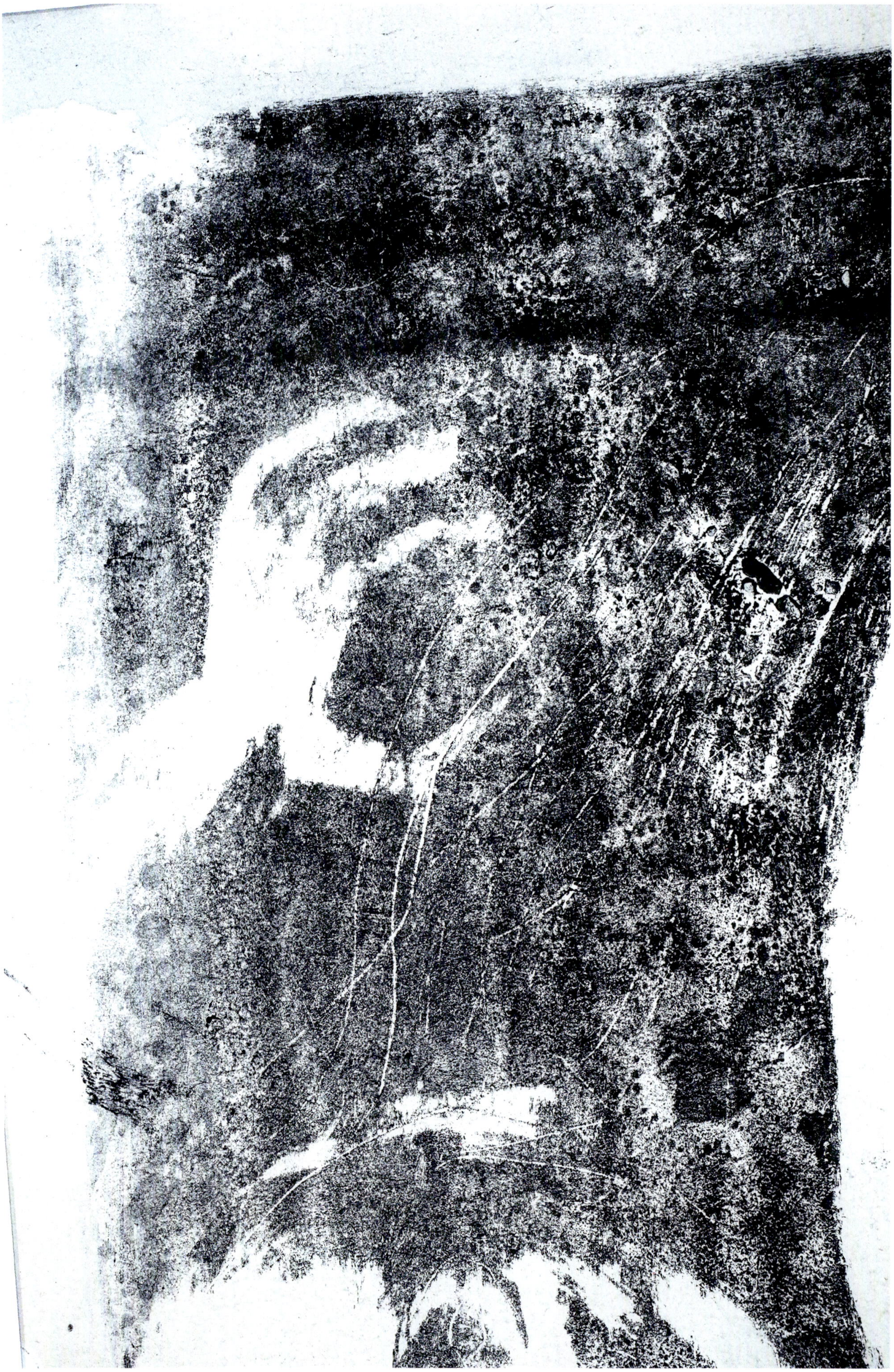

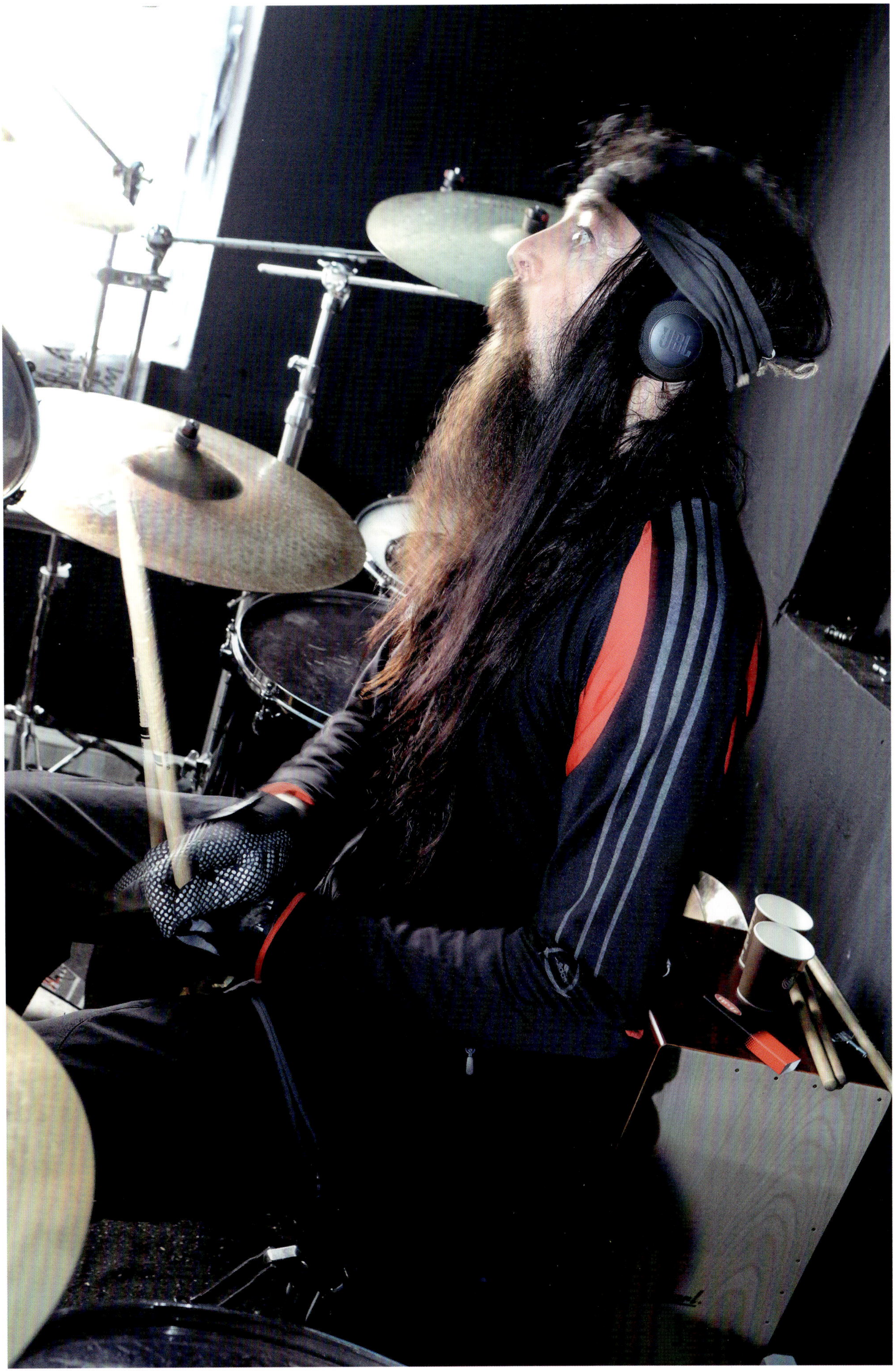

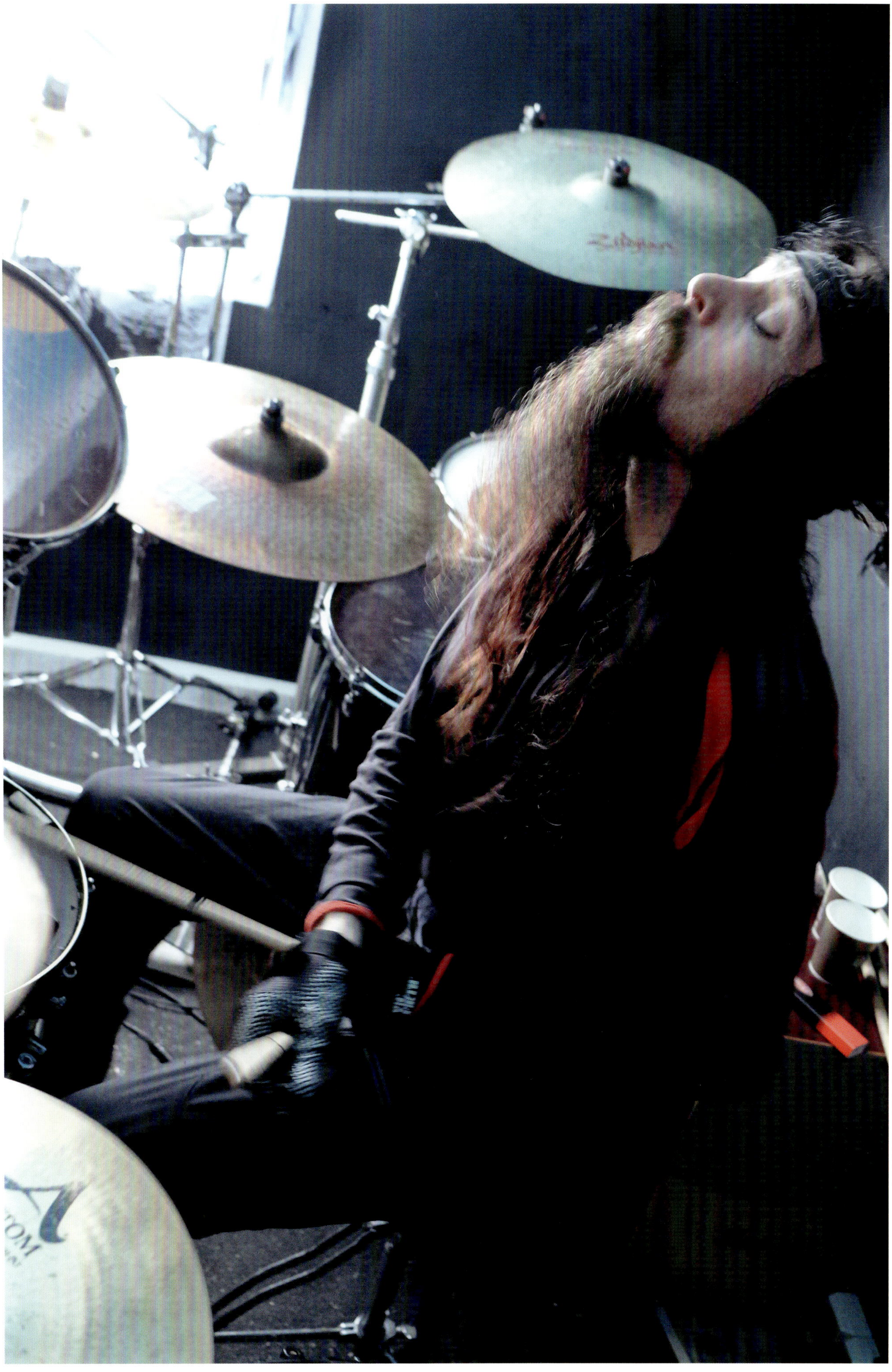

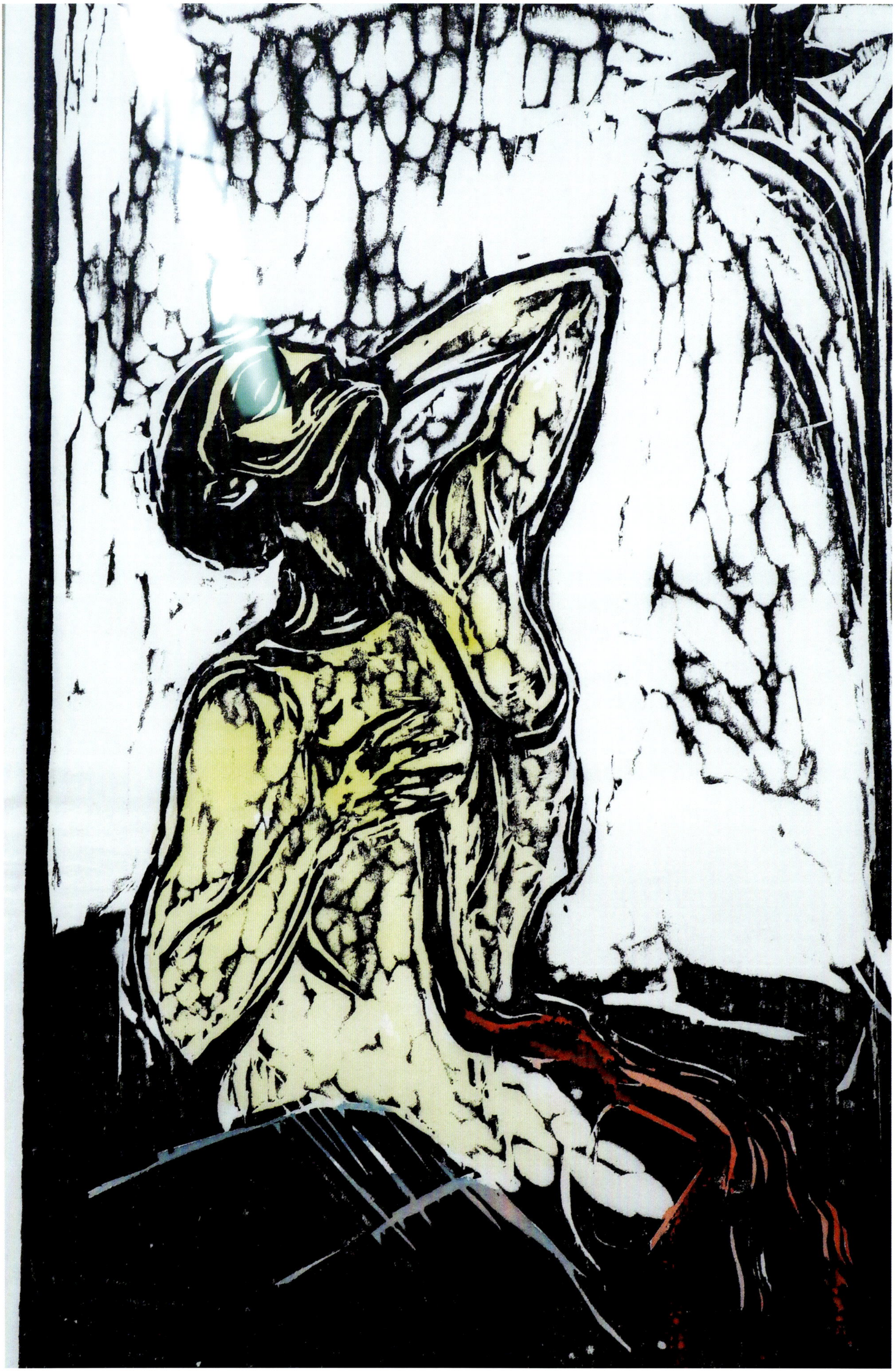

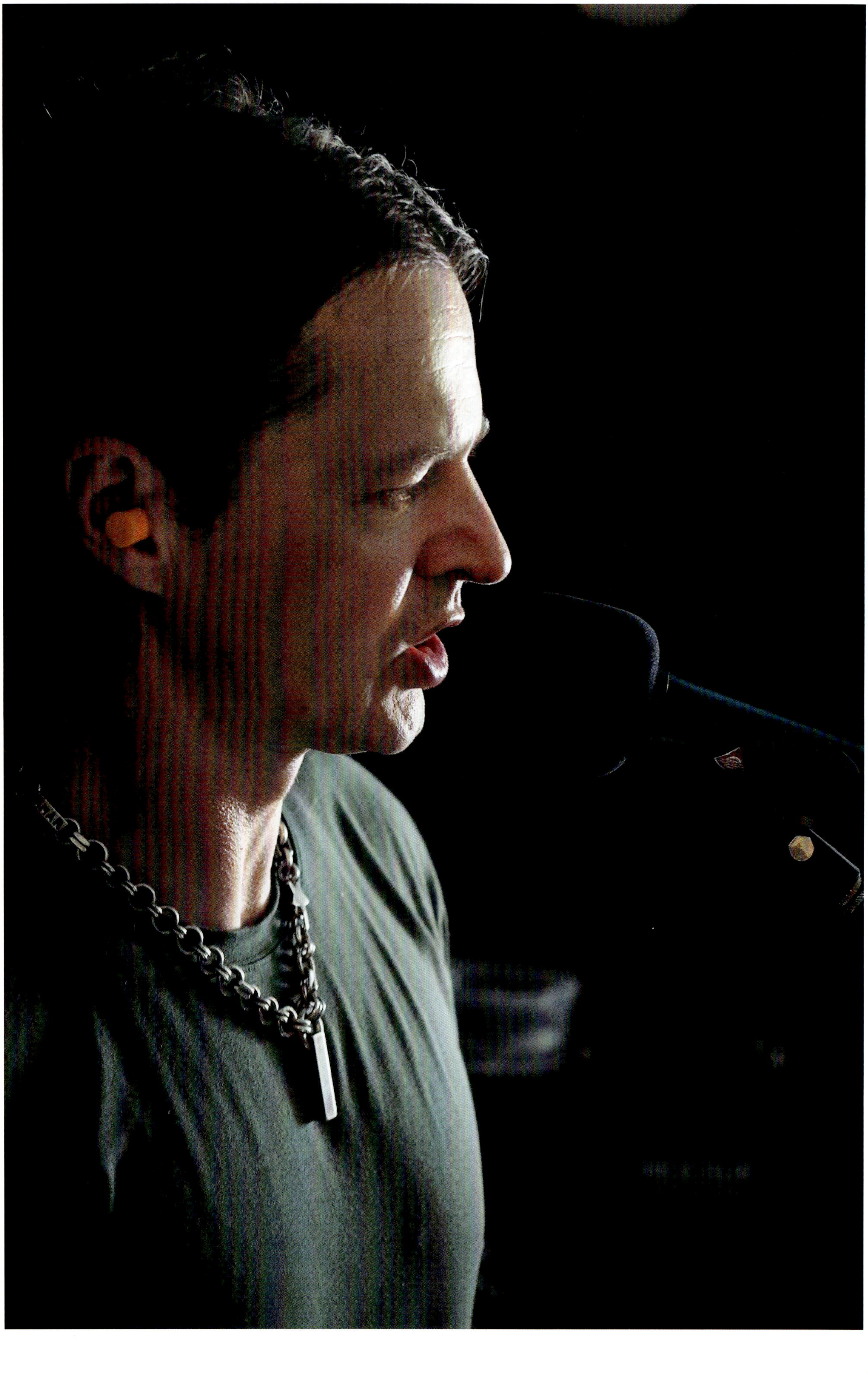

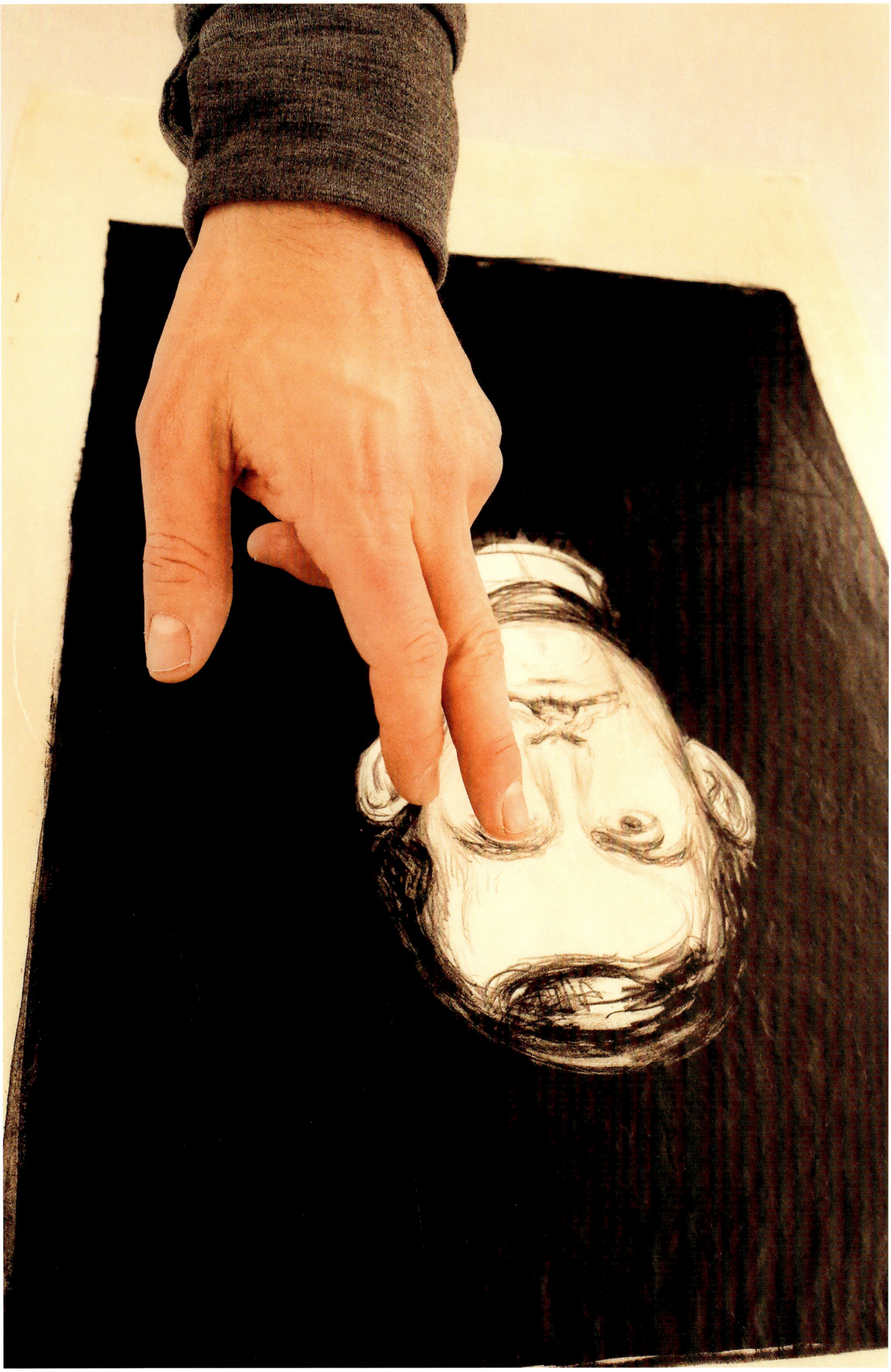

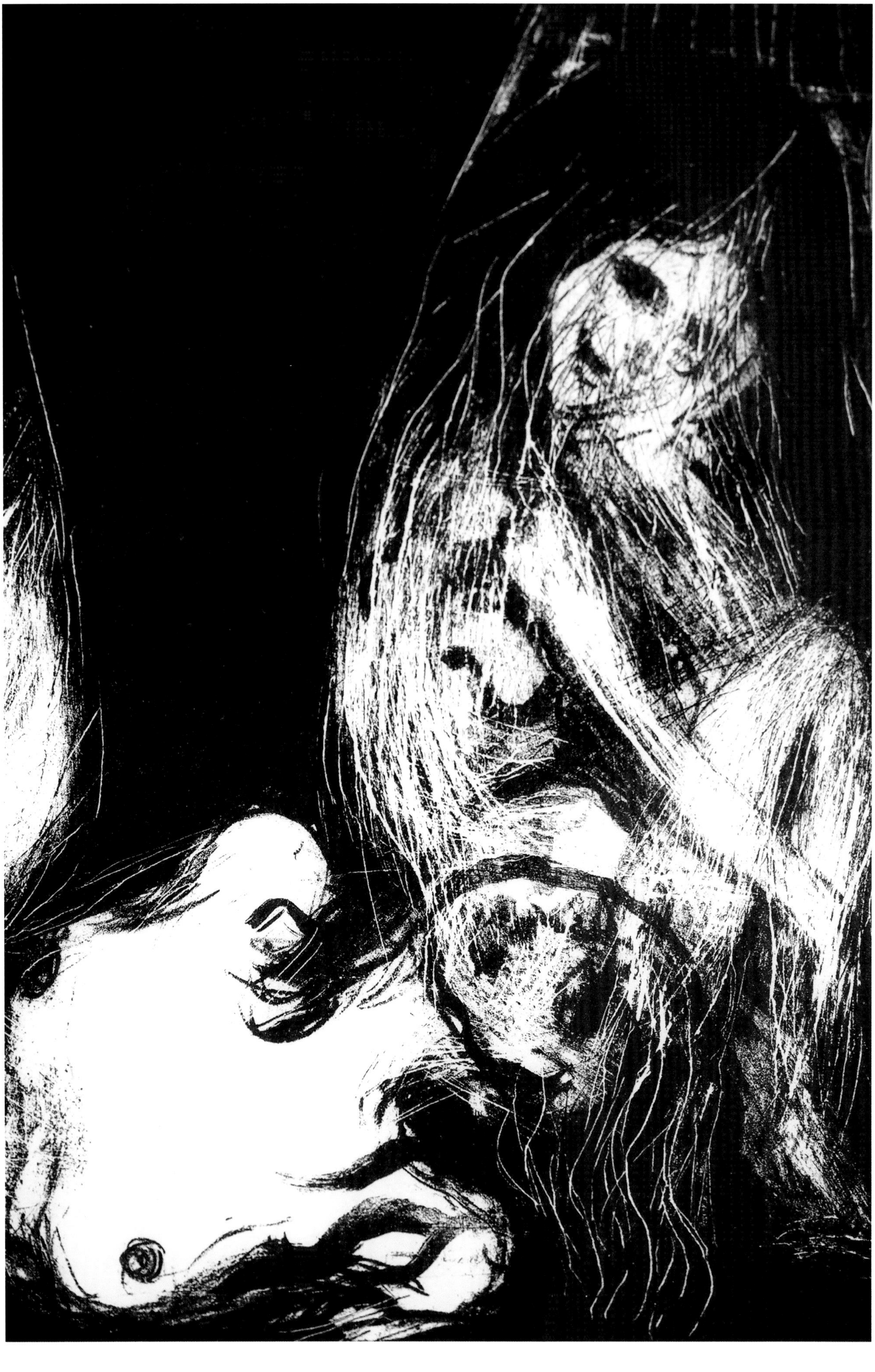

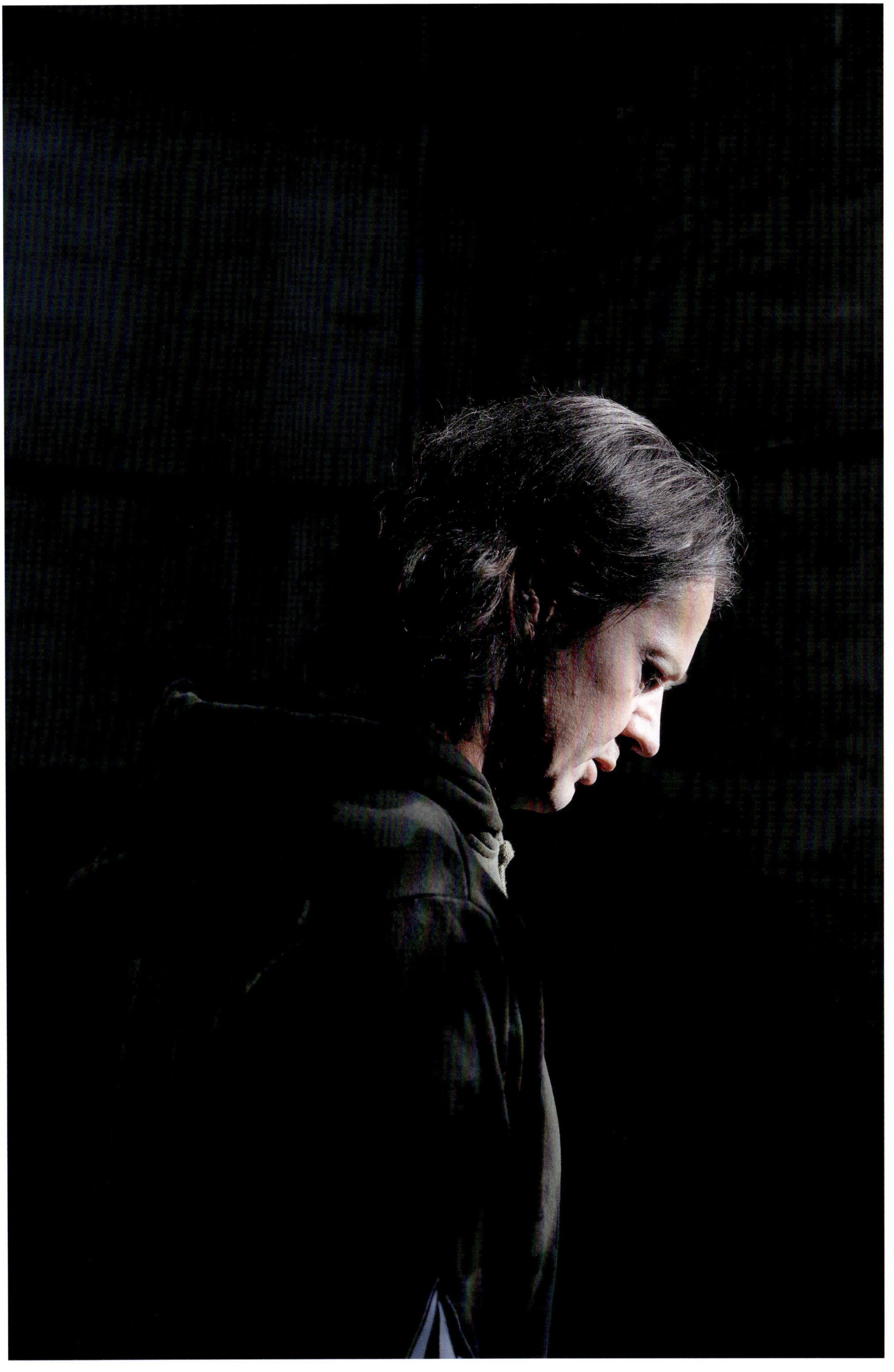

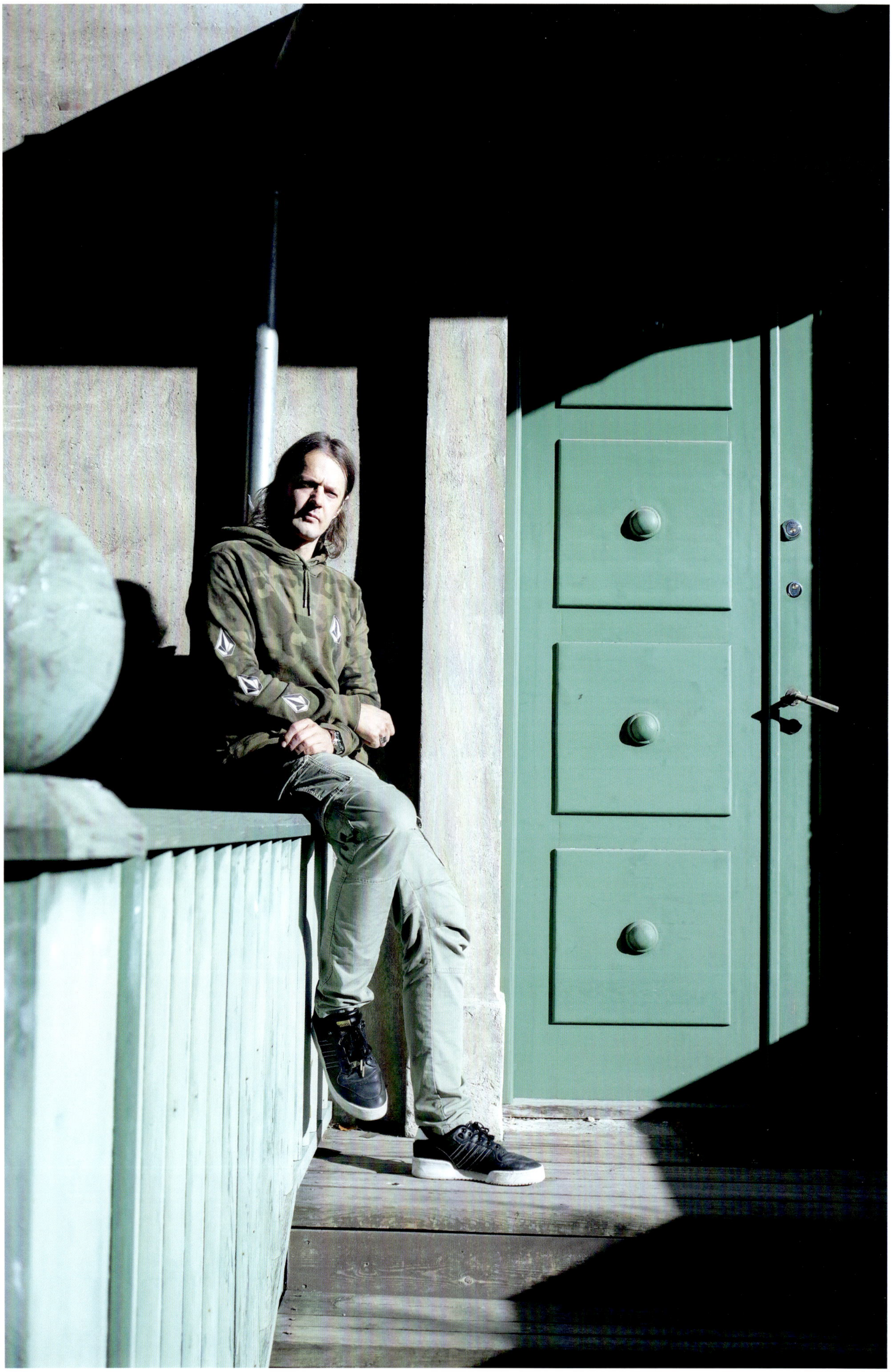

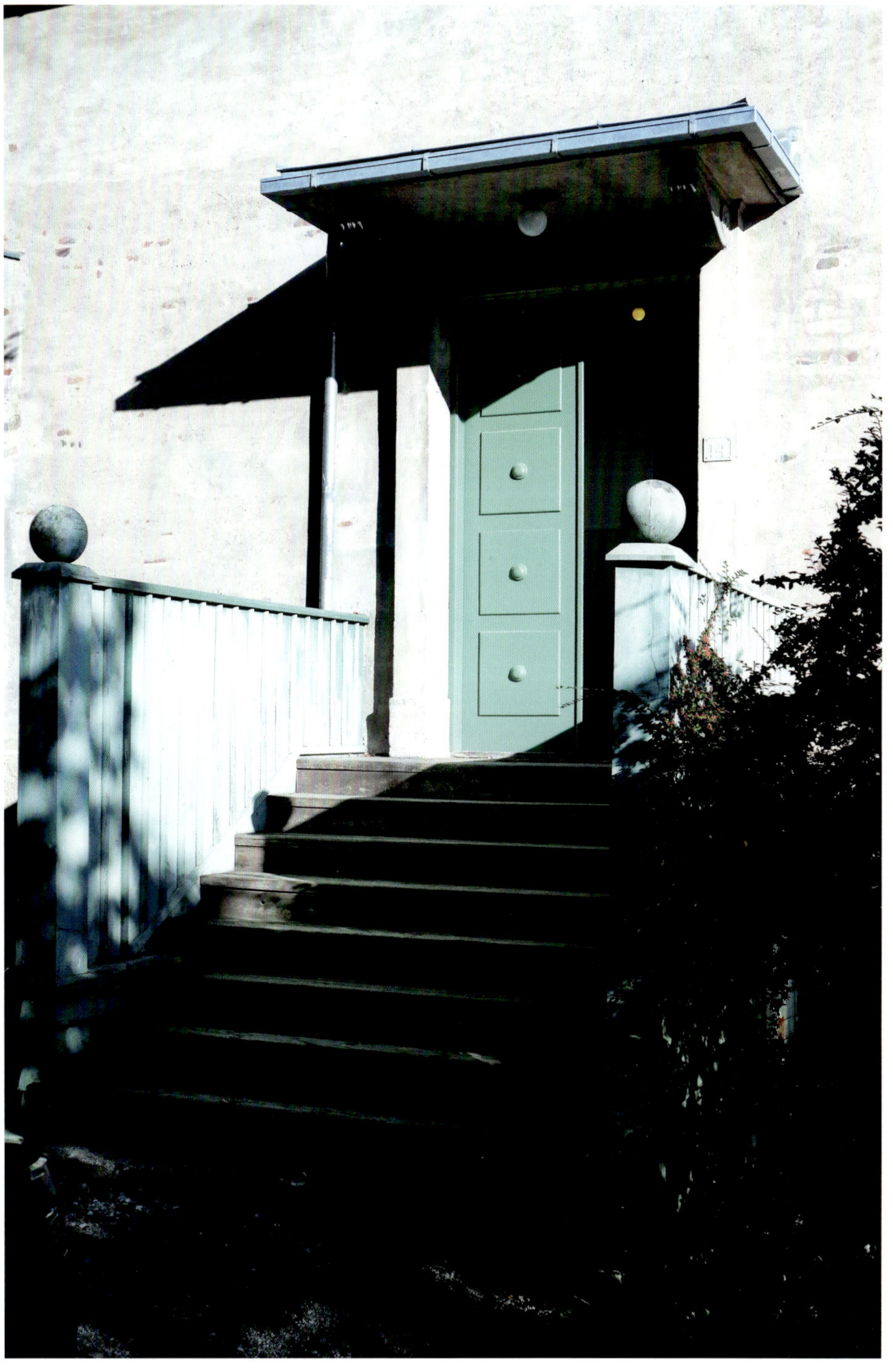

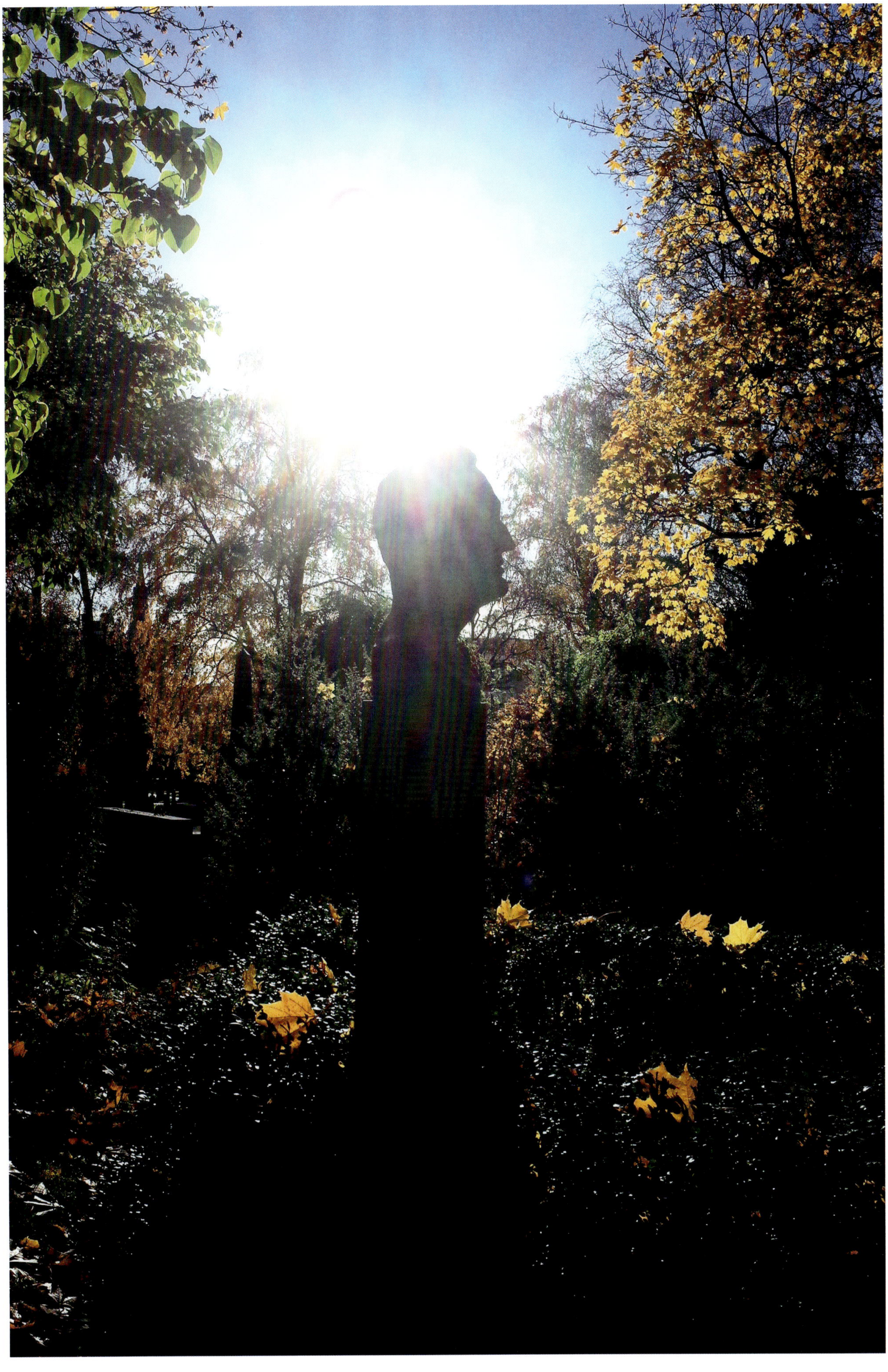

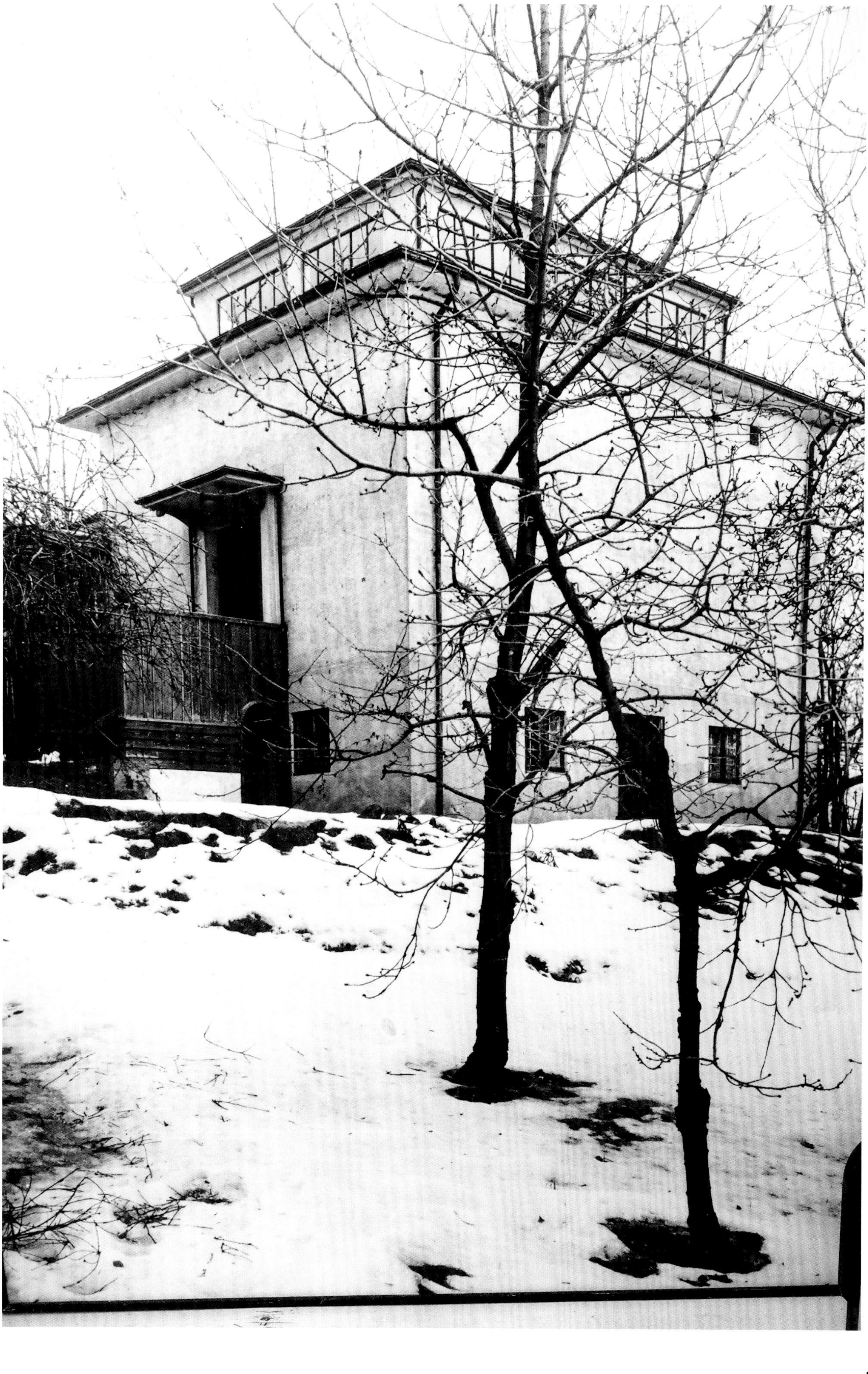

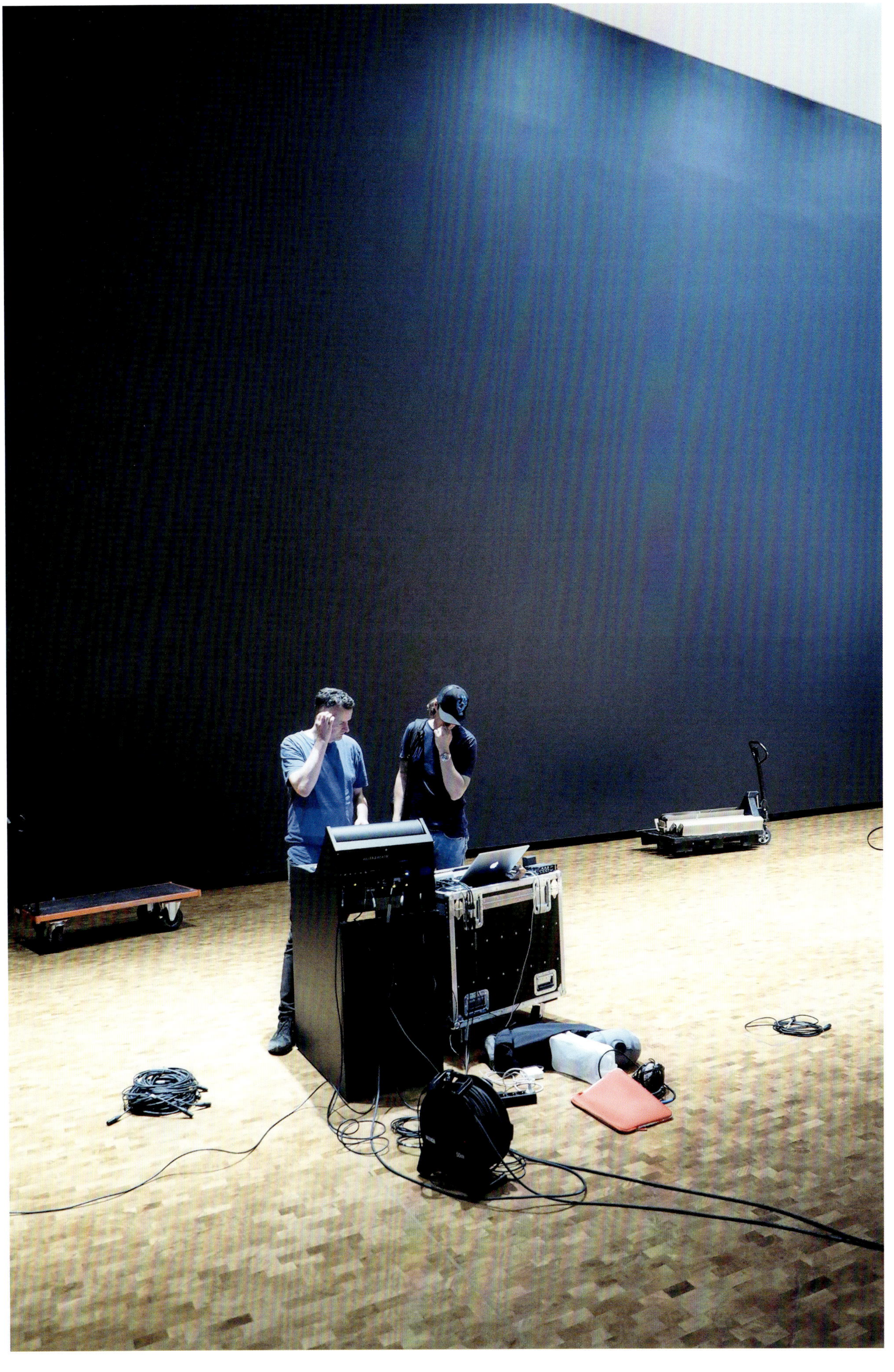

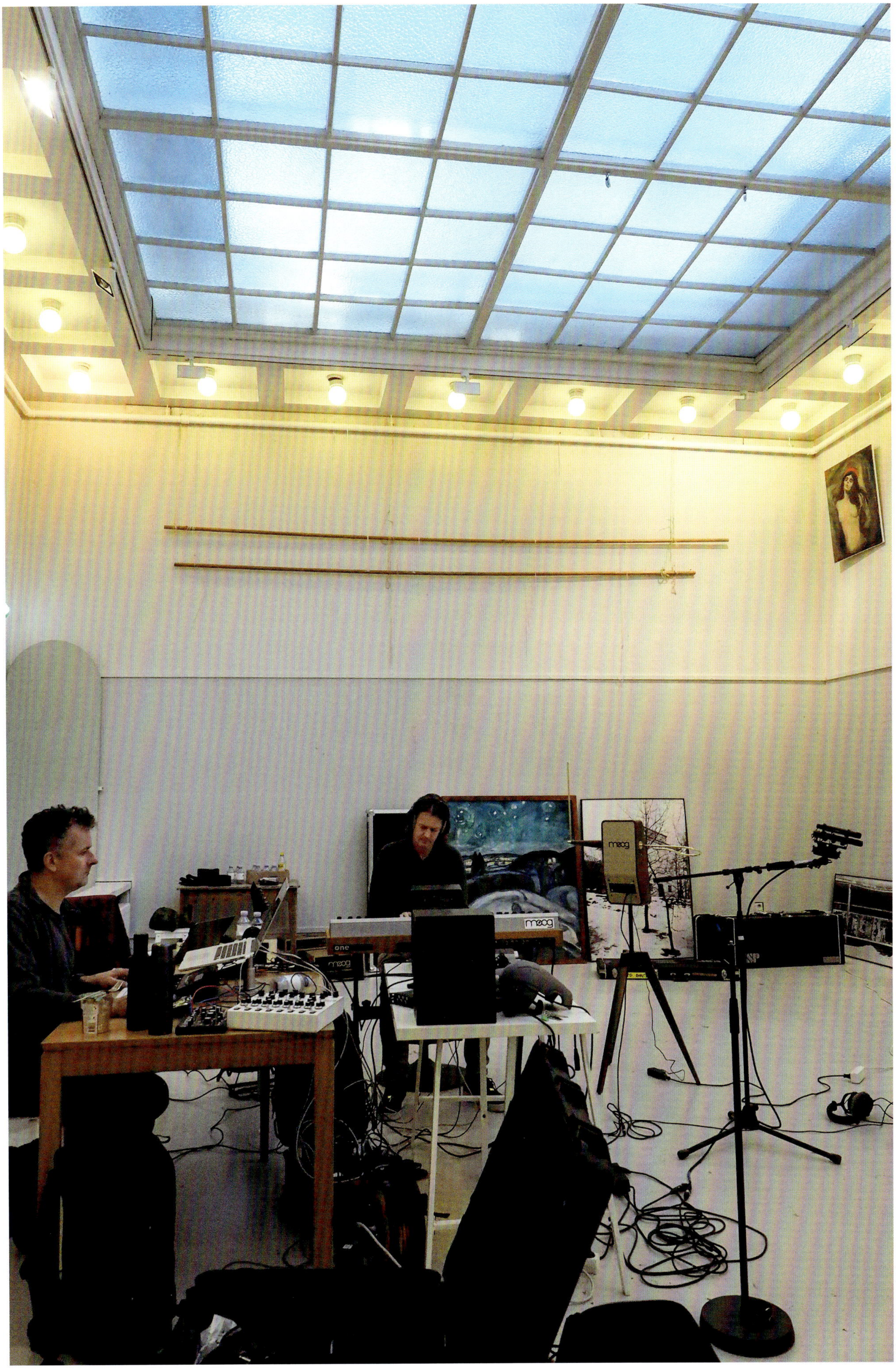

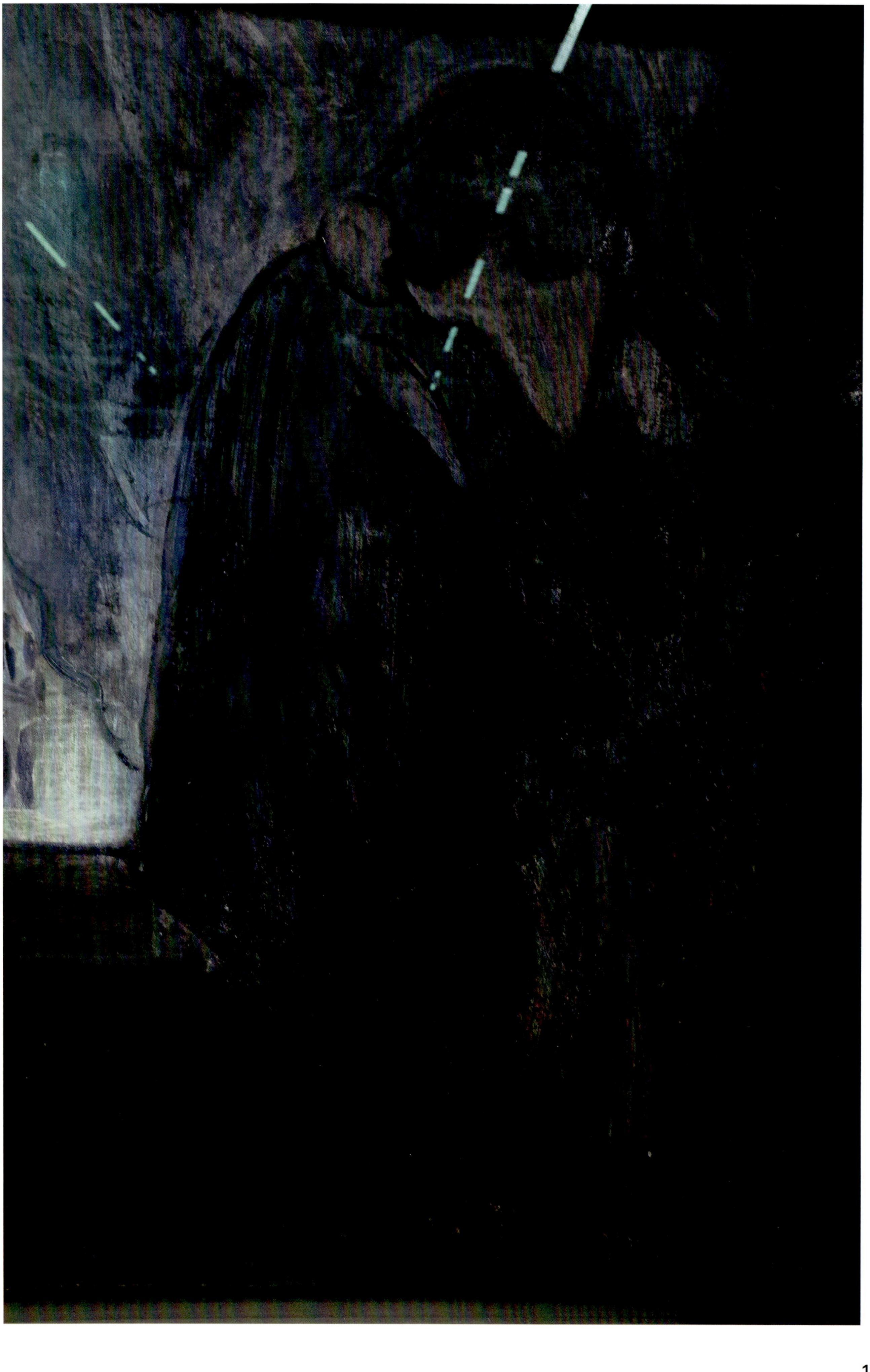

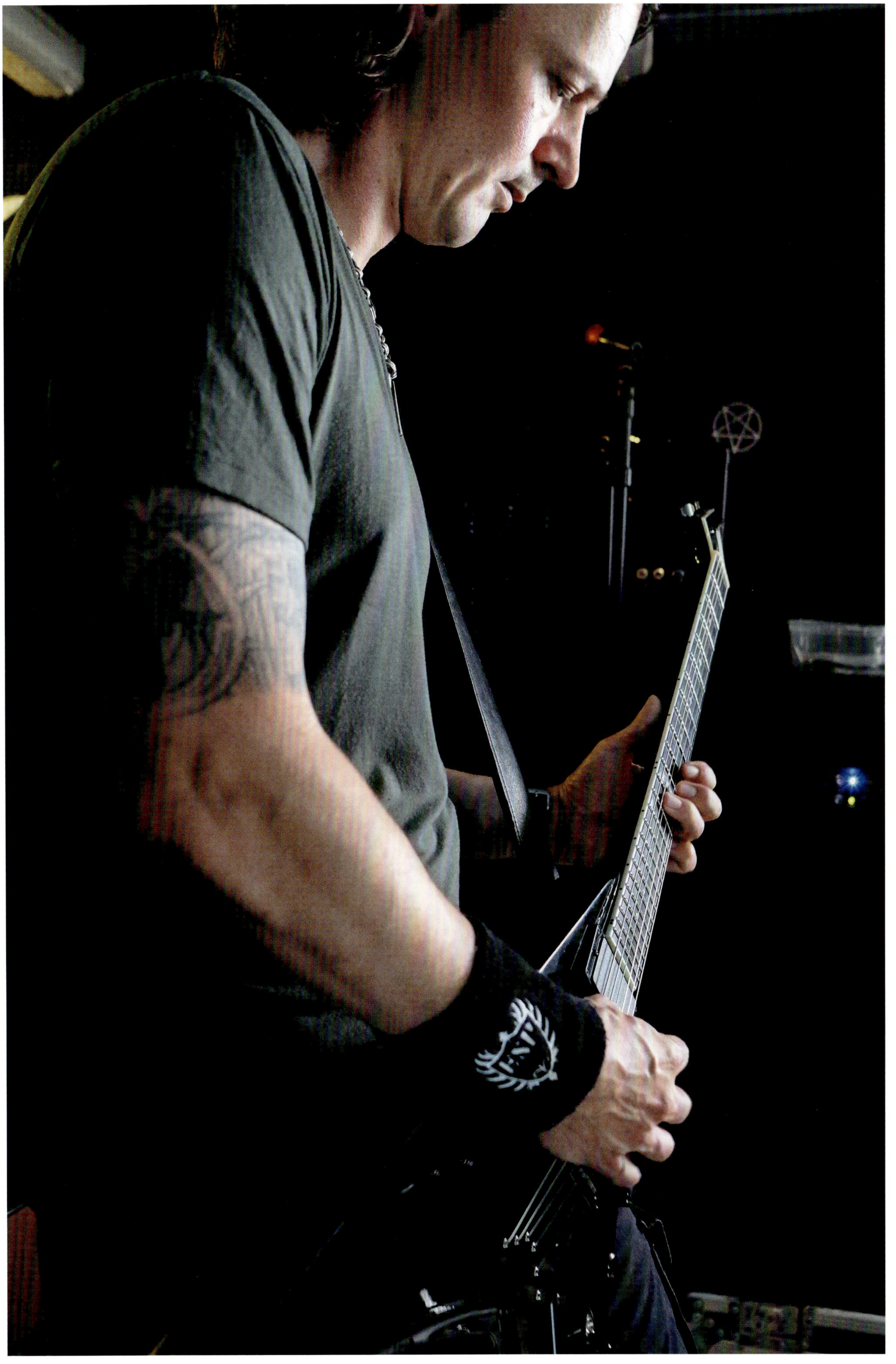

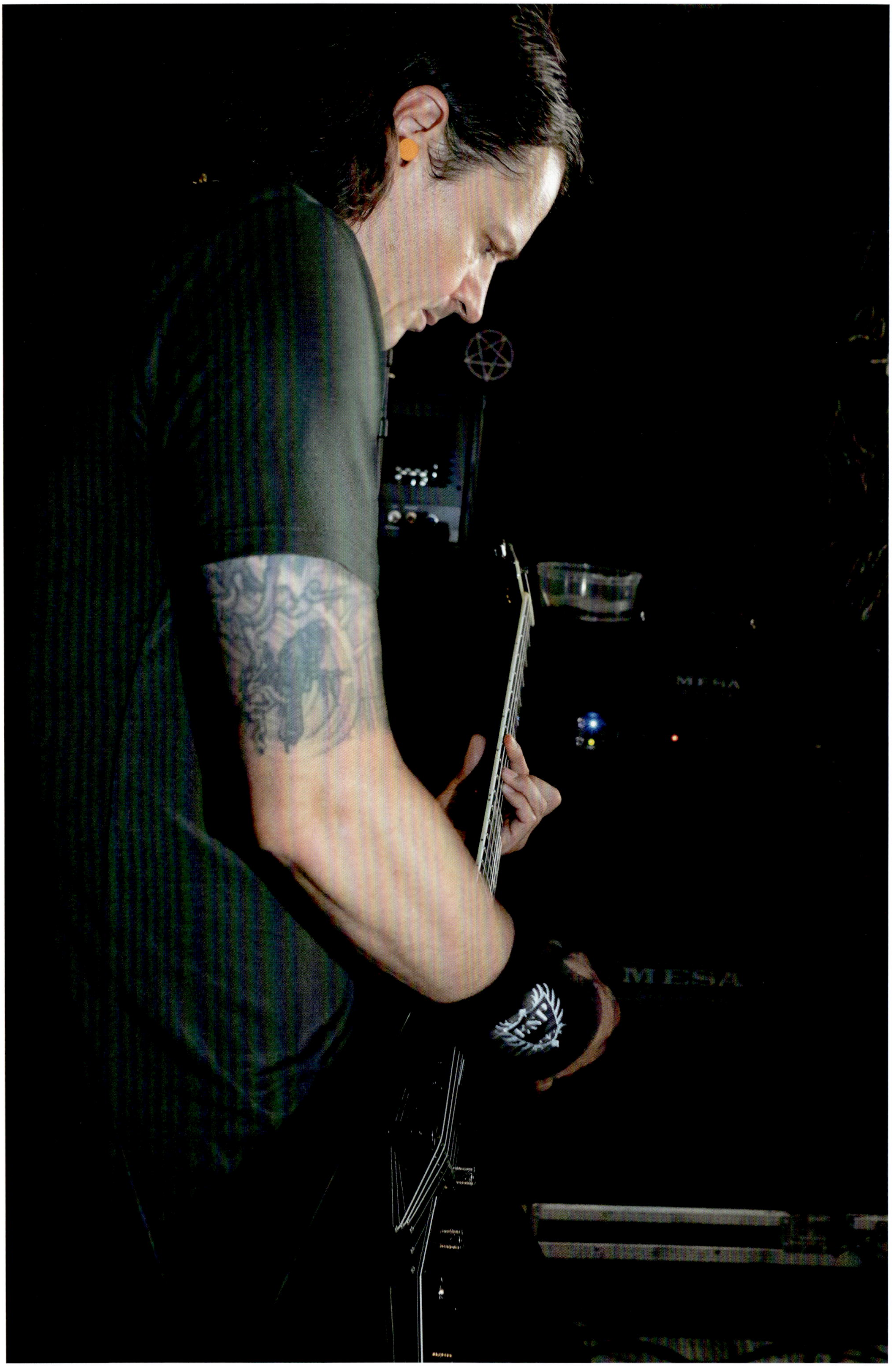
MESA
MESA

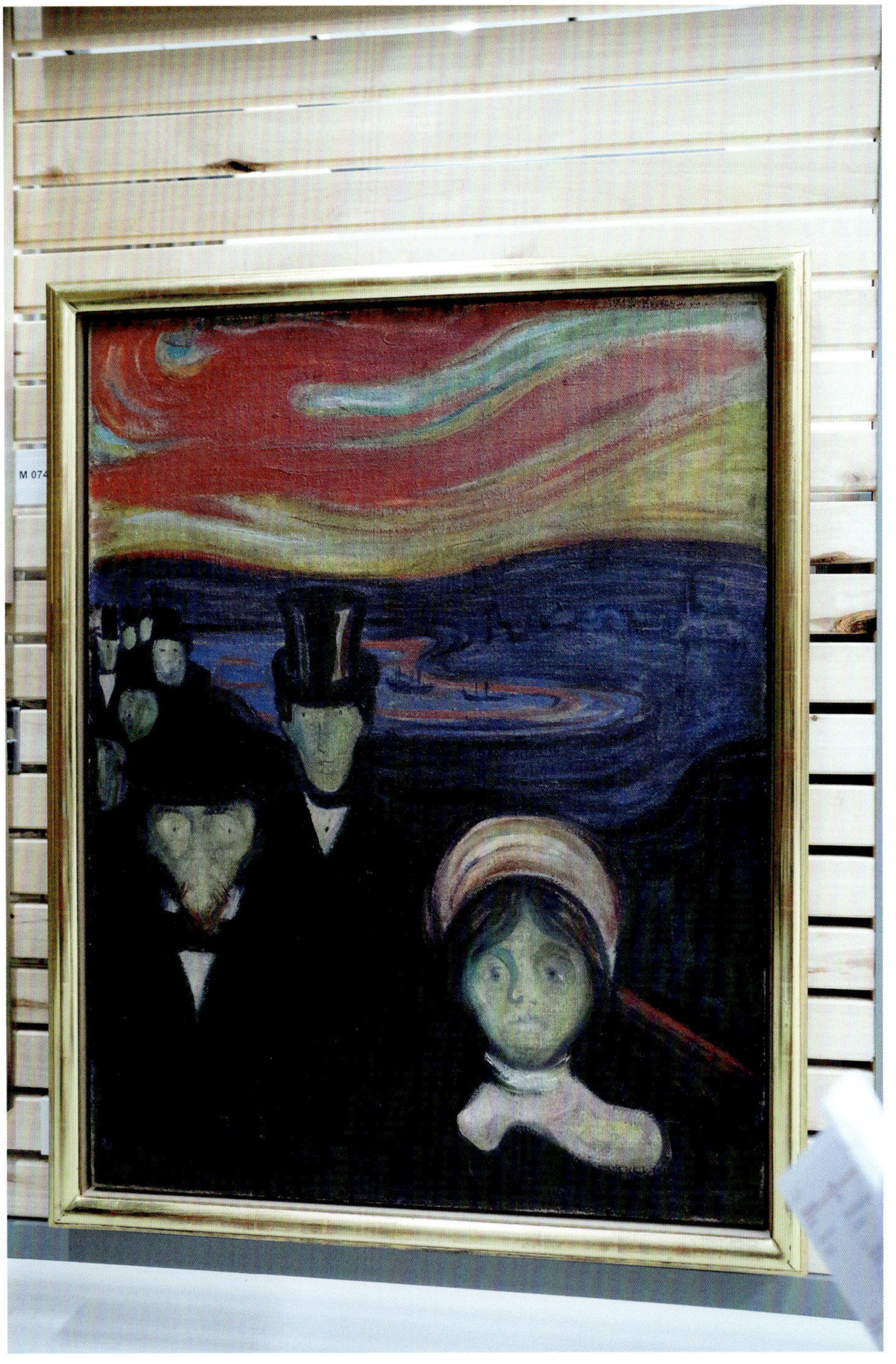

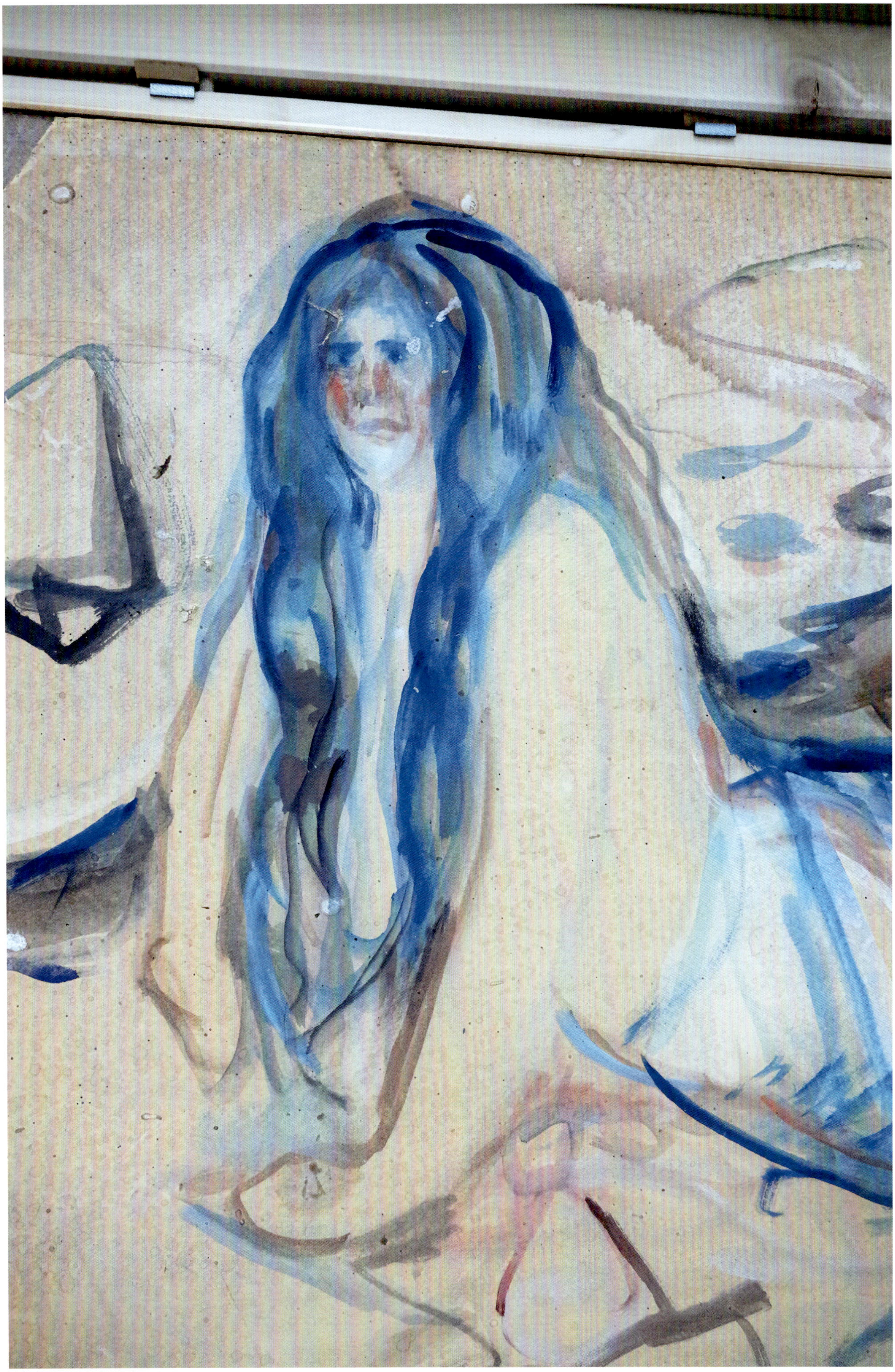

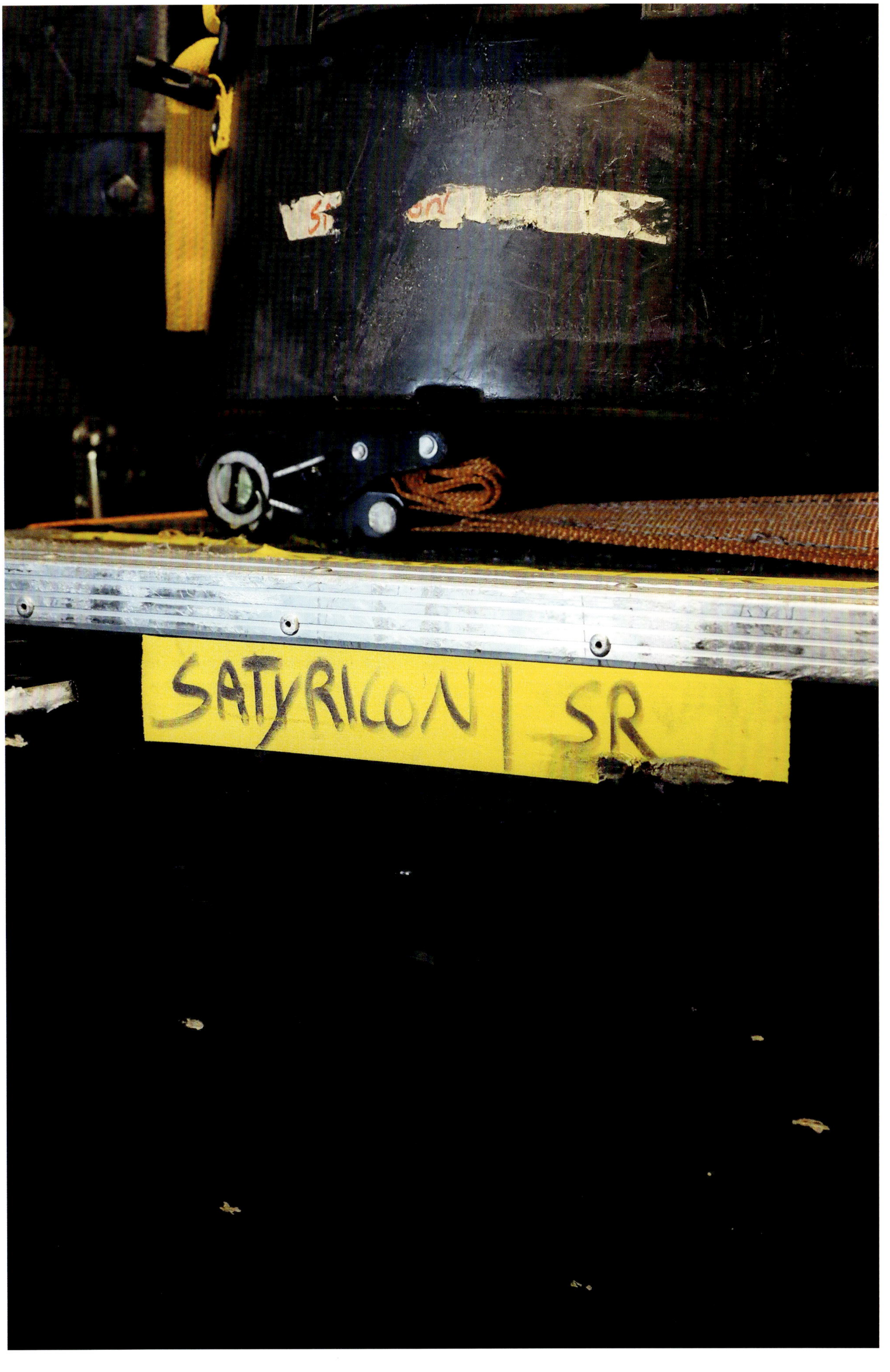
SATYRICON | SR

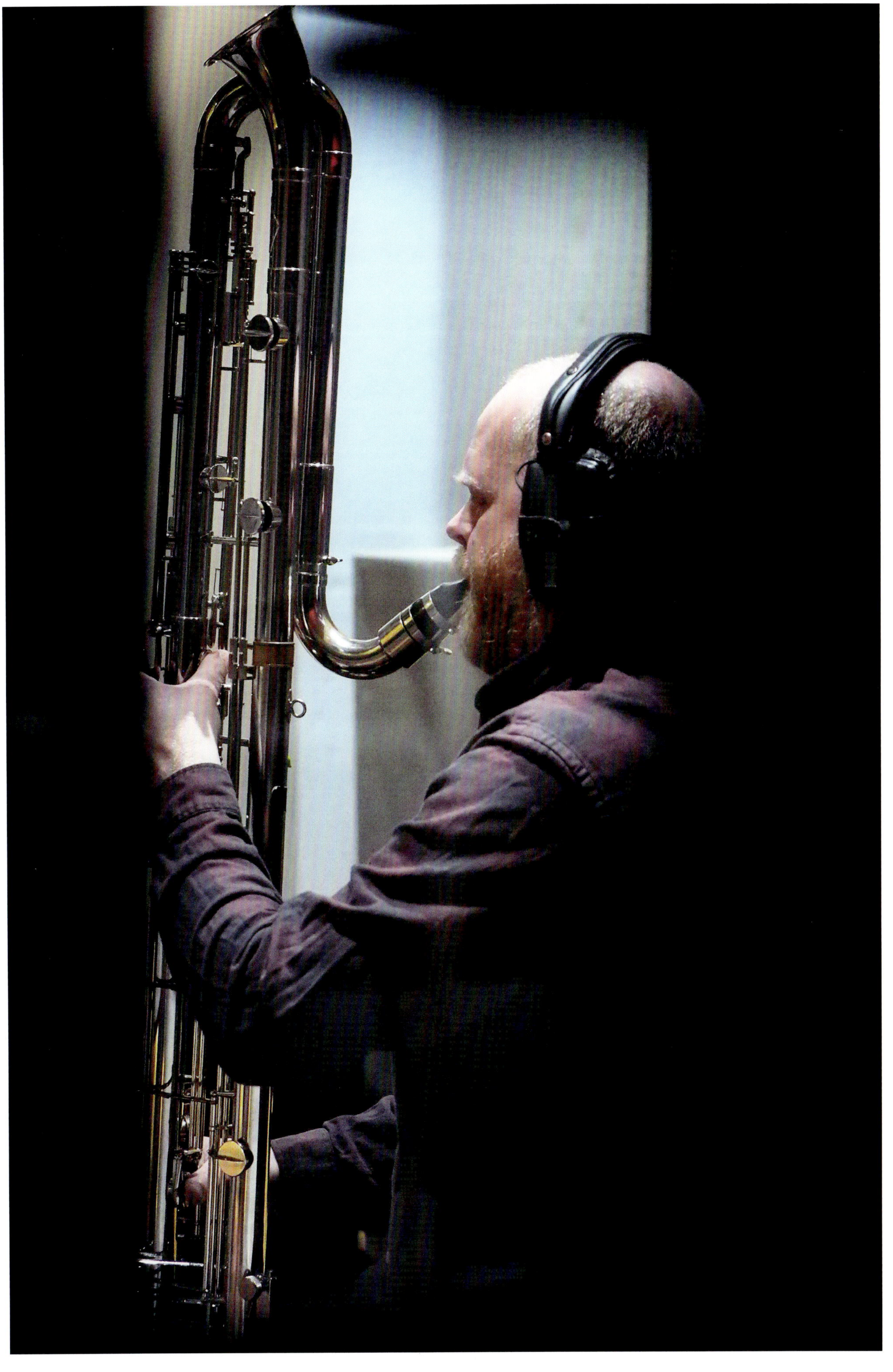

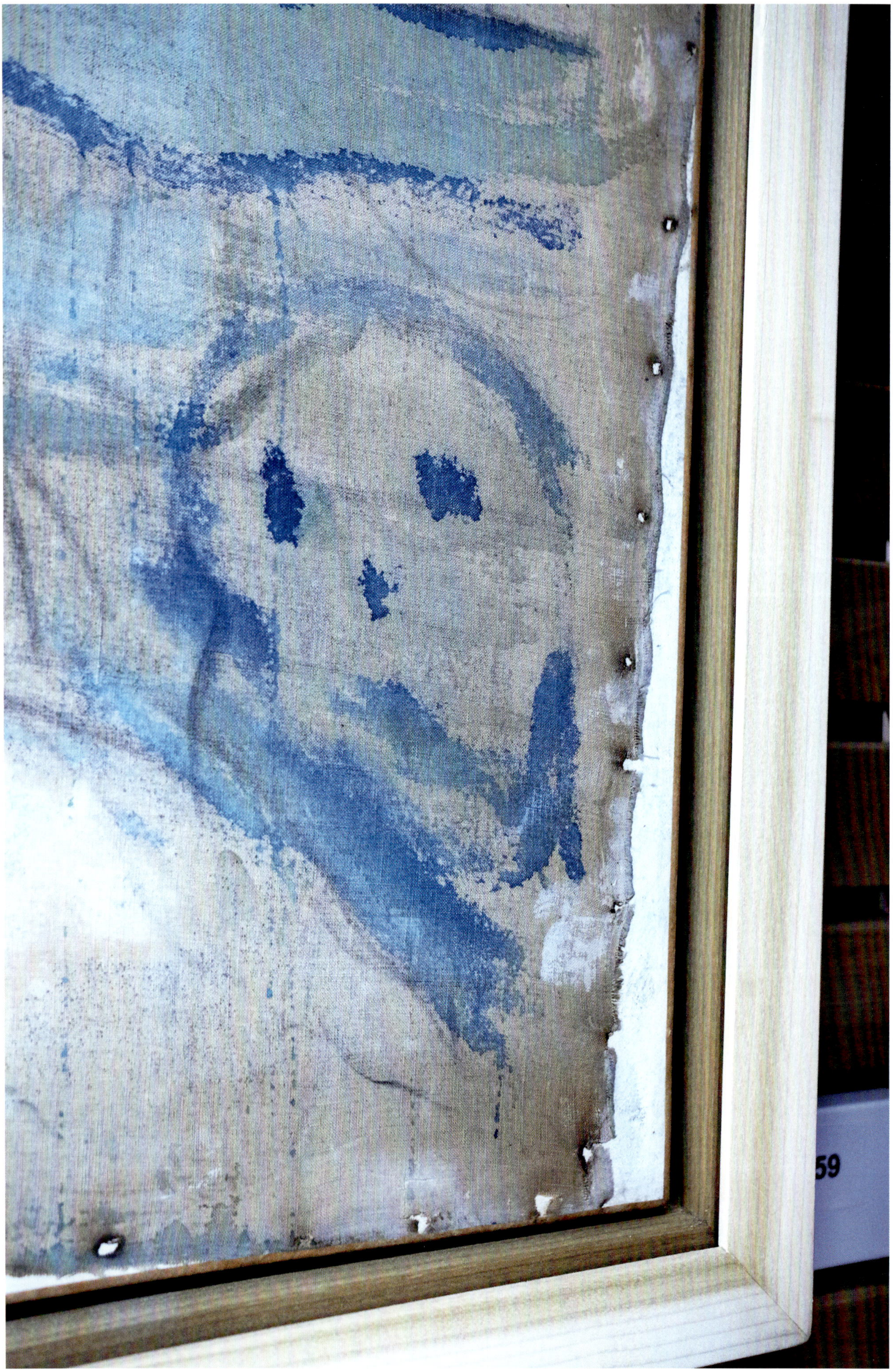

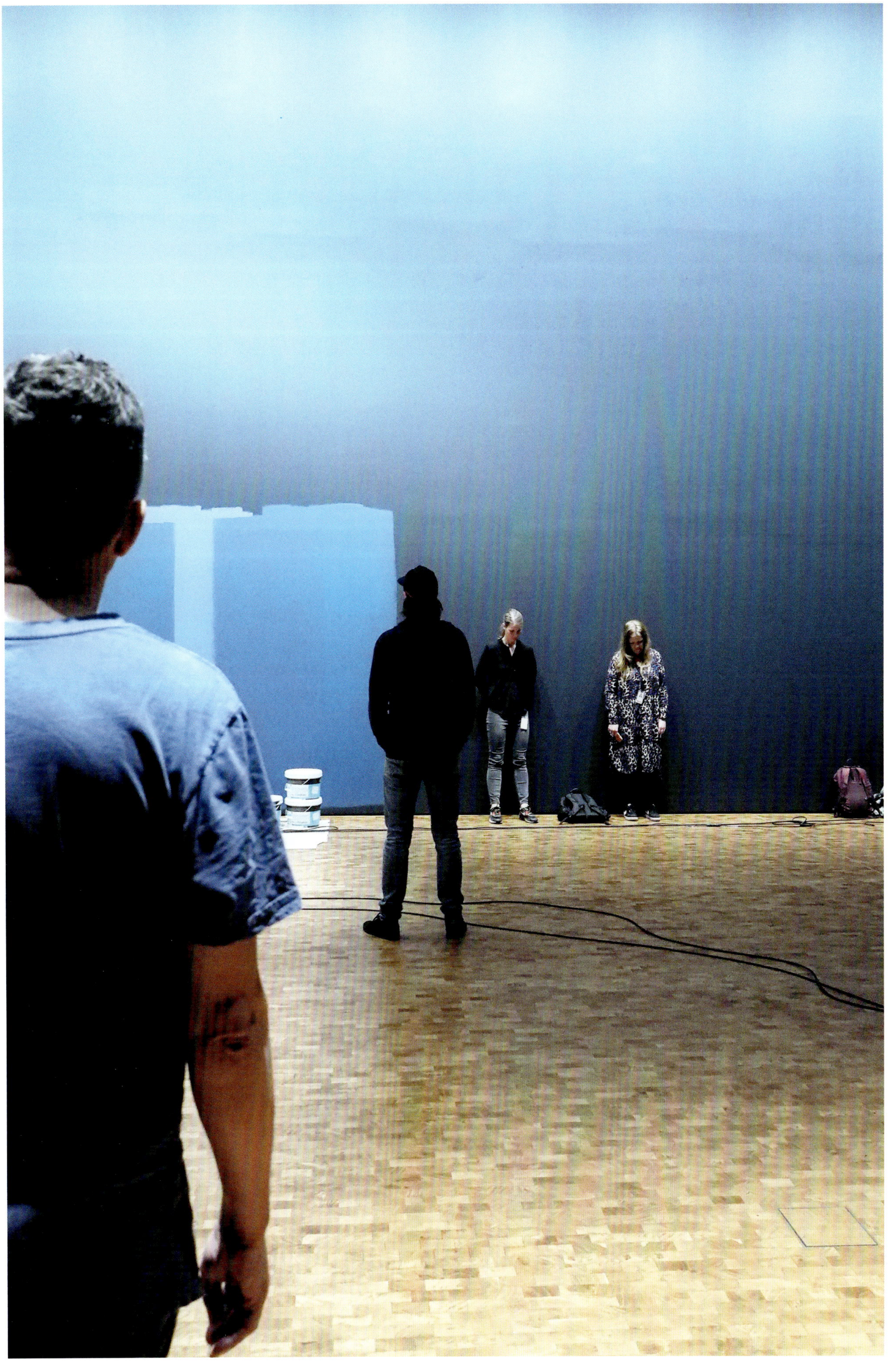

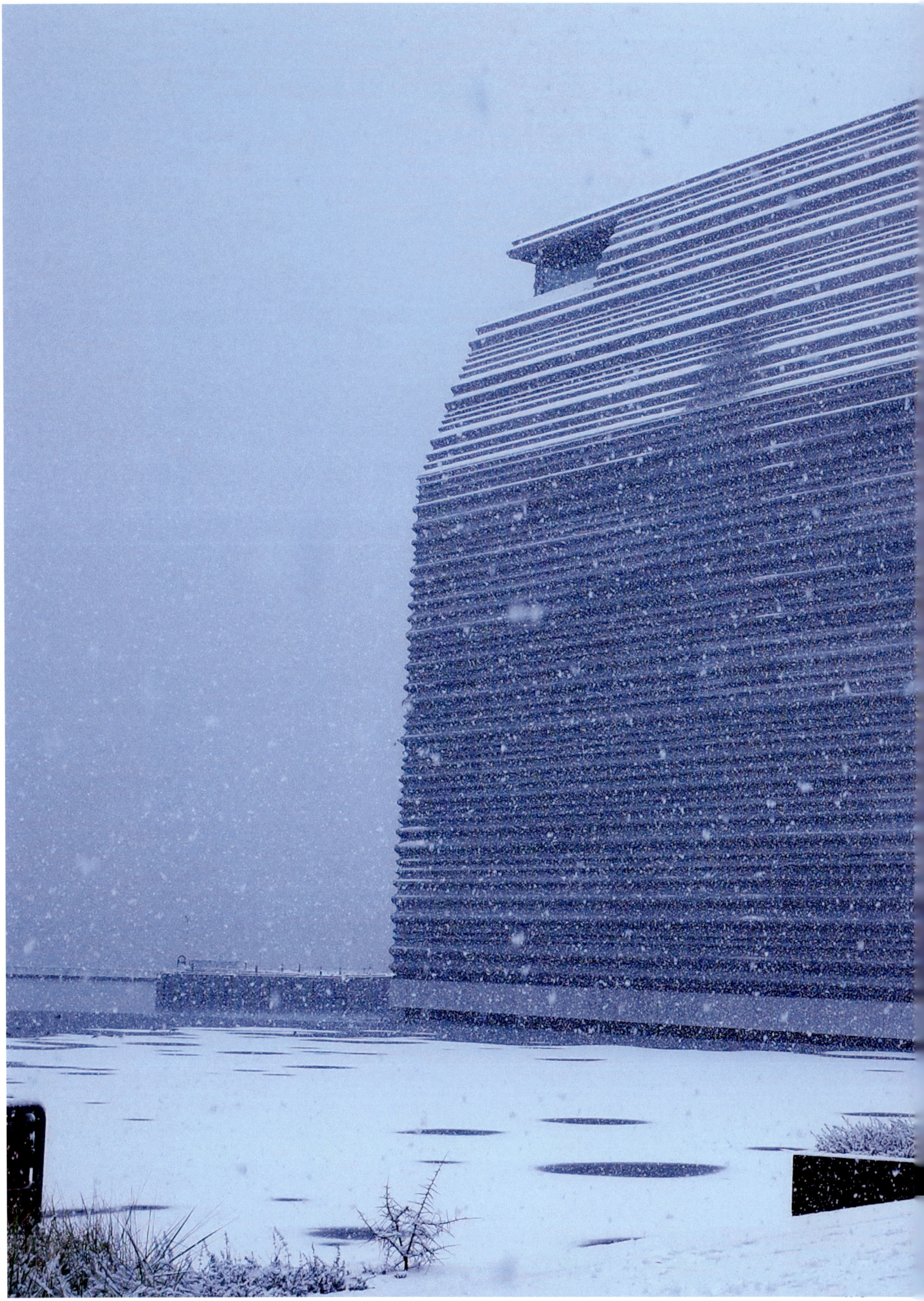

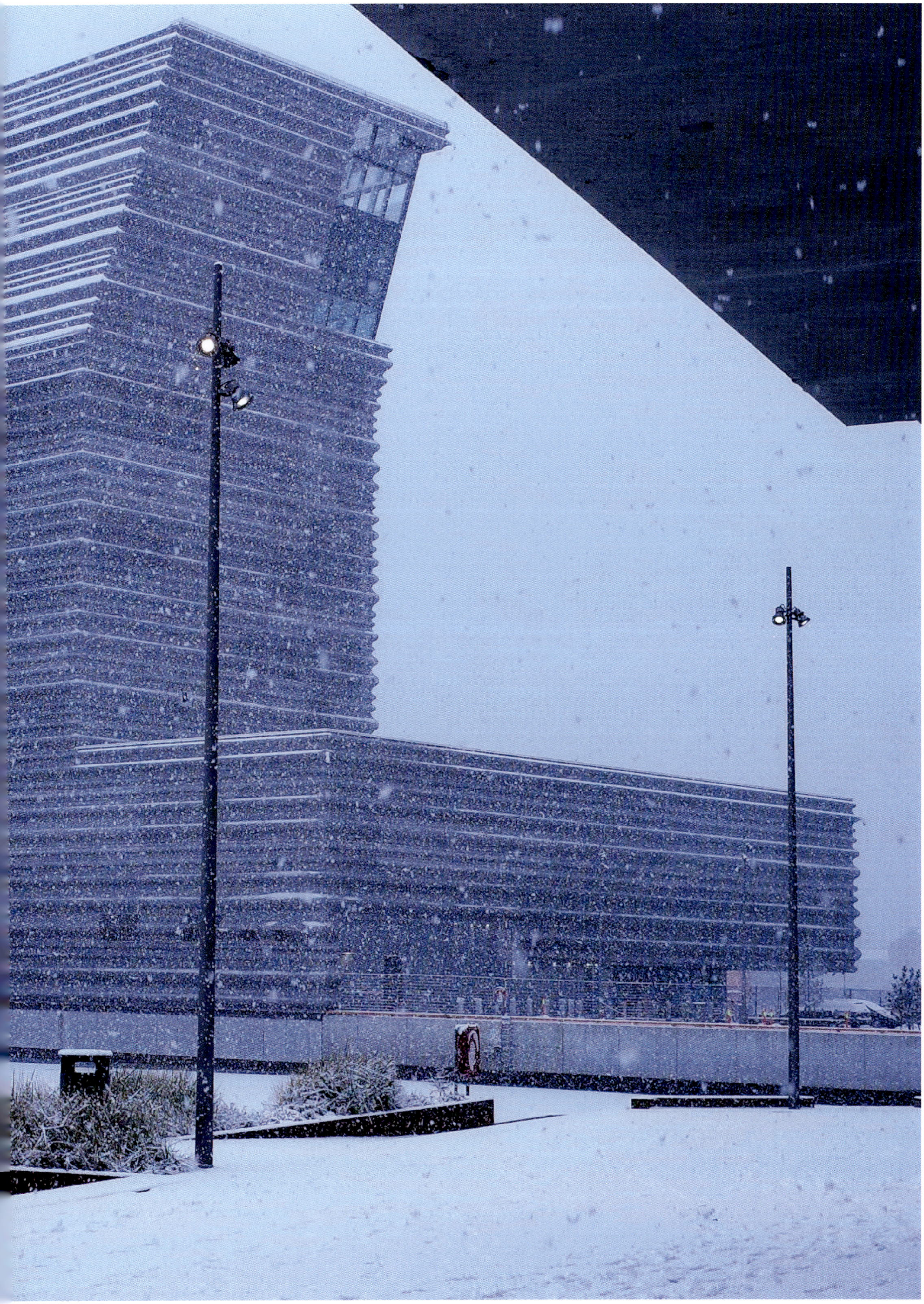

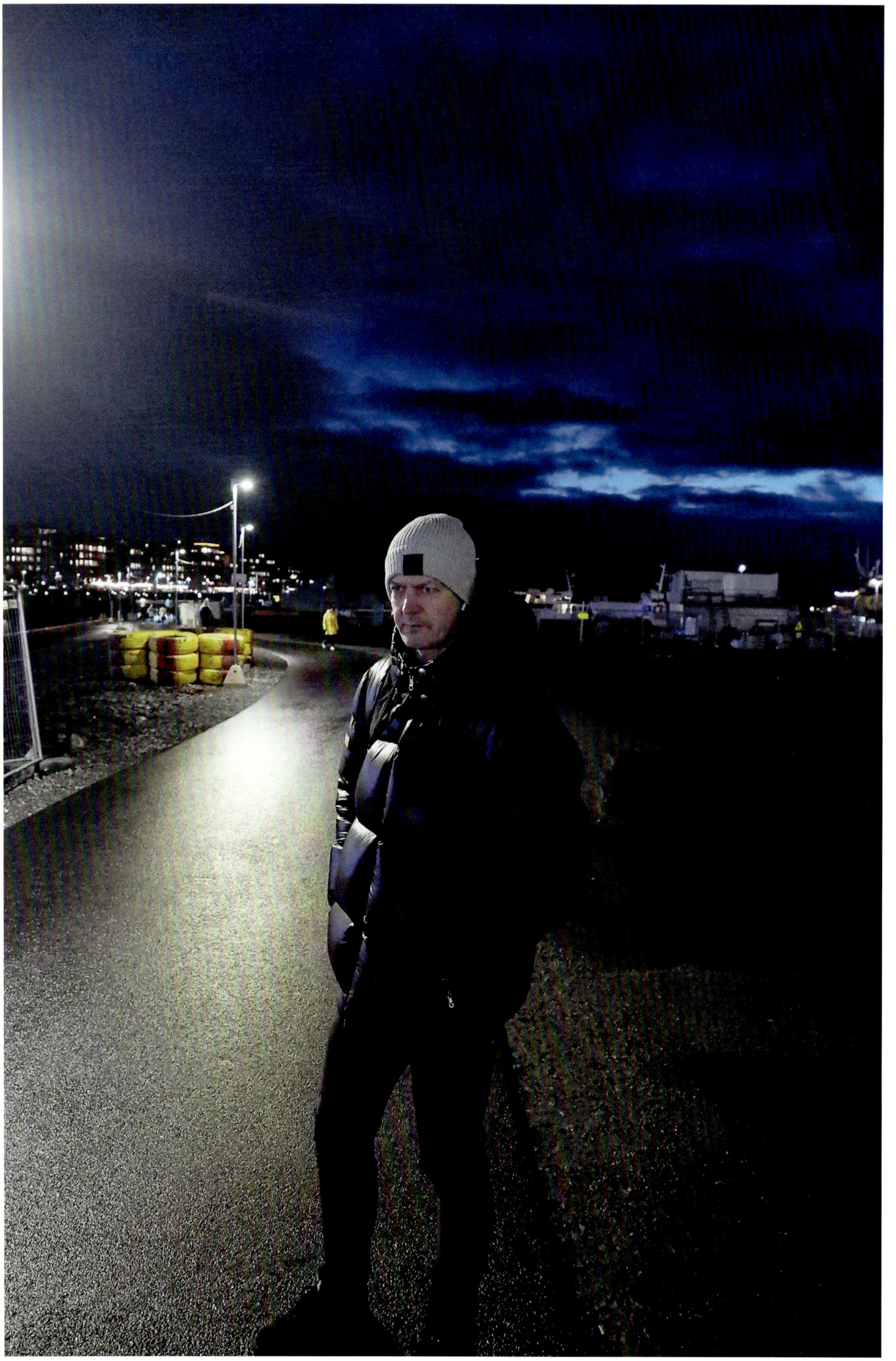

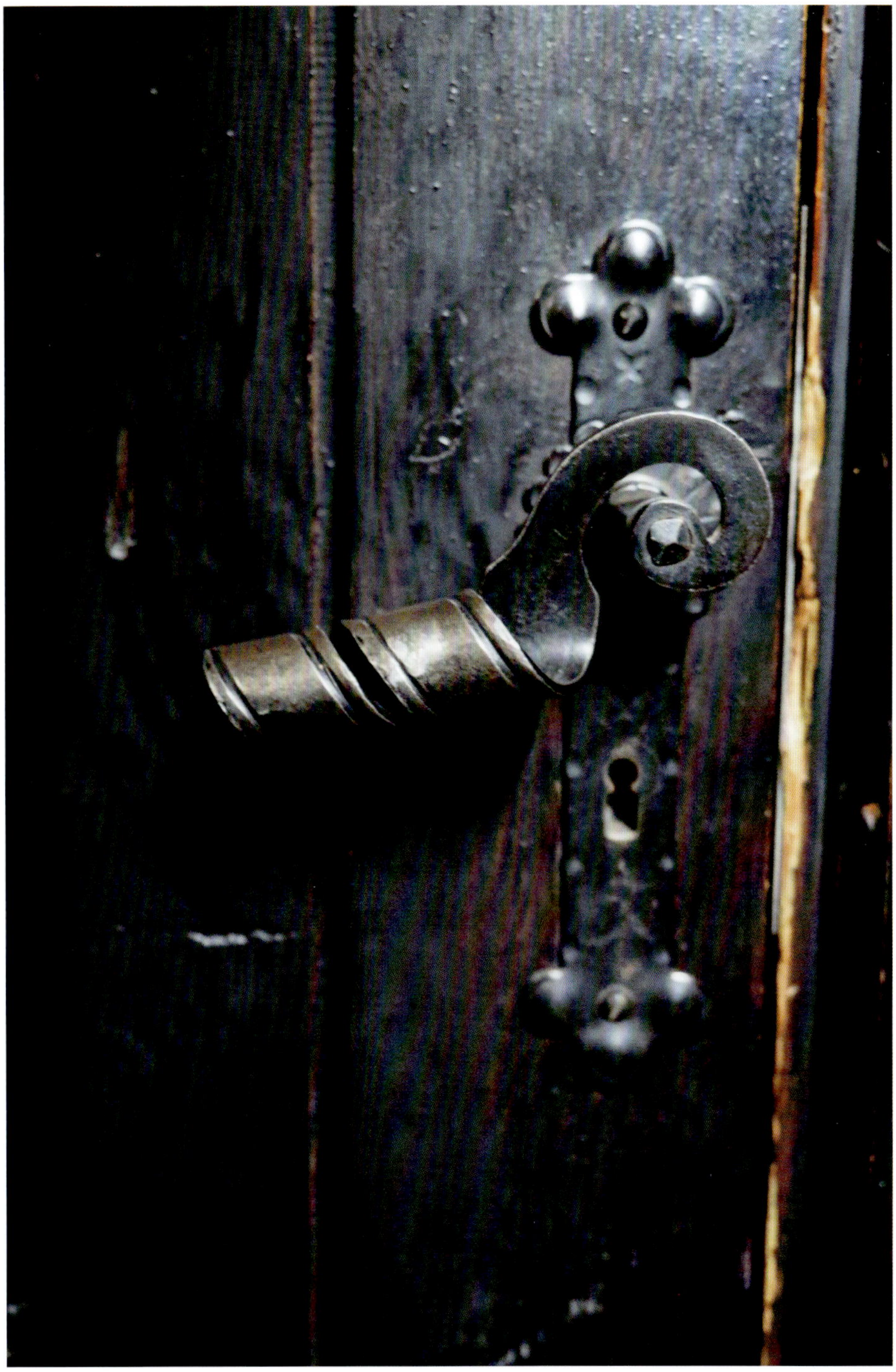

Afterword

Composition for Hand and Eye
Heidi Bale Amundsen

My pictures –
But there is always a progression and
never the same
– I build one image upon another one[1]

A photograph from a studio at Lysaker on the outskirts of Oslo depicts a pale hand playing with some guitar picks on a scratched, black tabletop (77). With the tendons taut as guitar strings, the hand has stiffened in mid-gesture, as if it were in the process of drawing the little slivers of plastic across the surface of the table. Additional picks lie strewn about, and on some of them the word "satyr" is barely visible; it is the stage name of Sigurd Wongraven, the lead singer of the black metal band Satyricon. A grinning skull can be glimpsed on other guitar picks – a detail from Edvard Munch's lithograph *Kiss of Death* (1899), which was reproduced on the cover of Satyricon's album *Deep Calleth upon Deep* (2017). Light from a source outside the photograph is reflected in the tabletop, so that the scratches appear as expressive pen strokes on coarse paper, whereas the guitar picks speak mutely of music. The intimated link between the visual and the musical at the core of Morten Andersen's *Satyricon & Munch* is thereby established even before one has opened the book.

Andersen's photographs document the twofold curatorial-compositional process from its inception and up until the exhibition, which carries the same name as this book and is on view at MUNCH from April to August 2022. The exhibition is a collaboration between Wongraven and the museum's curator Trine Otte Bak Nielsen, and consists of a selection of Munch's works and a musical piece. The music is written with these and with Munch's register of emotions as inspiration, and with the exhibition hall and the specific experience it sets the stage for in mind. The visual part of the project is composed of paintings and prints in various techniques, famous as well as unknown motifs including early and late works. There is however, despite the variation, a formal connection between the works, for instance in the use of colour and the repetition of Munch's characteristic undulating lines. All the exhibited Munch pictures are reproduced in this book, in addition to works that were considered but did not end up on the wall. Because the book is not about the final product, but about the journey which led from Wongraven's first visit to the storage spaces at the old Munchmuseet at Tøyen, via working in the recording studio with Munch's images on a screen on the wall, recordings with several musicians and sound checks in the exhibition hall, to the moment the musical composition was completed and the low, heavy wooden door to the studio at Lysaker was locked (131).

As a 15-year-old, photographer Morten Andersen (b. 1965) began taking pictures of friends in the music field, around the time punk gained a foothold in Norway. He continued to take pictures throughout the 1980s, photographing for music magazines like Puls and Beat. As opposed to prog rock, for example, which is characterised by knowledge of classical compositional theory and often a high level of instrumental technique, punk has a more unprocessed style inspired by the amateur's do-it-yourself approach. The influence from punk can also be traced in Andersen's photographic method. He is a fly on the wall rather than a director, and captures moments as they naturally arise, without cropping the pictures later. This approach gives his photographs a raw and spontaneous expression that suits his low-keyed confrontational and often oblique eye for situations: an a-ha poster in the black metal musicians' studio (78), a banana on a coiled wire next to a metronome, a laptop and pair of headphones (53), and the "thought bubbles" above Munch's sombre face in *Self-Portrait under the Mask of a Woman* (1893) – the playful result of the flash's reflection in the picture (33).

Andersen's visual expression is not only formed by punk culture, but also by the years he spent at the International Center of Photography in New York during the 1990s, where he studied under photographers such as Joan Liftin, Nan Goldin, Ken Schles and Larry Clark. They represent a subjective form of documentary that Andersen has developed further, beginning with the first of his 25 photobooks to date, *Fast City* (1999). That book represented a breakthrough for him as a photographer and is mentioned in the 3rd volume of Martin Parr and Gerry Badger's canonizing work *The Photobook. A History* (London: Phaidon Press, 2014). *Fast City* consists of grainy and confrontational photos of street scenes from Oslo, most of which were taken at night, in a style that is reminiscent of Daidō Moriyama's and William Klein's dynamic compositions. The book nevertheless represented something totally new at the time, as Andersen had included an occasional colour photograph, which creates a shift in tempo in the otherwise black and white structure. Eventually colour became his favoured mode of expression and *Satyricon & Munch* consists solely of colour photographs.

Even when the motifs are relatively static, as in this book, Andersen's background in music and street photography is tangibly present. Sound checks in the studio and the inspection of paintings can be considered somewhat sedentary activities, yet energy, resonance and an apparently vibrating atmosphere are expressed in several of the photographs; for instance, in the specks of dust that dance in a ray of light above a set of synthesizers (66), entwined feet in ankle socks during intense listening, like a physical key of G (86), and in the undulating lines in Munch's pictures (1, 32, 98) which reflect the sound waves visible on a screen in Satyricon's recording venue (58). Nevertheless, movement is implied first and foremost in the sequence of pictures, in the way the photographer links one picture to the next and deliberately focuses on resonance, progression and staging – strategies that have as much in common with music as with visual art.

The link between the photographic and musical sequences is also a repeated theme in Andersen's teacher Goldin's *The Ballad of Sexual Dependency* (1986). The book had a significant influence on the development of the contemporary photobook as an interactive form offering the reader an unlimited number of directions to read in. This way of figuring in the reader as a collaborator is also a premise for Andersen's photobooks. They do not confine the experience to a linear narrative that runs from the first to the last page, or to chronological narratives, but appear rather as networks of connections that readers must navigate on their own. Within these networks more than one path through the book is both possible and meaningful, and each image can be included in several different narratives.

In other words, the closed door in the book's last image (131) does not mark the end to the book's reading. For although the photograph marks the end of Satyricon's studio work, it simultaneously invites the reader to flip back through the pages to one of the book's first pictures, in which Wongraven poses in front of the same door (4). Unlike the picture at the back of the book, here one can see a door knocker shaped like a cross, from whence another narrative opens, about black metal's affinity for the occult. This narrative also includes the photograph of

Lucifer peeking out from behind a drum set (104), a picture of Eivind Buene wearing a demonic expression as he conducts (85) and the many pictures of skulls (79, 82, 128).

The musical composition that was created in front of Andersen's lens is more bound to a linear experience than the photobook is, yet it is composed so that the end of the piece is linked up to the work's beginning in both tone and theme. This means that the transition from the end to a new start is not audible when the work is performed repeatedly, without pause, in the exhibition room. This structure implies that the visitors will experience the music from the moment they enter the room until the moment they leave it, and that the experience of the composition will thus be different for each listener. The same applies to the exhibition, which is not confined to a specific sequence, but opens for visitors to return to pictures they have already seen. In a similar way, the experience of the photobook will be different for each reader. A majority will open the book on the first page, but my guess is that they will end up by leafing back and forth between the pages, as associations to images they saw at earlier stages appear.

Which specific connections people will dwell on, and the pace at which they will leaf through the book, will depend on which photographs and connections appeal most strongly to the individual reader. For me, it was the image of Satyricon drummer Kjetil "Frost" Haraldstad's dark hair and dramatically made-up eyes (15) reflected in the pale female figure with the equally large eyes in Munch's lithograph *The Urn* (1896, 16) that first made me slacken the pace of my reading. It had to do with striking visual qualities, but also with how the connection prompted a reflection on the awareness of death which underscores Munch's art as well as black metal. Connections of this kind are found on all levels in this book and shape the reading process without confining it to one possible outcome. However, there is undoubtedly a cohesiveness here, all the while a certain mood and rhythm run through the book. The photobook has an impressionistic and explorative receptiveness for reciprocity between pictures and music, and a constant disruption of the sequence in pictures of Satyricon's enormous selection of analogue synthesizers; an element the band has experimented with since the end of the 1990s, but which is otherwise uncommon in black metal.

The musical composition Satyricon has created for the exhibition is demanding, quite literally, as it takes nearly an hour to listen to it through to the end. Although photographs are direct references to actual events, to read this type of book is a similarly demanding exercise, since patterns and meanings first become visible over time, through repeated exposure to motifs and strategies. In *Satyricon & Munch* the continuous use of light as a narrative element is one such strategy, as are the photographs of automobiles, which underscore the process-oriented nature of the book. The same applies to the pictures of trees with a dense network of branches. Andersen weaves a similarly dense network in his book, but for the reader who takes the time, a liberating portrait of Satyricon emerges in the reading. Here the make-up and stage costumes are mainly replaced with t-shirts and shorts, and Andersen has deliberately distanced himself from the band's dark aesthetics, and from the traditional iconic character of portraits of bands.

A similarly untraditional approach characterises the book's treatment of Munch's pictures, which are often thought of as separate iconic artworks, but in this book appear in various versions and details, and in situations that pull and stretch their meanings. It applies for example to *Anxiety*, which appears both on a screen on the wall where the band practices (49), on a wall in the storage space at Tøyen (32) and as a reference to the bleeding sky that can be seen through the skylight in Satyricon's studio (57). This kaleidoscopic treatment of Munch's art is productive, because it opens a dimension in his oeuvre that has not been sufficiently dealt with, but which the artist himself put into words in a letter draft to the Swedish art historian Axel Romdahl.

In the letter, Munch writes that his pictures are never the same, but always stages in a progression, and it is this progression that Andersen's sensitive treatment of the transition from one picture to another brings to light in such a suggestive way. Munch does not add anything more about the process-oriented aspect of his work in his letter, but it is a fact that he returned continuously to the same scenes, made multiple versions of the same motifs and reworked his pictures several times. During his entire life he worked on the series *The Frieze of Life*, which *Anxiety* is linked to, without ever defining a final selection. The process-oriented element is present in Munch's pictures on an individual level as well. In the painted version of *Anxiety* (1894), for instance, Munch has used cadmium yellow, a type of paint that would later prove to be sensitive to light. This has caused the yellow areas of the picture to fade, flake and change colour, something Munch was not necessarily displeased about. In fact, he placed many of his pictures outdoors, where they were eroded by wind and rain, thereby developing in ways outside of his control.

In a particularly memorable photograph in the book, a long, tattooed arm reaches into the frame and barely touches one of Haraldstad's drums (100). The motif brings to mind God's hand reaching towards Adam in Michelangelo's ceiling painting in the Sistine Chapel (1508–12) to bestow life on the first human being. In a similar way, the hand's contact with the mute battery in the photograph animates the apparently frenetic drum solo which is documented in the following photographs (101, 102, 103). Similar rigid hand gestures are repeated several places in the book; in the make-up artist's delicate touch on Wongravens cheek (105), the photograph of conductor Buene gesticulating toward the musicians (84), and in the detail of Munch's lithograph *Desire* (1898, 106). In this context, the hand can be seen as a metaphor for the reader's hand, and as an invitation to pick up the book and leaf through it, thereby bringing to life Morten Andersen's dynamic composition for hand and eye.

1 Based on a quote by Edvard Munch: "mine billeder – / Men det er altid en utvikling og / aldrig det samme / – Jeg bygger et billede på et annet." Undated letter draft to Axel Romdahl, Göteborgs Konstmuseum. MM N 3359, Munchmuseet.

Pictures

1 Edvard Munch, *On the Waves of Love*, 1896 (cropped)
2 Munch's grave, Our Saviour's Cemetery, Oslo
3 Munch's grave, Our Saviour's Cemetery, Oslo
4 Outside the studio, Lysaker
5 Ila Boarding House, Oslo
6 Studio, Lysaker
7 Studio, Lysaker
8 Studio, Lysaker
9 En route to Åsgårdstrand
10 Munchmuseet, Tøyen
11 Ekely
12 En route to Åsgårdstrand
13 Munch's House, Åsgårdstrand
14 Munchmuseet, Tøyen
15 Ila Boarding House, Oslo
16 Edvard Munch, *The Urn*, 1896 (detail)
17 Studio, Lysaker
18 Munchmuseet, Tøyen
19 Munchmuseet, Tøyen
20 Studio, Lysaker
21 Studio, Lysaker
22 Edvard Munch, *The Magic Forest*, 1919–25 (detail)
23 Ila Boarding House, Oslo
24 Munchmuseet, Tøyen
25 Edvard Munch, *Kiss of Death*, c. 1930
26 Munchmuseet, Tøyen
27 Edvard Munch, *Desire*, 1898
28 Studio, Råde
29 Munchmuseet, Tøyen
30 Edvard Munch, *The Urn*, 1896
31 Munch's winter studio, Ekely
32 Munchmuseet, Tøyen
33 Edvard Munch, *Self-Portrait under the Mask of a Woman*, 1893 (cropped)
34 Studio, Råde
35 Munchmuseet, Tøyen
36 Ila Boarding House, Oslo
37 Tøyen
38 Ila Boarding House, Oslo
39 Munchmuseet, Tøyen
40 Edvard Munch, *Funeral March*, 1897 (detail)
41 Munch's winter studio, Ekely
42 Munch's House, Åsgårdstrand
43 Studio, Råde
44 View from the studio, Lysaker
45 Studio, Råde
46 Munch's winter studio, Ekely
47 Propeller Studio, Oslo
48 Propeller Studio, Oslo
49 Studio, Lysaker
50 View from studio, Lysaker
51 Munch's winter studio, Ekely
52 Ragnvald Væring, Edvard Munch in his winter studio, Ekely, 1938; Munch's winter studio, Ekely
53 Munch's winter studio, Ekely
54 Munch's winter studio, Ekely
55 Studio, Lysaker
56 Studio, Lysaker
57 View from studio, Lysaker
58 Studio, Lysaker
59 Studio, Lysaker
60 Studio, Lysaker
61 Propeller Studio, Oslo
62 Edvard Munch, *On the Waves of Love*, 1896
63 Sound check, MUNCH, Bjørvika
64 Munchmuseet, Tøyen
65 Sound check, MUNCH, Bjørvika
66 Studio, Lysaker
67 Sound check, MUNCH, Bjørvika
68 Studio, Lysaker
69 Studio, Lysaker
70 Propeller Studio, Oslo
71 Propeller Studio, Oslo
72 View from MUNCH, Bjørvika
73 Edvard Munch, *Funeral March*, 1897 (detail)
74 Munch's winter studio, Ekely
75 Studio, Lysaker
76 Studio, Lysaker
77 Studio, Lysaker
78 Studio, Lysaker
79 Edvard Munch, *Andreas Munch Studying Anatomy*, 1886 (cropped)
80 Studio, Lysaker
81 Studio, Råde
82 Edvard Munch, *Kiss of Death*, 1899 (cropped)
83 Studio, Lysaker
84 Propeller Studio, Oslo
85 Propeller Studio, Oslo
86 Studio, Lysaker
87 Studio, Lysaker
88 Ekely
89 Edvard Munch, *Under the Stars*, 1900–05 (cropped)
90 Munchmuseet, Tøyen
91 Studio, Lysaker
92 Edvard Munch, *Golgotha*, 1900 (detail)
93 Studio, Lysaker
94 Propeller Studio, Oslo
95 Studio, Lysaker
96 Sound check, MUNCH, Bjørvika
97 Propeller Studio, Oslo
98 Edvard Munch, *On the Waves of Love*, 1896 (cropped)
99 Munchmuseet, Tøyen
100 Studio, Råde
101 Studio, Råde
102 Studio, Råde
103 Studio, Råde
104 Studio, Råde
105 Make-up for promo video, Oslo
106 Edvard Munch, *Desire*, 1898 (detail)
107 Studio, Råde
108 Studio, Råde
109 Edvard Munch, *Blossom of Pain*, 1898 (cropped)
110 Studio, Råde
111 Munchmuseet, Tøyen
112 Edvard Munch, *The Urn*, 1896 (detail)
113 Munch's winter studio, Ekely
114 Munch's winter studio, Ekely
115 Munch's winter studio, Ekely
116 Munch's grave, Our Saviour's Cemetery, Oslo
117 Ragnvald Væring, Munch's winter studio, Ekely, late 1930s; Munch's winter studio, Ekely
118 Sound check, MUNCH, Bjørvika
119 Munch's winter studio, Ekely
120 Edvard Munch, *The Kiss*, 1897 (cropped)
121 Studio, Råde
122 Studio, Råde
123 Edvard Munch, *Anxiety*, 1894; Munchmuseet, Tøyen
124 Edvard Munch, *Mermaid on the Beach*, 1917 (detail)
125 Studio, Råde
126 Propeller Studio, Oslo
127 Edvard Munch, *The Human Mountain*, 1909 (detail)
128 Sound check, MUNCH, Bjørvika
129 MUNCH, Bjørvika
130 Bjørvika
131 Studio door, Lysaker

All pictures taken between January 2021 and February 2022

Published by MUNCH

Photographs © Morten Andersen

Head of Publications: Josephine Langebrekke
Editor: Heidi Bale Amundsen
Editorial Contributor: Karen Elizabeth Lerheim
Translations from Norwegian: Francesca M. Nichols
Artistic outline: Morten Andersen
Design: Kristoffer Busch

Front cover: Studio, Lysaker

Paper: Arctic Silk, Munken Print White
Typeface: Akkurat LL (Lineto)
Print and Binding: Narayana Press, Denmark

www.munchmuseet.no

ISBN: 978-82-93560-69-2

MUNCH thanks its sponsors and supporters